A TEENAGER'S GUIDE

HOW TO MANIPULATE YOUR WAY TO HAPPINESS

THIRTY-SEVEN EASY STEPS
IN
THE CARE AND FEEDING
OF
YOUR PARENTS

KEVIN M. DENNY M.D., M.P.H., M.A.

ILLUSTRATIONS BY
ANDREA EVANS WINTON

**This book is positively not to be sold to anyone over 18.
(Booksellers violating this prohibition will be prosecuted!)**

LIBRARY OF CONGRESS CATALOG CARD NUMBER 92-081556

ISBN 0-9633108-0-1

POEM: I'M A "SPECIAL" GIFT BY LARISA BERDICHEVSKY

PRINTED IN THE UNITED STATES OF AMERICA

ADDITIONAL COPIES OF THIS BOOK ARE AVAILABLE DIRECTLY FROM
THE PUBLISHER:

WARTHOG PUBLISHING
P.O. BOX 1000
CHOCOWINITY, N.C. 27817

PLEASE ADD $2.50 PER BOOK
FOR SHIPPING AND HANDLING

FOR ADDITIONAL COPIES:
PHONE 919-975-1001

2ND EDITION, DECEMBER 1995

OF NORTH CAROLINA

TO A GENERATION OF ADOLESCENTS WITH THE PATIENCE

TO TEACH ME HOW TO LISTEN.

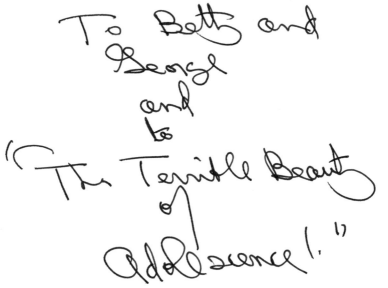

To Betty and
George
and
to
"The Terrible Beauty
of
Adolescence (, ")

K. M. D
Christmas
1995

INTRODUCTION

MY EDITOR SAYS I'VE "GOTTA HAVE" AN INTRODUCTION. I'M ALMOST FIFTY YEARS OLD AND I'M STILL GETTING THE "GOTTA HAVES" AND THE "GOTTA DOS"! WELL, I'D BETTER DO WHAT I GOTTA DO!

AS ONE YOUNG FRIEND SAID TO ME THE OTHER DAY: "GROWING UP IS HARD TO DO!" YES, AND SOMETIMES IT IS VERY LONELY TOO.

I WROTE THIS BOOK TO TRY TO HELP YOU THROUGH THE DIFFICULT TIMES ..... AND THE PAIN AND LONELINESS THAT GO WITH IT. EVEN IF I'M ONLY A PARTIAL SUCCESS, I HOPE IT WILL HAVE HELPED YOUR JOURNEY.

TABLE OF CONTENTS
THIRTY-SEVEN EASY STEPS

EASY STEP # 1

TIRED OF BEING ON RESTRICTION ...
MOM IS OUT-OF-CONTROL ... DAD IS BEING A JERK ...
GRADES SLIPPING ... GOT THE BLUES ...

EASY STEP #1

PARENTS ARE EASY TO PLEASE!

LIFE'S A BITCH....BUT PLEASING YOUR PARENTS CAN BE THE EASI-
EST THING YOU'LL EVER DO!

OK, GANG...GETTING STARTED IS ALWAYS THE HARDEST PART....
BUT YOU MUST HAVE PICKED UP THIS BOOK FOR SOME REASON.
(TIRED OF BEING ON RESTRICTIONS... MOM IS OUT OF CONTROL....
DAD'S BEING A JERK AGAIN....YOUR GRADES ARE SLIPPING AND
YOU'VE GOT THE "BLUES"?) SO LET'S GET GOING! WE'LL START
YOU OFF WITH THE EASIEST THING THERE IS TO UNDERSTAND.....
THAT IS, ONCE YOU'VE GOT THE IDEA!

PARENTS ARE EASY TO PLEASE!

NOW, WAIT ONE SECOND! PLEASE! JUST A FEW PRECIOUS SEC-
ONDS OF YOUR TIME BEFORE YOU THROW THIS BOOK DOWN
THINKING THAT I'M SOME KIND OF A MAJOR LUNKHEAD. GIVE ME
ANOTHER FIFTEEN SECONDS TO EXPLAIN. PLEASE! PLEASE!!

PLEASE! PLEASE! DON'T GIVE UP ON ME UNTIL AT LEAST
EASY STEP #3.

ALL THAT YOU HAVE TO DO TO MAKE YOUR PARENTS HAPPY IS BE:

PLEASANT

PRODUCTIVE

HUMANOID

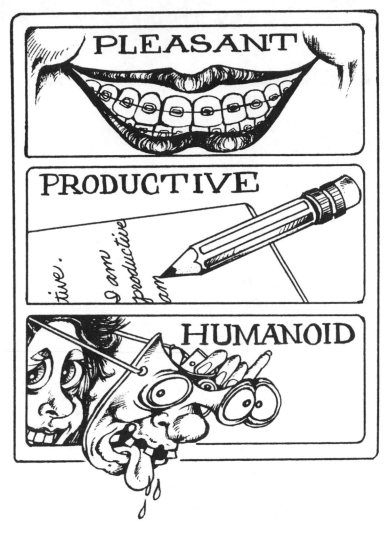

(TRUST ME....I WAS A PARENT WAY BEFORE I EVER BECAME A
PSYCHIATRIST...AND I WAS EVEN A KID ONCE, TOO.)

STILL WITH ME, KIDDO? GOOD...BECAUSE THIS CAN BE FUN!
YOU HAVE JUST COMPLETED EASY STEP #1!   DO YOU HAVE WHAT
IT TAKES TO GO TO EASY STEP #2?...........GOOD-BYE TO ALL YOU
WIMPS WHO LEAVE US NOW!!!

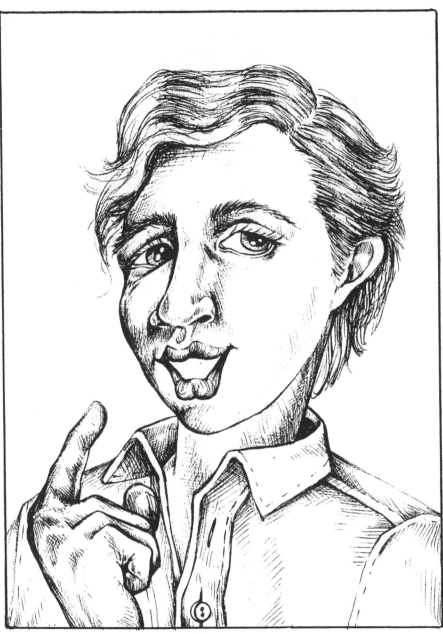

ALL THAT YOU HAVE TO DO TO MAKE YOUR
PARENTS HAPPY IS TO BE .....
PLEASANT, PRODUCTIVE AND HUMANOID!
O.K., WHAT'S THE TRICK HERE !

EASY STEP#2

A REPORTER ASKED," GROUCHO IF YOU COULD HAVE ANY ONE WISH IN THE WORLD GUARANTEED TO COME TRUE WHAT WOULD YOU WISH FOR?"

" HM-M-M ...," GROUCHO THOUGHTFULLY ANSWERED," TO BE SOMEONE ELSE!"

EASY STEP#2

THE TRICKY PART.....WHAT DOES IT TAKE TO BE PLEASANT, PRODUCTIVE AND HUMANOID?

GOOD! GLAD YOU'VE DECIDED TO COME ALONG FOR THE TRIP.

WHAT DOES IT TAKE TO SATISFY YOUR PARENT? WELL, THE ANSWER TO THIS CAN BE VERY EASY...YOU ALL KNOW A BUNCH OF KIDS THAT SEEM TO HAVE NO PROBLEM WITH IT. OR IT CAN BE VERY HARD. AND THAT BRINGS US TO THE NEXT BIG POINT:

LIFE WAS NEVER SUPPOSED TO BE FAIR!

SOME PEOPLE WERE BORN WITH BIG UGLY NOSES...OR AT LEAST THEY GOT THAT WAY PRETTY DARNED QUICK AFTER THEY WERE BORN. SOME PEOPLE HAVE BEAUTIFUL NOSES (BUT, KIDDO, REMEMBER A LOT IS IN THE EYE OF THE BEHOLDER)......THE KIND OF NOSES THAT YOU WOULD KILL FOR, OR GO TO A PLASTIC SURGEON FOR, IF YOU COULD.

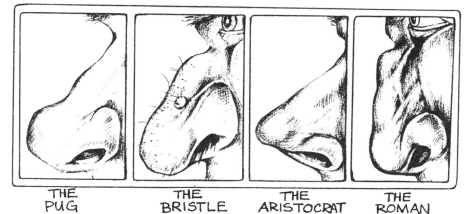

THE PUG   THE BRISTLE   THE ARISTOCRAT   THE ROMAN

IT IS THE SAME WITH PARENTS. SOME PEOPLE GOT A GREAT DEAL! YOU GOT WHAT YOU GOT. LIFE AIN'T FAIR! BUT SOME GOT WORSE AND YOU KNOW IT....SO FOR THE MOMENT, LET'S JUST ACCEPT THAT PARENTS ARE LIKE NOSES: FOR NOW, AT LEAST, YOU GOTTA WORK WITH WHAT YOU GOT.

CAN YOU SWALLOW THAT? IF YOU CAN'T, JUMP AHEAD TO EASY
STEP #35, WHICH TELLS YOU EVERYTHING YOU EVER WANTED TO
KNOW ABOUT SEX...BECAUSE THAT'S ABOUT ALL YOU ARE GOING
TO GET OUT OF THIS BOOK!

A REPORTER ONCE ASKED GROUCHO MARX, "IF YOU COULD HAVE
ANY ONE WISH IN THE WHOLE WORLD AND IT WAS GUARANTEED
TO COME TRUE, WHAT WOULD YOU WISH FOR?" GROUCHO
THOUGHT ABOUT IT FOR ONLY A BRIEF SECOND AND REPLIED, "TO
BE SOMEONE ELSE!"

(IF GROUCHO ISN'T IN YOUR VOCABULARY—ASK YOUR DAD.)

ABSURD? OF COURSE, IT IS..... WHEN SOMEONE ELSE SAYS IT, BUT
HOW MANY TIMES HAVE YOU WISHED IT FOR YOURSELF? IF YOU
ARE LIKE THE REST OF US, PROBABLY MORE THAN YOU CAN
COUNT. "OH I WISH I WERE JENNY....SHE HAS SUCH STRAIGHT
TEETH AND HER PARENTS ARE SO COOL!" (ADMIT IT....YOU DO IT
ALL THE TIME!)

OF COURSE IT'S ABSURD! WE ARE ALL STUCK WITH WHO WE ARE,
NOSES AND ALL (MINE HAS UGLY BLACK HAIRS GROWING OFF ITS
TIP THAT I CUT EVERY TIME THEY GET BAD ENOUGH TO BOTHER
ME!). SO WE PRETTY MUCH HAVE TO WORK WITH THE PARENTS
WE HAVE, EVEN IF THEY AREN'T PERFECT.

MOST PARENTS HAD CHILDREN TO MAKE THEM HAPPY.

OK, WHAT AM I TRYING TO SAY HERE? FIRST, I'M NOT TRYING TO SAY THAT PARENTS HAVE CHILDREN JUST TO MAKE THEMSELVES HAPPY. I'M TRYING TO SAY THAT WHEN MOST PARENTS HAVE KIDS, THEY PICTURE THEM GROWING UP TO BE BEAUTIFUL AND WONDERFUL PEOPLE THAT WILL ENRICH THEIR LIVES AND HAVE HAPPY LIVES OF THEIR OWN.

SURE, THERE ARE NASTY, MEAN-SPIRITED, GOOD-FOR-NOTHING PARENTS—YOU'D KNOW I WOULD BE LYING IF I TRIED TO TELL YOU THAT THERE WEREN'T. BUT, MOST PARENTS ARE DECENT PEOPLE, TRYING THEIR BEST. KIDS AND PARENTS ARE REALLY IN THE SAME BOAT, WHEN YOU COME RIGHT DOWN TO IT: NEITHER OF THEM WANT TO LIVE THEIR LIVES IN MISERY. THERE IS ENOUGH MISERY IN THE WORLD THAT MOST PEOPLE DON'T GO LOOKING FOR MORE.

I'VE BEEN THINKING... HOW DO I GET YOU TO TRUST ME? DON'T I LOOK LIKE SOMEONE YOU CAN TRUST?!?

LET ME TELL YOU ONE MORE LITTLE THING ABOUT PARENTS ....
WAIT, WAIT, STOP, HOLD ON A MINUTE—I'VE CAUGHT MYSELF
STARTING TO LECTURE YOU—MAYBE JUST LIKE YOUR PARENTS DO
TO YOU! I DON'T EVEN HAVE YOUR TRUST YET. I'M MAKING A BIG
MISTAKE (PARENTS DO THAT TOO.)

LET'S STEP BACK HERE A SECOND. YOU HAVE <u>ABSOLUTELY</u> NO
REASON TO TRUST ME YET. WE ARE ONLY IN EASY STEP #2 AND
I'VE ALREADY ASKED YOU TO ACCEPT AN AWFUL LOT. LET'S SLOW
UP.

I'VE BEEN THINKING, HOW DO I GET YOU TO TRUST ME? FIRST YOU
HAVE TO KNOW ME, OF COURSE. AND YOU'D BE A FOOL TO BE-
LIEVE ME JUST BECAUSE I SOUND NICE OR BECAUSE I'M A
PSYCHIATRIST.(TO BE HONEST WITH YOU, THERE ARE A LOT OF
ADULTS WHO DON'T SEEM TO TRUST ME BECAUSE I <u>AM A</u> PSYCHIA-
TRIST—BUT WE'LL GET MORE INTO ADULT PROBLEMS A BIT LATER!)

LUCKILY, THIS MORNING WHILE I WAS SHAVING (THAT'S A LIE...I
HAVE A BEARD) I GOT AN IDEA. WHO KNOWS ME THE BEST? WHO
COULD TELL YOU ABOUT ME IN A WAY THAT COULD BE USEFUL?
SUDDENLY, LIGHTNING STRUCK....WHO COULD TELL YOU BETTER
THAN MY OWN SON, HIMSELF SOON TO ESCAPE THOSE HORRIBLE
TEENAGE YEARS. I'M TELLING ANOTHER LITTLE LIE. WHAT ACTU-
ALLY HAPPENED WAS HE ASKED ME FOR MONEY FOR A SKI TRIP
AND I DECIDED TO MAKE HIM WORK FOR HIS MONEY. HERE IS
WHAT HE THINKS YOU OUGHT TO KNOW:

> SOMETIMES, I THINK MY FATHER WORKS AT BEING A BIT
> PECULIAR......AND I MUST SAY HE HAS GOTTEN QUITE GOOD
> AT IT BY NOW! SOME PEOPLE MIGHT EVEN SAY THAT HE
> HAS GONE A BIT BEYOND PECULIAR, INTO THE REALM OF
> THE ECCENTRIC.
>
> WHAT MIGHT HELP YOU TO KNOW IS THAT HE IS KIND, BUT
> SOMETIMES HE IS SO STUBBORN THAT THE KINDNESS TENDS
> TO GET LOST IN THE SHUFFLE. THERE WERE A LOT OF YEARS
> THAT I FOUND IT USELESS TO ARGUE WITH HIM, BUT I'VE
> LEARNED THAT SOMETIMES IT IS WORTH THE EFFORT,
> ESPECIALLY IF I FEEL I'M RIGHT. HE USUALLY FIGHTS FAIR
> AND MOST OF THE TIME WE ENJOY A GOOD "DISCUSSION",
> BUT IF HE IS TIRED OR IN A BAD MOOD, I KNOW THAT IT'S
> BEST JUST TO BACK AWAY. SOMETIMES I'M SURE HE LIKES
> TO ARGUE JUST TO SEE IF I'LL STAND UP TO HIM FOR WHAT
> I BELIEVE.
>
> IN SOME WAYS I GUESS YOU WOULD HAVE TO SAY HE IS OLD
> FASHIONED—LOTS OF TALK ABOUT HOW THINGS WERE IN

THE OLD DAYS! EVEN THOUGH WE KNOW THINGS WERE TOUGH IN THE OLD DAYS WE GET TIRED OF HEARING ABOUT IT SOMETIMES. BUT IN MANY WAYS HE IS RATHER LIBERAL AND "WITH THE TIMES." FOR INSTANCE, HE VERY SELDOM TRIES TO TELL US WHAT WE OUGHT TO BE DOING AND HE SEEMS TO GENUINELY WANT US TO MAKE THE BIG DECISIONS IN OUR LIVES FOR OURSELVES.

SOMETIMES, HE'S A BIT EMBARRASSING, LIKE WHEN WE ARE OUT AT DINNER AND HE DECIDES TO ACT UP. YOU KNOW THE KIND OF STUFF— NOT ACTING HIS AGE. SOMETIMES WE HAVE TO TELL HIM WE ARE LEAVING IF HE DOESN'T SHAPE UP AND A COUPLE OF TIMES WE HAVE ACTUALLY HAD TO LEAVE HIM SITTING ALONE.

I SUPPOSE HIS BEST CHARACTERISTIC IS HIS WILLINGNESS TO TAKE CHANCES AND NOT ALWAYS JUST BE "ONE OF THE CROWD". I GUESS THAT IS THE GOOD PART ABOUT HAVING A FATHER WHO IS A BIT OF AN ECCENTRIC! AS HE HAS TOLD US, "ONCE YOU MAKE ENOUGH MISTAKES IN YOUR LIFE, YOU DON'T QUITE WORRY ABOUT IT AS MUCH AS YOU USED TO". I THINK I NOW KNOW WHERE HE GOT A LOT OF THIS. DAD WAS ONLY SLIGHTLY OLDER THAN I AM NOW WHEN HE WENT TO AFRICA IN THE PEACE CORPS, RIGHT AFTER PRESIDENT KENNEDY WAS ASSASSINATED.
HE HAS TAKEN ME BACK THERE ONCE WITH HIM AND I CAN SEE HOW LIVING THERE WOULD AFFECT YOUR LIFE. YOU LEARN VERY QUICKLY THAT THE AMERICAN WAY OF LIFE IS NOT THE ONLY ALTERNATIVE AND , IN FACT, THERE ARE SOME THINGS ABOUT OTHER CULTURES THAT ARE BETTER THAN OUR OWN. FOR EXAMPLE, IN AFRICA IF ANYONE IN THE VILLAGE NEEDS HELP, LIKE BUILDING A NEW HOUSE, ALL THE PEOPLE OF THE VILLAGE WILL BAND TOGETHER TO HELP AND NO ONE TRIES TO BUILD A HOUSE BIGGER THAN HIS NEIGHBOR , JUST TO IMPRESS PEOPLE. EVERYONE HAS SO LITTLE THAT SHARING IS A WAY OF LIFE, WITHOUT IT THEY WOULD NOT SURVIVE!

OTHER THINGS I CAN TELL YOU ARE THAT DAD WORKS TOO HARD BUT SEEMS TO ENJOY HIS WORK. I SAY "SEEMS" BECAUSE HE NEVER TALKS TO US ABOUT HIS PATIENTS, SO WE JUDGE MOSTLY FROM HIS MOOD WHEN HE COMES HOME.HE EATS TOO MUCH AND SHOULD EXERCISE MORE...THAT'S WHY WE TRY TO LEAVE MOST OF THE YARD WORK FOR HIM. HE LOVES OLD MG CARS, IRISH MUSIC, VELVEETA CHEESE, THANKSGIVING, SUNDAY NAPS, AFRICAN MASKS, WRESTLING, "THE AMERICAN GLADIATORS", WARTHOGS, TRAVEL, BASEBALL, FLEA MARKETS, AND A GOOD BOOK. HE HATES DANCING, BALLET, OPERA, NINTENDO, ILL-BEHAVED KIDS, SNOBS, LIMA BEANS, CHRISTMAS, KNOW-IT-ALLS, LAZY PEOPLE AND CARS THAT DON'T RUN. IF WE REALLY WANT TO GET HIM MAD WE TEASE HIM ABOUT HIS INABILITY TO CARRY A TUNE OR POUND A NAIL IN STRAIGHT.

WE KNOW WHEN WE'VE TEASED HIM TOO MUCH WHEN HE BEGINS TO SAY THINGS LIKE "&*!@#$~!`^+$#". WHEN HE DOES, WE BACK OFF! WHEN HE'S REALLY ANGRY..... HE'S NOT A LOT OF FUN TO BE AROUND.

SURE, THERE ARE THINGS ABOUT HIM I'D LIKE TO CHANGE. AND, IN FACT, SOME OF THEM SEEM TO BE CHANGING AS HE GETS OLDER....LIKE A BULL ELEPHANT LEARNING THAT HE NO LONGER HAS TO TRUMPET HIS LOUDEST TO BE HEARD. BUT, I'VE PUT ENOUGH WORK INTO TRYING TO UNDERSTAND HIM THAT I WOULDN'T WANT HIM TO GO CHANGING TOO RADICALLY ON ME NOW. I THINK I'LL DO WELL TO KEEP WHAT I HAVE!

YOU KNOW WHEN I READ THAT DESCRIPTION OF ME AS SEEN BY MY OWN SON , IT STARTED ME THINKING (I'LL GET BACK TO THE MAIN SUBJECT REAL QUICK, I PROMISE.) "GOLLY HE REALLY KNOWS A LOT ABOUT ME." BUT THEN I THOUGHT ..."BUT IN A WAY HE DOESN'T REALLY KNOW MUCH ABOUT THE REAL ME AT ALL!" HOW MUCH DO YOU REALLY KNOW ABOUT YOUR PARENTS? (SEE EASY STEP #4, FOR A BUNCH MORE ON THIS!)

ANYWAY, BACK TO THE SUBJECT. WHERE WERE WE? OH, YES,I WAS JUST ABOUT TO TELL YOU ANOTHER WISE THING ABOUT PARENTS, JUST WHEN I REALIZED WE HAD A TRUST ISSUE BREWING.

THE OTHER THING I WANTED TO TELL YOU WAS:

MOST PARENTS ARE TRYING THEIR HARDEST..... HONEST, THEY ARE.

YOU ALL KNOW THAT TO DRIVE A CAR YOU HAVE TO PASS A TEST AND GET A LICENSE. TO PRACTICE MEDICINE YOU HAVE TO PASS TESTS AND GET A LICENSE. TO FLY A PLANE YOU HAVE TO PASS A TEST AND GET A LICENSE.

TO HAVE A KID YOU DON'T NEED A LICENSE AND YOU DON'T EVEN HAVE TO PROVE YOU KNOW WHAT YOU ARE DOING !

SO WHERE DOES THAT LEAVE US? I'LL TELL YOU WHERE THAT LEAVES US: WITH A WHOLE BUNCH OF AMATEUR PARENTS OUT THERE! THAT'S WHERE IT LEAVES US! (ARE YOU STARTING TO SEE WHY I WANT THIS BOOK KEPT OUT OF PARENTS' HANDS...I COULD BE IN BIG TROUBLE IF ANY OF THEM EVER HAPPENED TO READ THIS! KEEP IT HIDDEN UNDER YOUR BED! TREAT IT AS IF IT WERE A CONDOM! PLEASE, HELP KEEP ME OUT OF TROUBLE!) THANKS! I FEEL BETTER NOW AND CAN PROCEED WITH OUR TOPIC AT HAND:

PARENTS DON'T HAVE ALL THE ANSWERS JUST BECAUSE THEY ARE PARENTS.

BUT, PLEASE DON'T MAKE A BIG MISTAKE. REMEMBER:

JUST BECAUSE YOUR PARENTS AREN'T PERFECT;

IT DOES <u>NOT</u> MEAN YOU ARE EQUALS

NOW, KIDDO, THIS IS FAIRLY TRICKY BUSINESS BUT REAL IMPORTANT. PARENTS, FOR INSTANCE, MAY AT TIMES WANT TO TREAT YOU LIKE AN EQUAL, BUT WHEN PUSH COMES TO SHOVE, THEY REALLY SELDOM DO: FOR A SIMPLE REASON—THEY ARE THE PARENT AND YOU ARE THE NON-PARENT. SAVE YOURSELF SOME TIME—ACCEPT IT. IF YOU CAN ACCEPT IT, WITHOUT PROBLEMS, JUMP TO EASY STEP #4. IF IT GETS YOU KIND OF NAUSEATED JUST THINKING ABOUT IT, YOU'D BETTER READ THE NEXT EASY STEP, BEFORE YOU SKIP AHEAD.

... GOOGLESCHMIDT'S FIRST LAW...

EASY STEP # 3

GOOGLESCHMIDT'S FIRST LAW OF ASTRONUMEROLOGY:

THE ENTIRE WORLD DOES NOT
REVOLVE AROUND _____
(INSERT YOUR NAME ABOVE)

LET'S START THIS EASY STEP WITH A LITTLE EXPERIMENT. GO OUT TO THE KITCHEN AND GET A BUCKET OF WATER. FILL IT 3/4 FULL. TAKE YOUR RIGHT HAND AND MAKE A FIST. PLACE YOUR FISTED HAND INTO THE WATER UP TO YOUR ELBOW. CAREFULLY, WITH-DRAW YOUR ARM. NOW, CAREFULLY OBSERVE FOR THE HOLE THAT HAS BEEN LEFT BY WITHDRAWING YOUR ARM. OBSERVE CAREFULLY. NOTE THAT THE WATER IN THE BUCKET IS TOTALLY UNCHANGED EXCEPT FOR THE TINY DROPS OF WATER THAT REMAIN ON YOUR ARM AND THAT ARE NOW DRIPPING ON YOUR MOTHER'S NICE CLEAN FLOOR. (I'VE STOPPED MY LECTURING; I'M NOT GOING TO TELL YOU TO CLEAN IT UP.)

WHAT DID YOU LEARN FROM THIS EXPERIMENT? THE "HOLE" YOU LEFT BEHIND IS JUST ABOUT THE SAME HOLE THAT YOU WOULD LEAVE BEHIND IN THIS WORLD IF YOU WERE NOT HERE....THE SAME HOLE THAT ALL OF US WOULD LEAVE. HENCE, WE COME TO GOOGLESCHMIDT'S FIRST LAW OF ASTRONUMEROLOGY: THE WORLD DOES NOT ROTATE AROUND ANY ONE OF US; WE ARE JUST ONE SMALL, FAIRLY INSIGNIFICANT PART OF IT. AND, FURTHERMORE, WE ARE A SMALLER PART OF THE WORLD THAN ARE PARENTS, WHO HAVE BEEN AROUND LONGER AND HAVE PAID THEIR DUES IN THE "SCHOOL OF HARD KNOCKS".

GOOGLESCHMIDT'S FIRST LAW IN THE ORIGINAL GERMAN ACTUALLY SAID *"ES GIBT KEIN FREIES MITTAGESSEN , KIDDO."* WHICH ROUGHLY TRANSLATED MEANS: "THERE AIN'T NO SUCH THING AS A FREE LUNCH, KIDDO!"

NOW, THIS IS ANOTHER PLACE WHERE ADULTS TEND TO BLOW THEIR COOL..."THIS CRAZY PSYCHIATRIST IS TELLING OUR KIDS THAT LIFE IS MEANINGLESS AND THAT WHATEVER THEY DO IS MEANINGLESS. THEY ARE GOING TO START RUNNING AROUND COMMITTING SUICIDE.....THEY WON'T HAVE ANYTHING TO LIVE FOR!"

DON'T BELIEVE IT!. THAT IS PURE UNADULTERATED POPPYCOCK! IN FACT, IT'S WHEN YOU START TO LEARN THAT YOU ARE NOT SO DARNED IMPORTANT THAT YOU WILL START TO ENJOY LIFE MORE! (PLEASE, DON'T GO OUT AND CUT YOUR WRIST TO PROVE ME WRONG....WE REALLY WOULD MISS YOU! HONEST!

BUT, THIS ISN'T ALL YOUR FAULT. MANY PARENTS HAVE SPENT A LOT OF TIME TELLING YOU THAT EVERYTHING THEY DO IS FOR YOU....YOU HAVE A RIGHT TO COME TO BELIEVE IT. WE'VE HEARD IT.....I'VE SAID IT: "YOU DON'T APPRECIATE ALL THE THINGS I DO FOR YOU". OR," I WORK SIXTEEN HOURS A DAY, JUST SO YOU CAN HAVE AIR JORDANS. WHEN WAS THE LAST TIME YOU SAW ME SPEND ANY MONEY ON MYSELF——EVERYTHING I DO IS FOR YOU!"

UNFORTUNATELY, I'M NOT TOO SURE THAT PARENTS ARE GETTING MUCH SMARTER ABOUT THIS. MAYBE, YOU GUYS NEED HELP IN SMARTENING THEM UP. ARE ALL THE GOODIES MAKING YOU HAPPY? GO LOOK IN YOUR CLOSET.....IF YOU HAVE MORE THAN THREE PAIRS OF EXPENSIVE SHOES IN YOUR ROOM YOU MAY BE ONE OF THEM...... A SPOILED KID! BUT TRY ANOTHER QUESTION. WHAT WOULD YOU RATHER HAVE, ANOTHER PAIR OF SPIFFY

SHOES YOUR MOM OR DAD BUYS....(AND REMEMBER FOR EVERY PAIR OF HUNDRED DOLLAR PUMPJORDANS THEY HAVE TO WORK ABOUT TEN TO TWENTY EXTRA HOURS IF THEY HAVE AN AVERAGE TYPE JOB.)...OR WOULD YOU RATHER HAVE THEM SPEND MORE TIME WITH YOU AND YOUR LITTLE BROTHER? THEY PROBABLY ARE NOT GOING TO MAKE THE CHANGE, UNTIL YOU TELL THEM WHAT YOU WOULD PREFER. (WHY NOT START A FAD IN YOUR SCHOOL? "HEY, GANG. K-MART SNEAKERS ARE THE COOLEST...AND YOU CAN GET THEM WITH VELCRO STRAPS IN GREY OR BLACK! AND, BY THE WAY, MY DAD'S GOING TO THE ROCK CONCERT THIS WEEKEND WITH THE MONEY WE'VE SAVED".....WELL, OK, THAT MAY BE PUSHING IT A BIT, BUT STRANGE THINGS CAN HAPPEN WHEN YOU FOLLOW THESE 37 EASY STEPS!)

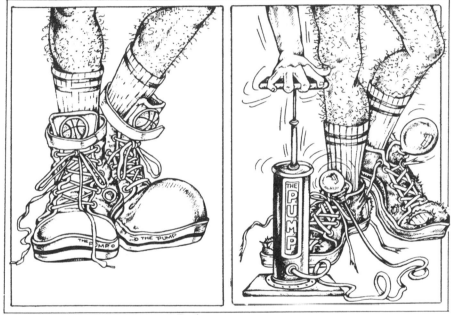

YOU COULD FEED A FAMILY OF 4 FOR A WEEK WITH WHAT A PAIR OF SOME SHOES COST . . . . SO-O-O-O, HOW ABOUT "PUMP YOUR OWN!"

ALLOW ME A SIDETRACK HERE. EVEN WITH K-MART SHOES AND SHIRTS WITHOUT THE LATEST BRAND NAME, YOU'D BE IN PRETTY GOOD SHAPE.

WHEN I WAS JUST A FEW YEARS OLDER THAN YOU...21, TO BE APPROXIMATELY EXACT, I LIVED IN AFRICA FOR TWO YEARS AND IT WAS THE BEST THING I EVER DID. I SAW PEOPLE BY THE THOU-SANDS WITH ONLY ONE SET OF CLOTHING......AND, YOU KNOW WHAT, THEY WERE SOME OF THE HAPPIEST PEOPLE I EVER MET IN MY LIFE! I'M NOT SAYING I WOULD EVER LIKE TO LIVE LIKE THAT, OR THAT I WOULD EVEN BE ABLE TO DO IT, BUT I LEARNED MORE IN THAT TWO YEARS, AWAY FROM MY FAMILY AND IN THE MIDDLE OF POVERTY, THAN I EVER LEARNED ANYWHERE ELSE IN MY LIFE. (TELL YOU WHAT, AFTER I COMPLETE THIS BEST SELLER, I'LL WRITE A BOOK ABOUT THAT EXPERIENCE FOR YOU. I GUARANTEE THAT YOU WON'T BELIEVE SOME OF THE STORIES! I GUESS I'LL HAVE TO DRAW ON SOME OF TRUST I'VE BUILT WITH YOU BY THEN TO GET YOU TO BELIEVE SOME OF IT!

SPEAKING OF TRUST, I GUESS I'M TRYING TO TELL YOU THAT I HAVE TRUST THAT YOU ARE NOT GOING TO JUMP OFF A BRIDGE JUST BECAUSE I'M BREAKING THE NEWS TO YOU THAT YOU ARE NO EXCEPTION TO GOOGLESCHMIDT'S FIRST LAW OF ASTRONUMER-OLOGY. IN FACT, STICK WITH ME FOR THE NEXT EASY STEP AND I'LL GIVE YOU THE GOOD NEWS ABOUT ALL OF THIS.

LET'S GET MOVING ON. SO FAR....SO GOOD? I'M HAVING FUN AND AM LOOKING FORWARD TO YOU STICKING WITH US. LET'S LEAVE GOOGLESCHMIDT BEHIND...HE WAS A CROCHETY OLD GUY ANY-WAY AND I DON'T THINK ANY OF YOU WOULD HAVE LIKED HIM! ALSO, IF YOU HAVE AN IQ HIGHER THAN A SALAMANDER ,YOU'VE GOTTEN EVERYTHING THAT HE HAD TO SAY BY NOW.

IF YOU'VE DRIED YOUR MOTHER'S KITCHEN FLOOR, LET'S PRO-CEED.

EASY STEP #4

EASY STEP #4

MY FATHER'S EYES ARE BROWN......
NO. NO. THEY'RE SORTA BLUE!

EVERY GENERAL KNOWS THAT THE FIRST RULE OF COMBAT IS:

KNOW THY ENEMY

COSTLY MISTAKES HAVE TAKEN PLACE WHEN THIS RULE HAS NOT
BEEN FOLLOWED. MAY I POINT YOU TO A GENERAL NAMED
CUSTER...WHO PAID FOR HIS LACK OF UNDERSTANDING OF THE
ENEMY WITH HIS LIFE. THE VIETNAM WAR CAN SERVE AS ANOTHER
SHINING EXAMPLE OF FAILURE TO UNDERSTAND THE FIGHTING
WILL AND CUNNING OF AN ENEMY.

ALTHOUGH I AM SURE YOU DO NOT VIEW YOUR PARENTS AS "THE
ENEMY" (AT LEAST ON A FULL-TIME BASIS) THE SAMPLE PRINCIPLE
HOLDS FOR LEARNING TO HANDLE THE MANIPULATIONS SET
FORTH IN THIS BOOK: LEARN WHO YOU ARE DEALING WITH.

THE FIRST IMPORTANT STEP IS GETTING TO KNOW WHO YOU ARE
DEALING WITH. HOW MUCH DO YOU KNOW ABOUT YOUR PARENTS?
WELL LET'S TRY TO FIND OUT! I NEVER FAIL TO BE AMAZED AT
HOW LITTLE SOME KIDS KNOW ABOUT THEIR PARENTS. TAKE THE
FOLLOWING LITTLE TEST AND SEE WHERE YOU STAND.

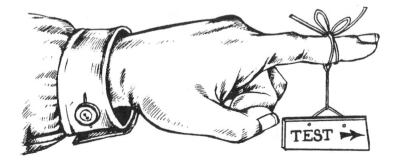

THE PARENT QUIZ

THE QUESTION	MOM	DAD
1. WHAT COLOR HAIR DO THEY HAVE?	☐	☐
2. WHAT COLOR EYES?	☐	☐
3. HAVE THEY STILL GOT THEIR APPENDIX?	☐	☐
4. HAVE THEIR TONSILS BEEN REMOVED?	☐	☐
5. DO THEY HAVE ALL THEIR OWN TEETH?	☐	☐
6. WHERE WERE THEY BORN?	☐	☐
7. DID THEY HAVE ANY BROTHERS OR SISTERS WHO DIED?	☐	☐
8. WHAT KIND OF WORK DID THEIR PARENTS DO?	☐	☐
9. WHAT EXACTLY IS THE WORK YOUR PARENTS DO?	☐	☐
10. WHAT IS THEIR FAVORITE COLOR?	☐	☐
11. DID THEY HAVE A PET GROWING UP?	☐	☐
WHAT WAS ITS NAME?	☐	☐
12. DID THEY EVER GET SUSPENDED FROM SCHOOL? WHY?	☐	☐
13. DID THEY EVER FAIL A SUBJECT? WHICH ONE?	☐	☐
14. WHAT WAS THE MOST EXCITING DAY OF THEIR LIFE?	☐	☐
15. WHAT WAS THE SADDEST DAY OF THEIR LIFE?	☐	☐
16. HAVE THEY HAVE BEEN DISAPPOINTED BY FRIENDS? HOW?	☐	☐
17. WHAT IS THE BIGGEST DISAPPOINTMENT OF THEIR LIVES?	☐	☐
18. WHAT DID THEY WANT TO BE WHEN THEY WERE GROWING UP?	☐	☐
19. WHO IS THEIR BEST FRIEND?	☐	☐
20. WHAT POLITICAL PARTY DO THEY BELONG TO? WHY?	☐	☐
21. DID THEY VOTE IN THE LAST ELECTION?	☐	☐
22. WHAT WAS THE LAST BOOK THEY READ?	☐	☐
23. WHAT IS THEIR FAVORITE TV PROGRAM?	☐	☐
24. WHAT IS THE BEST MOVIE THEY EVER SAW?	☐	☐
25. WHAT IS IT ABOUT YOU THAT UPSETS THEM THE MOST?	☐	☐
26. WHAT IS THE MOST EMBARRASSING MOMENT OF THEIR LIFE?	☐	☐
27. WHERE DID THEY GO ON THEIR HONEYMOON?	☐	☐
28. WHAT IS THEIR FAVORITE FOOD?	☐	☐
29. IF THEY HAD THREE WISHES...WHAT WOULD THEY BE?	☐	☐
30. IF THEY COULD HAVE ONLY 3 THINGS ON A DESERTED ISLAND..WHAT WOULD THEY BE?	☐	☐
31. WHAT WAS THE MOST DIFFICULT THING THEY FACED WITH THEIR DAD?	☐	☐
32. WHAT WAS THE MOST DIFFICULT THING THEY FACED WITH THEIR MOM?	☐	☐
33. IF THEY FOUND A BAG OF MONEY, WHAT WOULD THEY DO?	☐	☐
34. IF THEY COULD DO ONE THING OVER, WHAT WOULD IT BE?	☐	☐
35. WHAT WAS THEIR POSITION DURING THE VIET NAM WAR?	☐	☐
36. WHAT IS THEIR FEELING ABOUT THE VIET NAM WAR NOW?	☐	☐
37. WHAT ARE THE SONGS THEY WOULD LIKE AT THEIR FUNERAL?	☐	☐
38. WHAT ARE THEIR DREAMS FOR WHEN THEY RETIRE?	☐	☐
39. DO THEY FEEL THAT THEY HAVE BEEN GOOD ENOUGH PARENTS?	☐	☐
40. WHAT IS THEIR BIGGEST HEALTH FEAR?	☐	☐
41. DO THEY EVER GIVE MONEY TO BEGGARS ON THE STREET?	☐	☐
42. WHAT IS THE THING IN THEIR LIFE THEY ARE PROUDEST OF?	☐	☐
43. WHAT IS THEIR FAVORITE CHARITY?	☐	☐
44. WHAT DO THEY LIKE THE LEAST ABOUT THEMSELVES?	☐	☐
45. WHAT IS IT ABOUT YOU THAT THEY LIKE THE LEAST?	☐	☐
46. AT WHAT AGE WILL THEY NO LONGER LET YOU LIVE AT HOME?	☐	☐
47. IF THEY WON THE LOTTERY, HOW WOULD THEIR LIFE CHANGE?	☐	☐
48. IF THEY WERE INVITED TO FLY THE SPACE SHUTTLE, WOULD THEY?	☐	☐
49. WHAT IS THEIR FAVORITE MUSIC?	☐	☐
50. WHAT WOULD THEY WANT FOR YOU, ABOVE ALL ELSE?	☐	☐

(2 POINTS FOR EACH CORRECT ANSWER.....PERFECT SCORE 100)

WELL, WHAT DID YOU LEARN? DO YOU <u>REALLY</u> KNOW YOUR PAR-ENT?

IF YOU SCORED LOW, YOU ARE IN A DIFFICULT STARTING POSITION, BECAUSE IN ORDER TO OUT-MANEUVER (WOULD YOU PREFER OUT-MANIPULATE?) A FOE YOU HAVE TO KNOW THEM AS WELL AS YOU CAN.

FORTUNATELY, THIS IS USUALLY PRETTY EASY TO DO. AFTER ALL, WHAT IS THE ONE THING THAT PEOPLE WOULD RATHER TALK ABOUT THAN ANYTHING ELSE IN THE WORLD? YOU ARE RIGHT!

<u>THEMSELVES</u>!

YOUR MAJOR TASK THEN IS TO SET THE TIMING AND THE MOOD IN SUCH A WAY THAT THEY WILL BE READY TO TALK. INCIDENTALLY, ANOTHER GOOD TRICK IS TO <u>REALLY</u> WANT TO FIND OUT ABOUT THEM! YOU HAVE TO ADMIT IT——THERE ARE SOME PRETTY INTER-ESTING QUESTIONS ON THE LIST; SOME OF YOU MIGHT EVEN <u>REALLY</u> WANT TO KNOW THE ANSWERS TO. NEEDLESS TO SAY, I AM SURE YOU HAVE THOUSANDS OF OTHER QUESTIONS OF YOUR OWN YOU'D LIKE TO HAVE THE ANSWERS TO.

THE MORE YOU KNOW ABOUT YOUR PARENTS, THE BETTER PRE-PARED YOU'LL BE TO DEAL WITH THEM IN "COMBAT".

BUT, BACK TO THE GENERALS. THERE ARE TWO OTHER THINGS OF EQUAL IMPORTANCE THAT THEY ALL KEEP IN MIND WHEN DEALING WITH THE FOE:

ALWAYS RESPECT YOUR ENEMY

NEVER UNDERESTIMATE THE ENEMY

THE IMPLICATIONS OF THESE LAST TWO RULES OF "MILITARY CONDUCT" SHOULD BE CLEAR AND OBVIOUS TO ALL OF YOU. WHILE KNOWING YOUR OPPOSITION IS EXTREMELY IMPORTANT, IT IS NOT , BY ITSELF, ADEQUATE TO GUARANTEE VICTORY! YOU HAVE TO LEARN TO "THINK LIKE THE ENEMY", GIVING THEM CREDIT FOR ALL THEIR EXPERIENCE AND ABILITIES AND, PERHAPS MOST IMPORTANT, THE DEDICATION AND MOTIVATION THAT THEY HAVE TO FIGHT FOR THEIR CAUSE!

REMEMBER, YOUR PARENTS BELIEVE IN WHAT THEY ARE DOING AND ARE DEDICATED AND MOTIVATED TO DO THE BEST THAT THEY POSSIBLY CAN TO MAKE YOU, THEIR CHILD, THE BEST POSSIBLE PERSON THAT YOU CAN BE. RESPECT THEM AND DON'T UNDERES-TIMATE THEM! IF YOU FOLLOW THESE THREE IMPORTANT STEPS YOU'LL BE READY FOR THE "GREAT GAME."

 I'LL BET SOME OF YOU PROBABLY DIDN'T EVEN KNOW THE COLOR OF YOUR FATHER'S EYES.....BUT, I'LL BET YOU TOOK A CLOSER LOOK THE NEXT TIME YOU SAW HIM! TRUE CONFESSION TIME. I DIDN'T HAVE A CLUE WHAT A NICE MAN MY FATHER WAS UNTIL I WAS THIRTY-FIVE....AND THAT WAS THREE YEARS AFTER HE DIED!. DO YOURSELF A FAVOR——WORK AT FINDING OUT NOW, WHILE YOU CAN STILL ENJOY IT!.

SOMETIMES, THINGS GET SO BAD BETWEEN TEENS AND PARENTS THAT THEY ARE LIKE TWO PEOPLE STANDING IN A HUGE VAT WITH GASOLINE UP TO THEIR CHINS, EACH ONE HOLDING A PACK OF MATCHES SAYING, "I DARE YOU TO GO FIRST!"

WHICHEVER ONE GOES FIRST, IT IS A TOTAL DISASTER. MOST OFTEN THE PROBLEM IS THAT THEY DON'T KNOW EACH OTHER AND THEY CERTAINLY DON'T KNOW WHAT THEY NEED FROM EACH OTHER.

THIS BOOK IS ALL ABOUT LEARNING HOW TO THROW THE MATCHES AWAY...LEARNING TO KNOW THE OTHER PERSON!

"I DARE YOU TO GO FIRST."
"NO, I DARE YOU!"

EASY STEP #5

EASY STEP #5
SECRET POOP ON PARENTS

THIS EASY STEP <u>MUST</u> BE HIDDEN FROM PARENTS' SIGHT.

(IF I GET ONE LETTER FROM AN ANGRY PARENT, I WON'T BE YOUR FRIEND ANY MORE)

I'M SURE YOU ARE GOING TO SEE MY IMMEDIATE CONCERN HERE. AFTER ALL, SOME OF MY BEST FRIENDS ARE PARENTS! BUT THE POINT OF THIS EASY STEP IS JUST BETWEEN YOU AND ME....AND YOU JOLLY WELL BETTER KEEP IT THAT WAY! (A GOOD PLACE TO KEEP THIS BOOK OUT OF YOUR PARENTS REACH IS TO HIDE IT UNDER THAT PILE OF DIRTY CLOTHES IN YOUR CORNER THAT YOUR MOTHER TOLD YOU "CAN STAY THERE TILL IT ROTS.....I'M TIRED OF PICKING UP AFTER YOU ALL THE TIME!"
IF YOUR PARENTS ARE GETTING ON YOUR CASE AND WANT TO KNOW WHAT YOU ARE READING AND WHY THEY HEAR YOU LAUGH-ING IN YOUR ROOM (HAS THAT BECOME SUCH A STRANGE PHE-NOMENON IN YOUR HOME?) RIP OUT APPENDIX C AND GIVE IT TO THEM TO READ.....IT ISN'T EXACTLY THE FULL STORY BUT IT'S NOT REALLY A LIE EITHER, BUT IT OUGHT TO WORK TO SATISFY THEIR CURIOSITY AND GET THEM OFF YOUR BACK.

THE POINT OF THIS SECTION IS THAT ALTHOUGH YOUR PARENTS ARE BOSS AND THE WORLD DOES NOT SPIN ON YOUR CELESTIAL AXIS (I'M GOING TO START USING FANCY WORDS NOW, AS MOST OF THE ILLITERATES HAVE TOSSED THIS BOOK IN THE WASTE BASKET BY THIS POINT.), THE FOLLOWING IS ALSO TRUE:

IN MANY WAYS,
YOU ARE SMARTER THAN YOUR PARENTS

"PARENTS HAVE HAD A LOT MORE YEARS TO GET "STUPID"!

THE REASON FOR THIS IS SIMPLE: YOUR PARENTS HAVE HAD A LOT MORE YEARS TO GET STUPID THAN YOU HAVE!

WANT PROOF OF THE SOMETIMES SUPERIOR INTELLIGENCE OF A TEENAGER OVER A PARENT? OK. CONSIDER THE VCR....HOW MANY PARENTS DO YOU KNOW WHO ARE CAPABLE OF SETTING THE THING SO THAT THEY CAN RECORD A PROGRAM THAT WILL BE SHOWN AT A PARTICULAR TIME TWO DAYS FROM NOW? HOW MANY OF YOU KNOW? I THINK MY POINT HAS BEEN MADE! ON THE OTHER HAND, HOW MANY OF YOU KNOW HOW TO FILL OUT AN INCOME TAX RETURN OR OVER-HAUL A DIESEL ENGINE....SO DON'T GET TOO COCKY TOO SOON!.

ALRIGHT, HOW DO WE APPLY THIS LITTLE-KNOWN FACT: KIDS UNDER-STAND SOME THINGS PARENTS DON'T?

WELL, LET'S TRY ANOTHER EXAMPLE. HOW MANY TIMES HAS ONE OF YOUR PARENTS SAID TO YOU, "OK, THAT'S ENOUGH! YOU'RE TRYING TO MANIPULATE ME!."

AND YOU, OF COURSE, REPLY, "NO, MOM, I'M NOT TRYING TO MANIPU-LATE YOU!"... AND THEN, UNDOUBTEDLY YOU WITHDREW INTO YOUR ROOM TO CONTEMPLATE YOUR OWN POWERLESSNESS AND INABILITY TO GET YOUR MOTHER TO UNDERSTAND YOU.

WELL, THAT'S REASONABLE, BECAUSE YOU HAVEN'T BEEN USING YOUR NOGGIN. YOU GOT OUTSMARTED! WHY DIDN'T YOU REPLY, "OF COURSE, I'M TRYING TO MANIPULATE YOU, BUT IT APPEARS THAT AT

THE MOMENT I'M DOING A PRETTY LOUSY JOB OF IT."

THIS NATURALLY BRINGS US TO ANOTHER IMPORTANT POINT:

WHAT IS SO BAD ABOUT MANIPULATION?

SOMEWHERE ALONG THE WAY, MANIPULATION HAS GOTTEN A BAD RAP. WE ALL MANIPULATE EVERY DAY OF OUR LIVES. YOUR PARENTS MANIPULATE. IF YOUR FATHER MANAGES PEOPLE AT WORK HE IS MANIPULATING ALL DAY. (IN FACT, THAT MAY BE WHY HE IS SO TIRED WHEN HE GETS HOME AT NIGHT!) I'VE BEEN MANIPULATING YOU FOR FIVE EASY STEPS! I'M TRYING TO MANIPULATE YOU INTO BELIEVING I'M SOMEONE YOU CAN TRUST! .... BY THE WAY, HOW AM I DOING? WELL, YOU ARE STILL HERE, AREN'T YOU!

SO HOW DID MANIPULATION GET SUCH A BAD REPUTATION FOR ITSELF? I BET IT STARTED WITH ADAM AND EVE. ONE OF THEM MANIPULATED THE OTHER INTO EATING THAT APPLE. (I WON'T SAY WHO WAS THE MANIPULATOR AND WHO WAS THE MANIPULATEE AT RISK OF BEING CALLED A SEXIST, ESPECIALLY AS ADULTS ALREADY HAVE PROBABLY LABELED ME AS A "TEENIST". SO WHY IS MANIPULATION SO BAD? MY GUESS IS BECAUSE IT HAS ALWAYS BEEN DONE SO POORLY! ANOTHER WAY OF SAYING THIS IS TO ASK WHAT IS THE DIFFERENCE BETWEEN A "MANAGER" AND A "MANIPULATOR".

I THINK THAT THE ANSWER IS THAT THE MANAGER IS A BETTER MANIPULATOR THAN THE MANIPULATOR. (READ IT AGAIN, ...I THINK IT WILL MAKE SENSE TO YOU IF YOU LET IT SINK IN FOR A MINUTE....AFTER ALL, YOU ARE NO IDIOT IF YOU'VE MADE IT THIS FAR).

MANAGERS ARE SMOOTH OPERATORS! AFTER THEY HAVE MANIPULATED SOMEONE INTO DOING SOMETHING, THE MANIPULATEE SAYS, "THANKS, BOSS. YOU ARE A REAL KEEN FELLOW." AFTER A MANIPULATOR WALKS AWAY, THE SAME PERSON WOULD SAY "THAT SOB!! HE THINKS HE CAN CONTROL ME. HE THINKS HE OWNS ME JUST BECAUSE HE PAYS MY SALARY!"

THE REST OF THIS BOOK IS ABOUT MAKING YOU A BETTER MANIPULATOR!

EASY STEP# 6

WELL, ENOUGH ABOUT ME. LET'S TALK ABOUT YOU.....
WHAT DO <u>YOU</u> THINK ABOUT ME?

BEFORE I INTRODUCE YOU TO DR. DENNY'S SCHOOL OF CREATIVE MANIPULATION, I HAVE A CONFESSION TO MAKE, DEAR READER....

I'M STARTING TO LIKE YOU! AT FIRST I THOUGHT THAT MAYBE YOU WERE A BIT OF A JERK. I THOUGHT THAT MAYBE YOU WERE ONE OF THOSE BOOKWORMS WHO TRIES TO FIND ALL THE ANSWERS TO LIFE'S PROBLEMS IN A BOOK.....THE KIND THAT SPENDS SATURDAY AFTER-NOONS IN THE LIBRARY!!! BUT, IF YOU ARE STILL WITH ME, YOU'VE PROBABLY LAUGHED AT A FEW OF MY CORNY JOKES AND HAVE REALIZED THAT I'M REALLY ON YOUR SIDE. (DON'T WORRY, NO ONE LAUGHS AT MORE THAN 43.6% OF MY STUPID JOKES, AT THE BEST OF TIMES!)

I ALSO HAVE A CONFESSION TO MAKE. I WORK WITH OVER 200 TEEN-AGERS A YEAR AND THERE ARE VERY FEW THAT I LIKE WHEN I FIRST MEET THEM....IT ALWAYS TAKES ME A WHILE TO SCRAPE AWAY THE SURFACE PHONINESS OF A TEENAGER AND DISCOVER WHAT IS REALLY SPECIAL ABOUT THEM.

LET ME TELL YOU WHAT I THINK I'VE FIGURED OUT ABOUT YOU AND WHY I'M STARTING TO LIKE YOU.

<u>FIRST</u>, AT TIMES YOU ARE IN A LOT OF PAIN, OR YOU WOULDN'T BE READING THIS.

<u>SECOND</u>, THERE IS PROBABLY NO ONE IN THE WORLD, EXCEPT MAYBE A BEST FRIEND WHO HAS A LOT OF PROBLEMS OF HIS OR HER OWN, WHO KNOW HOW MISERABLE YOU FEEL INSIDE AT TIMES. (THANKS FOR SHARING IT WITH ME!)

<u>THIRD</u>, YOU REALLY WANT TO GET HELP.

<u>FOURTH</u>, YOU DON'T ALWAYS KNOW HOW TO GO ABOUT GETTING HELP.

<u>FIFTH</u>, AT TIMES, YOU HAVE A WAY OF MAKING THINGS A LOT MORE COMPLICATED THAN THEY REALLY ARE.

<u>SIXTH</u>, YOUR PARENTS ARE PROBABLY PRETTY TOUGH COOKIES SOMETIMES.

<u>SEVENTH</u>, YOU PROBABLY HAVE MADE SOME MISTAKES...AND SOME OF THEM HAVE BEEN WHOPPERS!

EIGHTH, THERE REALLY IS A NEAT KID INSIDE OF YOU.

SO, LET ME TELL YOU HOW I PICTURE YOU. YOU'VE GOT A NICE SMILE...BUT NOT TOO MANY PEOPLE HAVE SEEN IT LATELY. YOU PROBABLY FEEL YOU LOOK AWFUL...AND YOU ARE PROBABLY RIGHT, AS YOU HAVE LOST SOME OF YOUR SPARKLE. YOU'VE GOT SOME ZITS AND THEY ARE MAKING YOU EMBARRASSED TO GO OUT AND YOU THINK YOU ARE UGLY. (I ONCE SKIPPED SCHOOL FOR A DAY BECAUSE I CUT MYSELF THE FIRST TIME I TRIED TO SHAVE....TOLD MY MOTHER I HAD A STOMACH ACHE AND SHE FED ME HORRIBLE-TASTING MEDICINE ALL DAY.) INCIDENTALLY, ZITS GO WITH FEELING DOWN....DON'T ASK ME HOW IT WORKS, IT JUST HAPPENS. YOU ARE A LITTLE SHY WHEN YOU ARE NOT WITH COMFORTABLE FRIENDS AND YOUR BIGGEST FEAR IS GETTING UP IN FRONT OF THE CLASSROOM AND GIVING A PRESENTATION. YOU ARE SENSITIVE... PROBABLY A BIT OVER-SENSI-TIVE AND YOUR FEELINGS ARE HURT EASILY. YOU WORRY MORE ABOUT OTHERS MORE THAN YOURSELF. WHEN ONE OF YOUR FRIENDS HAS A PROBLEM THEY COME TO YOU BECAUSE YOU ARE A "GOOD LISTENER", BUT SOMETIMES YOU ARE AFRAID TO TELL YOUR PROBLEMS TO OTHERS BECAUSE YOU DON'T WANT TO OVERBURDEN THEM. YOU HAVE A BROTHER OR SISTER WHO YOU WISH WASN'T SUCH A CREEP BUT YOU HOPE YOU MAY BE ABLE TO BE FRIENDS SOME DAY.

SOME DAYS YOU FEEL YOU JUST CAN'T DO ANYTHING RIGHT...AND YOU ARE PROBABLY RIGHT! (AND, BY THE WAY, WELCOME TO THE HUMAN RACE.) A LOT OF TIMES YOU FEEL ALONE, EVEN WHEN YOU ARE WITH PEOPLE AND SOMETIMES ALL YOU WANT IS TO BE ALONE. SOME TIMES YOU JUST FEEL BAD AND YOU DON'T KNOW WHY.

WHEN YOU ARE FEELING GOOD, YOU CAN BE GIDDY AND YOU HAVE A REAL FUNNY LAUGH THAT PEOPLE MAKE FUN OF ....BUT IT ALSO GETS OTHER PEOPLE LAUGHING.
YOU'VE GOT SOME REAL SPECIAL TALENTS, BUT SOMETIMES YOU ARE TOO SHY TO SHOW THEM. YOU HAVE FANTASIES AND DREAMS BUT SOMETIMES YOU ARE AFRAID TO TALK ABOUT THEM BECAUSE YOU MIGHT FAIL TO REACH THEM. (YOU WANT TO BE A ROCK STAR OR A MOUNTAIN CLIMBER OR BALLET DANCER OR A NEUROSURGEON....OR ALL OF THEM TOGETHER, BUT YOU ARE AFRAID TO TELL PEOPLE BECAUSE THEY WILL LAUGH AT YOU OR TELL YOU THAT YOU CAN NEVER MAKE IT.)
YOU LIKE CATS, DOGS,RABBITS BUT HATE SNAKES IF YOU ARE A GIRL. YOU LIKE SNAKES BUT HATE CATS AND RABBITS IF YOU ARE A GUY AND YOUR OLD COON DOG IS YOUR BEST FRIEND AT TIMES.

ONE OTHER THING....EVEN IF I'M ONLY 50% RIGHT ABOUT YOU, YOU ARE STARTING TO FEEL A LITTLE BETTER, JUST KNOWING THAT MAYBE YOU AREN'T SO WEIRD AFTER ALL.

OK, LET'S GET ON WITH OUR LESSONS IN CREATIVE MANIPULATION!

So... LET ME TELL YOU HOW I PICTURE YOU...

MOM...I'M NOT READY TO TALK ABOUT IT
RIGHT NOW...I WANT TO CLEAN-UP
THE KITCHEN FIRST...MOM...
MOM...MOM

EASY STEP #7

WAIT A MINUTE MOM!!! I'M NOT READY TO TALK ABOUT IT WITH YOU RIGHT NOW....I WANT TO CLEAN UP THE KITCHEN FIRST!

LET'S GET DOWN TO WORK ON THIS MANIPULATION. THOSE OF YOU EXCEEDING THE LOWLY SALAMANDER IN NATIVE INTELLI-GENCE HAVE PROBABLY ALREADY FIGURED OUT WHAT THIS EASY STEP IS ALL ABOUT:

WHEN IN TROUBLE: DO THE UNEXPECTED

HOW MANY TIMES HAVE YOU HEARD ONE OF YOUR PARENTS TALKING ABOUT YOU AND SAYING, "I KNOW HIM LIKE A BOOK."...WELL, MAYBE IT'S TIME TO THROW AWAY THE BOOK!

LISA WAS A FOURTEEN-YEAR-OLD WHO ASKED FOR HELP IN GROUP THERAPY. SHE SAID, "I'M GOING HOME THIS WEEKEND AND I'M REALLY SCARED BECAUSE EVERY TIME MY MOTHER AND I GET INTO A DISAGREEMENT I GET REAL ANGRY AND UPSET AND NEED TIME TO THINK ABOUT WHAT TO SAY TO HER. SHE ALWAYS GETS MAD AND SAYS, "NO, YOU ALWAYS RUN AWAY. WE HAVE TO TALK ABOUT THIS RIGHT NOW!"

SHE ASKED, " CAN ANYONE HELP ME HOW TO DEAL WITH IT IF IT COMES UP AGAIN THIS WEEKEND?"

ONE OF THE OTHER GIRLS IN THE GROUP SPOKE UP. "YOU KNOW THAT SAME THING USED TO HAPPEN TO ME ALL THE TIME! LET ME TELL YOU WHAT I DID. ONE DAY MY MOTHER GOT REAL MAD AT ME BECAUSE MY BOYFRIEND KEPT ME OUT TOO LATE THE NIGHT BEFORE. IT WAS A SATURDAY MORNING AND I KNEW THAT SHE WAS BOILING MAD...IN FACT, SHE GOT ME OUT OF BED EARLY AND SAID, 'YOU AND I HAVE SOME TALKING TO DO, YOUNG LADY'...YOU ALL KNOW HOW THEY SAY IT! I HAD JUST AWAKENED AND KNEW WHAT I HAD COMING BUT I WASN'T READY FOR IT.
MY MOTHER WANTED TO HAVE IT OUT WITH ME ON THE SPOT. I KNEW I WOULDN'T BE ABLE TO HANDLE IT RIGHT THEN. LUCKILY I WAS AWAKE ENOUGH TO THINK CLEARLY AND I SAID TO HER, "MOM, I NOTICED THE STACK OF DISHES IN THE KITCHEN LAST NIGHT WHEN I CAME IN. HOW ABOUT IT IF I GET UP AND CLEAN UP THE KITCHEN FIRST AND THEN WE CAN TALK ABOUT LAST NIGHT?" YOU SHOULD HAVE SEEN THE LOOK ON HER FACE...AT FIRST SHE STAYED FURIOUS AND THEN SHE STARTED LAUGHING AND SAID,

'ALRIGHT, YOU'VE GOT A DEAL, BUT DON'T THINK THIS IS GOING TO GET YOU OUT OF ANYTHING.' YOU WOULD BE AMAZED AT THE AMOUNT OF THINKING YOU CAN DO SCRUBBING POTS AND PANS. BY THE TIME WE SAT DOWN, I WAS READY TO HANDLE IT AND SHE WAS IN A MUCH BETTER FRAME OF MIND. I STILL GOT RESTRICTION THAT NIGHT, BUT IT DIDN'T RUIN MY WHOLE WEEKEND."

LISA RESPONDED, "WELL, THAT MIGHT HAVE WORKED FOR YOU; BUT YOU DON'T KNOW MY MOTHER!"

A YOUNG MAN IN THE GROUP SPOKE UP. "I HAD YOUR PROBLEMS TOO. I FELT I COULD NEVER WIN, BECAUSE I ALWAYS GOT TOO ANGRY TO TALK WHEN MY MOTHER WANTED ME TO. THEN, ONE DAY WHEN WE WERE GOING AT IT, I SAID TO HER, 'YOU KNOW MOM, WHEN IT GETS LIKE THIS I FEEL LIKE A WEASEL....I FEEL TRAPPED AND LIKE I HAVE TO BITE AT YOUR ANKLES!' IT STRUCK HER FUNNY AND SHE STARTED LAUGHING AND SAID , 'THEN GO TO YOUR ROOM FOR TEN MINUTES, BUT WHEN YOU COME BACK YOU'D BETTER BE A PUSSY CAT.' I DID AND WE HAD A DISCUSSION RATHER THAN A FIGHT. NOW, EVERY TIME I TELL MY MOTHER I'M FEELING WEASELLY, MY MOTHER KNOWS WHAT I'M TRYING TO TELL HER."

ANOTHER YOUNG MAN ASKED LISA "WHAT KIND OF AN ANIMAL DO YOU FEEL LIKE WHEN YOUR MOTHER DOES THAT TO YOU?"

SHE STOPPED AND THOUGHT FOR A MOMENT AND SAID, "A CROCODILE...I MAY LOOK PEACEFUL, BUT IF SOMEONE COMES UP TO ME I'LL SNAP THEIR HEAD OFF!"

WHEN SHE CAME BACK, EVERYONE WANTED TO KNOW HOW IT HAD GONE FOR LISA AND SHE SAID, "THERE WEREN'T ANY DISHES TO CLEAN BUT I WAS ABLE TO TELL HER I FELT LIKE A CROCODILE AND SHE LEFT ME ALONE UNTIL I HAD CHANGED INTO A KOALA BEAR!"

THINK ABOUT OUR BASIC PRINCIPLES:
- **PLEASING PARENTS IS EASY.**
- **LIFE IS NOT SUPPOSED TO BE FAIR.**
- **MOST PARENTS ARE TRYING THEIR HARDEST.**
- **PARENTS AREN'T LICENSED TO KNOW HOW TO HANDLE EVERYTHING.**
- **YOU AND YOUR PARENTS ARE NOT EQUAL.**
- **GOOGLESCHMIDT'S FIRST LAW OF ASTRONUMEROLOGY.**
- **KIDS ARE SMARTER THAN THEIR PARENTS.....UPON OCCASION.**
- **WHEN IN TROUBLE: DO THE UNEXPECTED.**

CAN YOU SEE HOW THE TEENS IN THIS GROUP APPLIED EVERY ONE OF THESE PRINCIPLES?

HAD LISA LEARNED TO BECOME A MANIPULATOR? YOU ANSWER THAT ONE!

SOME MOODS ARE
IN LIKE A WEASEL — OUT LIKE A
PUSSYCAT ; OR IN LIKE A CROCODILE—
OUT LIKE A KOALA BEAR!

EASY STEP #8

... IN A CONFLICT – HOW ABOUT "MANIPULATING"
A <u>WIN</u> / <u>WIN</u> SITUATION
(JUST – HOPEFULLY NOT IN THE ABOVE MANNER.)

EASY STEP #8

HOW TO APOLOGIZE AND REALLY MEAN IT......
EVEN IF YOU DON'T REALLY MEAN IT!

REMEMBER, YOU ARE NOT GOING TO WIN THEM ALL...IF FACT, THE CARDS ARE STACKED AGAINST YOU (THAT IS SIMPLY A FACT IF YOU ARE WILLING TO ACCEPT THE BASIC RULES). BUT YOU SHOULD BE ABLE TO LEARN TO WIN MORE THAN YOU ARE WINNING AT THE PRESENT TIME. BUT YOU ARE GOING TO HAVE YOUR LOSSES. THIS EASY STEP PROVIDES SIMPLE ADVICE:

IF YOU AREN'T GOING TO WIN THEM ALL.....
LEARN TO BE A GOOD LOSER.

YOU SHOULDN'T HAVE TO BE A YOUNG EINSTEIN TO UNDERSTAND THIS ONE. TAKE YOUR LUMPS WHEN YOU HAVE TO...YOU MAY WIN THE NEXT ONE, IF YOU PLAY YOUR CARDS BETTER.

BUT STOP AND THINK HERE A SECOND, KIDDO. WE ARE TALKING "WINNERS" AND "LOSERS" HERE! IS THAT <u>REALLY</u> THE WAY IT HAS TO BE? WHAT HAPPENED IN LISA'S CASE? WAS THERE A "WINNER" AND A "LOSER"?

OH, WISE YOUNG ONE! WHAT IS YOUR ANSWER? SEEMS TO ME THERE WERE TWO "WINNERS" IN HER SITUATION. CERTAINLY HER MOTHER MADE OUT AS WELL AS SHE DID IN THE DEAL. HOW DID WE EVER GET TO THE POINT WHERE WE HAD TO SEE A "WINNER" AND A "LOSER" IN EVERY SITUATION WHERE THERE IS A CONFLICT?

MAYBE, IT IS FROM THE "LAW OF THE JUNGLE": LIONS EAT ANTELOPES, NO MERCY GIVEN. MAYBE, FROM FOOTBALL: EVERY COACH TELLS HIS PLAYERS,"A TIE IS LIKE KISSING YOUR COUSIN. WE'RE GOING OUT THERE TO WIN!" MAYBE, BECAUSE THAT'S THE WAY IT HAS ALWAYS BEEN DONE IN YOUR FAMILY!!!

LET US RETURN TO OUR QUESTION: WHAT IS WRONG WITH MANIPULA-TION? (I SURE HOPE THAT YOU ARE NOT READING THIS INSTEAD OF DOING YOUR MATH HOMEWORK, KIDDO. ANOTHER LIE....THERE ARE MILLIONS OF GOOD MATH BOOKS AND NOT SO MANY GOOD BOOKS ABOUT LIFE! KEEP READING, YOU CAN DO THE MATH TOMORROW .... ANYWAY, IF YOU ARE KEEPING THIS BOOK HIDDEN LIKE I ASKED, YOUR PARENTS WON'T BE ABLE TO BLAME IT ON ME AND ,IN FACT, THEY ARE PROBABLY THRILLED BECAUSE THEY THINK YOU ARE UP DOING MATH HOMEWORK!) I THINK MOST PEOPLE PICTURE THAT IN MANIPULATION THERE IS A "WINNER" AND A "LOSER" AND , FURTHERMORE, MANIPULA-TION IS A MATTER OF THE STRONGER PERSON FORCING THEIR WILL UPON THE WEAKER ONE. CERTAINLY A LOT OF THIS GOES ON! AND

THERE ARE A LOT OF PEOPLE WHO CALL THEMSELVES MANAGERS WHO ARE PATHETIC BECAUSE THIS IS HOW THEY TRY TO OPERATE. MAYBE, ITS MORE THE LAW OF SURVIVAL THAN THE LAW OF THE JUNGLE. (WATCH, I'LL GET A LETTER NOW FROM SOME DOPEY ADULT ACCUSING ME OF PUSHING EVOLUTION DOWN INNOCENT ADOLESCENTS' THROATS!)

BUT IF IT IS THE "LAW OF SURVIVAL", THERE ARE SOME INTERESTING THINGS HAPPENING. IF THE STRONG ARE EATING THE WEAK; WHY AREN'T THE WEAK ADAPTING? WHY AREN'T YOU KIDS LEARNING HOW TO DEAL WITH YOUR PARENTS BETTER?

ONE OBVIOUS REASON: YOU HAD NOT READ THIS SOON-TO-BE-FAMOUS BOOK!. BUT ANOTHER THING SHOULD BE MENTIONED WHICH IS FAR MORE IMPORTANT......THERE IS NO WAY I KNOW OF THAT KIDS ARE TAUGHT HOW TO DEAL WITH THEIR PARENTS AS GOOD MANIPULATORS. DO YOU KNOW OF ANY SCHOOL COURSE ON IT? WOULD YOUR TEACHERS GIVE YOU THE STRAIGHT POOP....AFTER ALL YOUR PARENTS' TAXES PAY THEIR SALARIES AND THEY CAN GET THEMSELVES FIRED IF THEY BECOME CONTROVERSIAL. IMAGINE A TEACHER TEACHING A KID TO FIGHT WITH HIS PARENTS! I IMAGINE THAT TEACHER WHO DID THAT WOULD GO DOWN THE TUBES PRETTY DARNED QUICK! WELL, KIDDO, I WORK FOR YOU...YOU BOUGHT MY BOOK. YOU PUT THE BREAD ON MY TABLE! I'LL GIVE YOU STRAIGHT POOP!

WHAT ELSE DO YOU WANT TO KNOW? LET ME TRY TO TAKE SOME GUESSES ON WHAT YOU WANT TO KNOW IN THE EASY STEPS THAT FOLLOW. I'M SURE I'M NOT GOING TO BE ABLE TO COVER EVERYTHING, BUT JUST KEEP THE SIMPLE BASIC PRINCIPLES IN YOUR MIND AND I THINK YOU'LL DO JUST FINE.

LET'S TALK MORE ABOUT SOME OF THE THINGS THAT BUG PARENTS MOST IN THE NEXT FEW EASY STEPS AND SEE WHETHER WE CAN FIGURE OUT SOME WAY TO MANIPULATE OURSELVES IN TO "WIN-WIN" SITUATIONS.

BY THE WAY, THERE ARE NO TWO WORDS THAT PARENTS LIKE BETTER THAN:

I'M SORRY

BUT A WORD TO THE WISE....DON'T OVER-USE IT. YOU CAN RUN INTO THE SAME PROBLEM AS WHEN YOU TELL YOUR GIRLFRIEND OR BOYFRIEND YOU LOVE THEM TOO OFTEN.....IT CAN LOSE ITS MEANING! AND, IF YOU TELL THEM YOU LOVE THEM; YOU SURE BETTER ACT LIKE YOU DO OR IT WILL COME BACK TO HAUNT YOU.

MY ESTIMATE IS THAT YOU CAN ONLY GET AWAY WITH SAYING "I'M SORRY" ABOUT THIRTY TIMES A YEAR WITHOUT BACKING IT UP WITH SOME REAL CHANGE IN YOUR BEHAVIOR. DON'T PUSH YOUR LUCK TOO FAR....AN ANGRY PARENT IS MUCH HARDER TO MANIPULATE THAN A HAPPY ONE! THAT'S THE WAY IT IS AND THE WAY IT WILL ALWAYS BE— AND YOU CAN TAKE THAT TO THE BANK WITH YOU!.

You can probably only get away with saying "I'm sorry" 30 times a year.

EASY STEP #9

SO ! YOUR PARENTS THINK YOUR FRIENDS ARE JERKS!

THIS IS A PRETTY COMMON PROBLEM, ISN'T IT?

MY GUESS IS THAT BIGGEST REASON FOR THIS IS THAT ADULTS BASE SO MANY OF THEIR OPINIONS ON FIRST APPEARANCE. (REMEMBER, THIS COMES FROM THE GUY WHO TOLD YOU THAT HE DOESN'T LIKE MOST TEENAGERS WHEN HE FIRST MEETS THEM!) SO I KNOW WHAT I'M TALKING ABOUT ON THIS ONE.

YOUR PARENTS PROBABLY HAVE BEGUN GIVING UP ON TRYING TO CONTROL WHAT YOU WEAR OR HOW YOU LOOK....WITHIN CERTAIN LIMITS, OF COURSE!. BUT, I THINK THAT THEY FEEL THAT OTHER PARENTS SHOULD SOMEHOW BE DOING A BETTER JOB WITH THEIR KIDS! DON'T LOOK FOR THE LOGIC....IT'S NOT REALLY THERE!

SO WHAT I THINK HAPPENS A LOT IS THAT YOUR FRIENDS SENSE THEY ARE NOT APPRECIATED BY YOUR PARENTS AND THEY BACK AWAY FROM TRYING TO GIVE THEM A "SECOND OPINION". HOW ARE WE GOING TO MANIPULATE OUR WAY TO SUCCESS IN THIS CASE?

BY NOW, I ASSUME THE WHEELS IN YOUR HEAD HAVE BEGUN TO SPIN.

HAVE YOU EVER SAT DOWN AND LOOKED INTO YOUR MOTHER'S PRETTY BLUE (OR ARE THEY BROWN?) EYES AND ASKED EXACTLY WHAT IT IS THAT SHE DOES NOT LIKE ABOUT YOUR FRIEND? IS IT HIS CLOTHES? HIS MANNERS? HIS HAIR? THE SAFETY PIN THROUGH HIS CHEEK? THE SCHOOL HE GOES TO?

BE READY FOR SOME—"THERE IS JUST SOMETHING ABOUT HIM" ANSWERS, BUT YOUR PARENTS REALLY OUGHT TO BE ABLE TO DO BETTER THAN THAT ..... ESPECIALLY IF YOU ARE BEING COOL AND APPROACHING THEM IN THE RIGHT WAY, FOLLOWING BASIC PRIN-CIPLES WE HAVE BEEN WORKING ON.

WHAT NEXT? ONCE YOU HAVE THE LAY OF THE LAND; DO THE UNEX-PECTED. HAVE YOUR FRIEND CUT HIS HAIR? NO, OF COURSE NOT...A FRIEND WOULD NEVER ASK YOU TO DO THAT JUST TO SATISFY HIS PARENTS, WOULD HE? BUT THINK THE UNEXPECTED!

I'M GOING TO SIT HERE AND TYPE OUT THE FIRST CRAZY IDEAS THAT COME INTO MY HEAD. I'LL BET YOU YOUR NEXT WEEK'S ALLOWANCE THAT ONE OF THEM WILL WORK FOR YOU. LET'S CALL YOUR FRIEND OSCAR (DOES ANYONE STILL NAME THEIR KID THAT....WHAT A DIRTY TRICK!). LET'S SAY THAT HE IS AN AVERAGE

STUDENT BUT LOOKS KIND OF MORONIC SOMETIMES. EVEN HIS FRIENDS ADMIT HE IS AN AIRHEAD AT TIMES. HE LIKES DUNGEONS AND DRAGONS, FOOTBALL, HORROR MOVIES, MOTORCYCLES AND HEAVY METAL. HE'S QUIET, SOMEWHAT SHY AND AWKWARD AROUND ADULTS. HE HAS SOME PROBLEMS WITH HIS PARENTS BUT HE'S NOT A TROUBLE-MAKER, THOUGH ,ONE NIGHT, HE AND YOU DID GET INTO SOME TROUBLE TOGETHER.....LET'S SAY YOU TRIED OUT SOME BEER WHILE YOUR PARENTS WERE AWAY AND HE BARFED ON YOUR MOTHER'S NEW WHITE CARPET. (AM I GETTING CLOSE TO HOME?) HE REALLY WOULD LIKE YOUR PARENTS TO LIKE HIM, BUT DOESN'T HAVE A CLUE HOW TO GO ABOUT IT.

WE'LL ASSUME YOU WANT TO BE HIS FRIEND, EITHER HIS GUY FRIEND OR HIS GIRL FRIEND.

OK, TWENTY MINUTES WORTH OF QUICK IDEAS AND THEN I'M OFF TO BED ...I'VE ALREADY SPENT ABOUT FOUR HOURS LONGER WITH YOU TONIGHT THAN I HAD EXPECTED.....I MUST BE REALLY STARTING TO LIKE YOU!

TIMER IS SET....HERE I GO.

> TELL YOUR PARENTS THAT OSCAR AND YOU WILL BE FIXING DINNER FOR THEM SATURDAY. (LOOK UP RECIPE FOR VEAL OSCAR AND TELL YOUR PARENTS HE INVENTED IT! (PLEASE CONSULT APPENDIX A FOR THE RECIPE FOR "VEAL OSCAR")

> ASK YOUR PARENTS TO PLAY D&D WITH YOU AND OSCAR JUST ONE NIGHT....I'M SURE THEY'LL GET HOOKED.

> GET OSCAR TO TAKE YOUR MOTHER FOR A RIDE ON HIS MOTOR-CYCLE.

> RENT A TUXEDO FOR OSCAR ONE NIGHT.

> WORK SHARE.....HELP WITH HOUSEWORK AT OSCAR'S AND HAVE HIM TRIM THE BUSHES WITH YOU AT YOUR HOUSE.

> SHOW YOUR PARENTS OSCAR'S REPORT CARD TO PROVE THAT HE IS A GOOD STUDENT.

> GET OSCAR TO ASK YOUR MOTHER IF HE CAN GO TO HER CHURCH WITH HER SUNDAY BECAUSE HE ISN'T GETTING ENOUGH OUT OF HIS PARENT'S CHURCH.

> (SEVEN MINUTES USED SO FAR)

> HAVE OSCAR BRING SOME OF HIS MUSIC AND EXPLAIN TO YOUR MOTHER THE DIFFERENCE BETWEEN SATANISM AND HEAVY METAL (FOR LAUGHS, TRY TO GET HER TO PLAY IT BACKWARDS ON HER RECORDER TO SEARCH FOR SUBLIMINAL MESSAGES.) TELL YOUR FATHER THAT OSCAR AND YOU WOULD LIKE TO GO

WHERE HE WORKS SOME DAY TO LEARN MORE ABOUT WHAT HE DOES.

HAVE OSCAR CARRY "THE COMPLETE WORKS OF SHAKESPEARE" THE NEXT TIME HE COMES OVER. (MAKE SURE HE READS AT LEAST ROMEO AND JULIET, BEFORE HE COMES.)

(TWELVE MINUTES USED)

ARRANGE AN EVENING FOR YOUR PARENTS TO MEET OSCAR'S PARENTS.

OSCAR AND YOU CAN TAKE YOUR PARENTS TO A MOVIE ... PREFERABLY ONE IN FRENCH WITH SUBTITLES ... PRETEND OSCAR DOESN'T NEED THE SUBTITLES!

HAVE OSCAR TELL YOUR PARENTS THAT THEY INTIMIDATE HIM

HAVE OSCAR BE THE ONE TO SUGGEST THAT YOU TAKE YOUR GOOFY LITTLE BROTHER WITH YOU NEXT TIME YOU GO SOME-WHERE.

MAKE SURE THAT OSCAR'S FAVORITE FOOTBALL TEAM IS THE SAME AS YOUR FATHER'S.

(EIGHTEEN MINUTES DOWN)

MAKE SURE THAT YOUR MOTHER KNOWS THAT OSCAR'S UNCLE IS A MISSIONARY IN AFRICA. (HAVE HIM ASK HER TO SAVE OLD CLOTHES FOR THE LEPERS)

TELL OSCAR NOT TO CHEW GUM, TO LOOK YOUR PARENTS STRAIGHT IN THE EYE WHEN HE TALKS TO THEM AND NOT TO MUMBLE. ("YES SIR" AND "NO MAM", WOULD BE OVERKILL.)

HAVE OSCAR SHOW YOUR PARENTS HIS BOY SCOUT MERIT BADGES.

TIME'S UP! I'M OFF TO BED. IF I WON THE BET, PLEASE SEND YOUR NEXT WEEK'S ALLOWANCE TO THE FOLLOWING ADDRESS:
> CREATIVE MANIPULATION
> POST OFFICE BOX 145
> BRYSON CITY , NEBRASKA 23432

GOOD NIGHT! REMEMBER: PRACTICE, PRACTICE, PRACTICE.

BYE - BYE OSCAR,
...BACK WHERE YOU CAME FROM
(MUST LOOK-WHILE PICKING YOUR NOSE.)

EASY STEP #10

SO, WHAT IF YOUR FRIEND
<u>REALLY</u> IS A JERK?

OK, SO WHAT IF OSCAR REALLY IS A JERK....SO DITZY THAT HE CAN'T EVEN ACCOMPLISH ONE THING ON THAT LIST THAT WE STAYED UP SO LATE LAST NIGHT COMPLETING?

FIRST NEWS FIRST...IF HE REALLY IS A JERK—HARD CORE— GIVE UP ON TRYING TO GET YOUR PARENTS TO LIKE HIM. IT WILL BE A TOTAL WASTE OF TIME! ARRANGE TO MEET HIM AT WENDY'S AND YOUR LIFE WILL BE A MUCH HAPPIER PLACE FOR BOTH YOU AND YOUR PARENTS ... BUT THERE IS ANOTHER QUESTION, PROBABLY MORE IMPORTANT IN THE FULL SCOPE OF THINGS: IF OSCAR REALLY IS A JERK, WHAT ARE YOU GETTING OUT OF HANGING AROUND HIM?

SIMPLE...BUT TRICKY ...QUESTION FIRST. WHAT IS YOUR DEFINI-TION OF A FRIEND? YEAH. YEAH. SOMEBODY YOU LIKE BEING AROUND. SOMEONE WHO WILL HELP YOU. SOMEONE YOU SHARE INTERESTS WITH. SOMEBODY TO DO THINGS WITH. THOSE ARE THE OBVIOUS...BUT WHAT IS THE TRUE DEFINITION OF A FRIEND.

I TREAT ADULTS TOO. (IT WOULD MAKE ME CRAZY TO JUST WORK WITH YOU TEENAGERS ALL THE TIME!!!) A MAN AND HIS WIFE, WHO HAD BEEN SEPARATED FOR SEVERAL YEARS WERE TRYING TO GET BACK TOGETHER AND HAD ASKED MY HELP. HE KEPT SAYING THAT THEY HAD TO BE FRIENDS BEFORE THEY COULD BE LOVERS; SHE SAID IT WAS THE OTHER WAY AROUND—THEY HAD TO BE LOVERS AGAIN FIRST AND THEN THEY WOULD BECOME FRIENDS.

THEY GOT INTO A HEATED DISCUSSION ABOUT THIS...AT HOME, YOUR PARENTS MIGHT LABEL IT AN ARGUMENT. I ASKED THEM TO STOP AND THINK FOR FIVE MINUTES AND THEN TOGETHER COME UP WITH THEIR ABSOLUTE BEST DEFINITION OF A "FRIEND". THEY WORKED HARD AND CAME UP WITH THIS DEFINITION, WHICH I HAVE BEEN USING EVER SINCE:

A FRIEND IS SOMEONE WHO YOU CAN TRUST IN YOUR HEART WOULD NEVER DO ANYTHING TO DELIBERATELY HURT YOU.

TWO QUESTIONS:

> HOW DOES YOUR FRIEND OSCAR FIT THIS DESCRIPTION?
>
> IS IT POSSIBLE THAT YOUR PARENTS COULD ACTUALLY FIT THE DEFINITION OF A FRIEND?

CHOOSING FRIENDS IS A TRICKY BUSINESS. HAVE YOU MADE THE RIGHT CHOICE WITH OSCAR? CAN YOU TRUST HIM? DOES HE DO THINGS THAT HURT YOU IN ONE WAY OR ANOTHER? DOES HE EVER DELIBERATELY DO THINGS THAT GET YOU MAD OR AREN'T IN YOUR BEST INTERESTS?

LET'S FOCUS ON A KEY WORD: DELIBERATELY.

THERE ARE TWO ASPECTS TO THIS. FIRST, IF HE DELIBERATELY HURTS YOU...WHY ARE YOU STILL HANGING AROUND HIM? ARE YOU LOONEY TUNES OR TOTALLY INSECURE? IS OSCAR THE BEST THAT YOU THINK YOU CAN DO? YOU MUST NOT THINK MUCH OF YOURSELF IF YOU SELECT AS A FRIEND SOMEONE WHO DOESN'T GIVE A HOOT ABOUT YOU AND WOULD EVEN SET OUT TO HURT YOU. SEND OSCAR BACK WHERE HE CAME FROM! THERE ARE PLENTY OF PEOPLE OUT THERE WHO ARE READY TO LIKE YOU AND TREAT YOU BETTER. BYE-BYE, OSCAR. DO NOT PASS "GO"...DO NOT COLLECT $200!

BUT THERE IS A MUCH MORE IMPORTANT POINT ABOUT THIS WHOLE THING. IF YOU HAVE A FRIEND, IN OUR TRUE SENSE OF THE WORD, AND THEY HAVE DONE SOMETHING TO HURT YOU OR MAKE YOU FEEL BAD, YOU CAN GO BACK TO THEM AND SAY, "OSCAR, (LET'S BRING OUR OLD FRIEND BACK...I SERIOUSLY DOUBT YOU WOULD BE HANGING AROUND WITH OSCAR IN THE FIRST PLACE IF THERE WASN'T SOMETHING KIND OF NEAT ABOUT HIM) OSCAR, OLD BUDDY. I WANT YOU TO KNOW THAT WHAT YOU SAID TO ME THE OTHER NIGHT HURT ME! I AM HOPING THAT YOU DID NOT DO IT DELIBERATELY BECAUSE YOU ARE MY FRIEND; BUT, BECAUSE YOU ARE MY FRIEND I'M TRUSTING YOU WOULD REALLY WANT TO KNOW HOW IT MADE ME FEEL AND IT MADE ME FEEL BAD!

OK, ITS OSCAR'S MOVE NOW!

WHAT ARE HIS CHOICES? I CAN THINK OF ONLY A COUPLE:

> A. REGGIE YOU ARE A TWIT; I DID DO IT TO HURT YOU!!!
> B. GOLLY-WOLLY, REG OLD BUDDY, I HAD NO IDEA IT HAD BOTHERED YOU. I WASN'T TRYING TO HURT YOU..HONEST I WASN'T.

AS YOU MAY HAVE NOTED, THE TITLE OF THIS BOOK IS "THIRTY-SEVEN EASY EASY STEPS IN THE CARE AND FEEDING OF YOUR PARENTS". WE ARE NOT TALKING ABOUT THE "CARE AND FEEDING OF FRIENDS"...

SOMEONE ELSE CAN WRITE THAT ONE. LET'S RETURN TO THE MA-
NIPULATION OF PARENTS!

SO, REGGIE...(.HOPE IT DIDN'T BOTHER YOU TOO MUCH FOR ME TO
CALL YOU THAT—I NEED TO KNOW WHO I'M TALKING TO!)....HOW DO
WE APPLY THIS TO DEALING WITH YOUR PARENTS? WELL, IF YOU CAN
BELIEVE THAT YOUR PARENTS CAN BE YOUR FRIENDS, IT DOESN'T
SEEM TO ME THAT THERE IS AN OUNCE OF DIFFERENCE!

SO HERE IS YOUR QUESTION OF THE HOUR:

DO YOU THINK THAT YOUR PARENT ARE OUT TO DELIBERATELY MAKE YOUR LIFE MISERABLE?

IF YOU HAVE ANSWERED "YES".....STOP READING BECAUSE YOU NEED
GOOD PROFESSIONAL HELP RIGHT NOW! CALL SOMEONE YOU TRUST
OR GO TO THE YELLOW PAGES OF YOUR PHONE BOOK AND LOOK
UNDER "PSYCHIATRIST" "PSYCHOLOGIST" OR "SOCIAL WORKER" . DO
IT NOW, NOT THREE WEEKS FROM NOW! YOU AND YOUR FAMILY NEED
HELP RIGHT AWAY!

IF YOU HAVE ANSWERED "NO" AND YOU GENUINELY FEEL THAT YOUR
PARENTS CAN BE YOUR FRIENDS....THEN YOU CAN WRITE THE LAST
PART OF THIS EASY STEP #10 BY YOURSELF.

HAVE FUN. I'LL SEE YOU AGAIN IN THE NEXT SECTION!

EASY STEP #11

EASY STEP #11

MY DAD IS IVY LEAGUE......
I'M SHOOTING FOR THE MAJOR LEAGUE

JUST BECAUSE YOUR PARENTS AREN'T OUT TO GET YOU, IT DOESN'T NECESSARILY MEAN YOU HAVE A LOT IN COMMON.

NOW LET ME GIVE YOU THE BOTTOM LINE FIRST FOR THIS EASY STEP:

YOU ARE NOT A CLONE:
YOUR GOAL HAS TO BE TO BE YOU!!!

YOU'VE HEARD IT A MILLION TIMES:" WE JUST WANT DEBBIE TO DO HER BEST AT WHAT SHE DOES! WE DON'T WANT TO MAKE HER DECISIONS FOR HER."

UNFORTUNATELY, PARENTS ARE NATURAL BORN TALKERS AND THEY ARE OFTEN "TALK THE TALK" ON THIS ONE..... BUT THEY ARE NOT ALWAYS SO GOOD AT "WALKING THE WALK"!

AS LONG AS YOU TELL THEM YOU WANT TO BE A DOCTOR OR A LAWYER OR A TEACHER... ALL GOES PRETTY SMOOTHLY. BUT YOU ALL KNOW WHAT HAPPENS TO THEM WHEN YOU TELL THEM YOU WANT TO BE A ROCK STAR OR YOU WANT TO JOIN THE CIRCUS... INSTANT HISSY FIT!

I WAS LUCKY. MY PARENTS NEVER TOLD ME WHAT THEY WANTED ME TO BE. THEY LET ME CHOOSE FOR MYSELF...... AND IT HAS TAKEN ME FOURTY-EIGHT YEARS TO FIND OUT WHAT I'VE WANTED TO BE AND I'M HERE AND HAPPY... AT LEAST A SIGNIFICANT CHUNK OF THE TIME!

WHAT ARE THE MESSAGES THAT YOUR PARENTS ARE GIVING YOU? ARE THEY GIVING YOU MIXED MESSAGES: "WE WANT YOU TO DO WHATEVER MAKES YOU HAPPY: BUT IT BETTER INCLUDE COLLEGE, GRADUATE SCHOOL AND WELL BEHAVED LITTLE GRANDCHILDREN FOR US TO ENJOY ON HOLIDAYS!"?

KNOCK OFF THE PARENT BASHING. WE ARE JUST TELLING IT LIKE IT IS: EVERY PARENT WOULD LOVE THEIR CHILD TO GROW UP TO BE THE PRESIDENT! THE JOB COMES WITH LOTS OF EGO SATIS-FACTION AND A FREE PLACE TO STAY WHEN YOU ARE IN WASHING-TON!

BUT WHAT PARENTS REALLY WANT IS TO SEE THAT YOU ARE USING ALL OF YOUR TALENTS AND THAT YOU ARE BEING PRODUC-TIVE. SURE, THEY WANT THE BEST FOR YOU....YOU'LL WANT THE SAME FOR YOUR KIDS. BUT WHAT DO YOU DO WHEN IT APPEARS THAT YOUR PARENTS ARE TRYING TO CONTROL YOU RATHER THAN GUIDE YOU?

FIRST POINT. PARENTS HAVE TO LEARN AS WELL...<u>LIFE IS NOT FAIR</u>. FAIR IS WHERE YOU GO ONCE A YEAR TO SEE THE HORSES AND THE COWS AND THE PIGS AND THE COUNTY'S BIGGEST WATERMELON AND "ZORCAN" THE HERMAPHRODITE! "STEP RIGHT UP!!! YOU WON'T BELIEVE YOUR EYES!!! ONE SIDE OF HIM IS MALE AND THE OTHER SIDE OF HER IS FEMALE!!!!....HURRY! HURRY! NEXT SHOW STARTS IN SEVEN MINUTES!!!!! HURRY! HURRY! DON'T MISS THE SPECTACLE!"

SO PARENTS HAVE TO GET REAL TOO. NOT EVERY KID IS GOING TO BE THE PRESIDENT!

POINT TWO. ALL YOU CAN REALLY DO IS WORK YOUR LITTLE BUTT OFF AT WHATEVER IT IS YOU WANT TO BE. IT WILL TAKE TEN THOUSAND HOURS OF PRACTICE TO BE A BALLERINA! IT WILL TAKE TWENTY YEARS OF STUDY TO BECOME A DOCTOR! (SOME OF US NEEDED EVEN MORE TIME TO "GET IT RIGHT"). NO ONE WILL HIRE A WELDER UNLESS THAT PERSON CAN PROVE THEY HAVE "PAID THEIR DUES" AND THAT THEY KNOW WHAT THEY ARE DOING.

IF EVERYBODY HAD A PH.D.; WHO WOULD DO THE REAL WORK?!?

ON THE OTHER HAND, I GET AN ANXIETY ATTACK EVERY MONDAY MORNING WHEN I LOOK AT THE GARBAGE PILED UP NEXT TO MY GARAGE AND WONDER, "WHO WOULD TAKE OUT MY GARBAGE, IF EVERYBODY HAD A PH.D.? WHO WOULD FIX MY ROOF IF EVERYONE BECAME A LAWYER OR AN ACCOUNTANT?" IT'S A SCARY THOUGHT....I HATE TAKING OUT THE GARBAGE! I'D RATHER CLEAN THE BATHROOM! I'M TERRIFIED OF HEIGHTS....WHO COULD I GET TO CLEAN MY GUTTERS IF EVERYONE BECAME OVER-EDUCATED AND STOPPED DOING THE THINGS WE ALL NEED DONE.

I KNOW MY POINT IS A BIT FUZZY HERE...ALL THAT I AM SAYING IS THAT THE CHOICE OF WHAT YOU WILL BECOME IS YOURS!—AND YOU HAVE TO MAKE A NEW COMMITMENT TO THAT GOAL EVERY DAY OF YOUR LIFE. AND NOW THE CLIMAX!!!!......IF YOUR PARENTS SEE YOU DOING THIS, THEY WILL BE VERY HAPPY, INDEED AND YOUR LIFE WILL BE EASIER....BUT NOT HASSLE FREE.

LIFE IS <u>NOT</u> FAIR...<u>THIS</u> IS A FAIR !!!

FOLLOW ME TO THE NEXT EASY STEP......YOU ARE GOING TO HATE IT, BECAUSE WE ARE GOING TO TALK ABOUT SOMETHING THAT EVERY TEENAGER HATES!

EASY STEP #12

EASY STEP #12

I WANT IT NOW...RIGHT NOW
AND
IF I CAN'T HAVE IT RIGHT NOW...........
I DON'T WANT IT AT ALL!!!!

ALL BUT THE VERY SLOWEST OF YOU ALREADY KNOW WHAT THIS "EASY STEP" IS ALL ABOUT: DISCIPLINE, PATIENCE, DELAYED GRATI-FICATION, HARD WORK, DETERMINATION, MOTIVATION.....ALL THOSE THINGS THAT MADE OUR NATION GREAT. ALL THOSE THINGS THAT MAKE A TEENAGER CRINGE!

YOU KNOW THE STORY: "WHEN I WAS YOUR AGE I WALKED TEN MILES TO SCHOOL, SNOW OVER MY HEAD, UPHILL BOTH WAYS!"

SORRY, MY FRIEND, BUT I'M AFRAID YOU ARE GOING TO FIND ME A BIT HARD- NOSED IN THIS SECTION. I NEVER PROMISED THAT YOU WERE GOING TO LIKE EVERYTHING THAT I HAD TO SAY, DID I?

FOR THE RECORD....MY STORY IS EVEN WORSE. I GOT UP EVERY DAY OF THE YEAR AT 5:30 TO DELIVER NEWSPAPERS, OFTEN IN THREE-FOOT-HIGH SNOW, BEFORE I WENT TO SCHOOL!

I THINK MANY KIDS TODAY ARE SPOILED, SELF-CENTERED, AND ALWAYS LOOKING FOR THE EASIEST WAY OUT. MY ONLY CONSO-LATION IS THINKING THAT THE LAZIEST OF THE LOT ARE GOING TO BE THE ONE'S COLLECTING MY GARBAGE IN FIVE YEARS!

KIDS TODAY HAVE MORE THAN THEY NEED AND KEEP WANTING MORE! (ALRIGHT, I'VE MADE A FEW ENEMIES NOW...BUT REMEM-BER THAT WE ARE AT EASY STEP #12 NOW...YOU SHOULD HAVE EXPECTED TO HEAR A FEW THINGS YOU DIDN'T LIKE WELL BEFORE THIS!) ALSO, I DON'T BLAME YOU. I'LL TAKE ANYTHING THAT IS GIVEN TO ME. ALSO, THE TIMES HAVE CHANGED RADICALLY....I DIDN'T NEED A CAR BECAUSE THERE WERE SO MANY THINGS TO DO IN MY OWN NEIGHBORHOOD AND I HITCH HIKED TO HIGH SCHOOL EVERY DAY—SOMETHING I WOULDN'T LET MY OWN KIDS DO IN THIS DAY AND AGE OF WEIRDOS.

BUT I AM NOT GOING TO DISGUISE WHAT I'M TRYING TO SAY. I THINK A LOT OF YOU HAVE GOTTEN TOO MUCH, TOO EASILY AND I'M NOT SURE WHAT IT IS GOING TO DO TO YOUR ABILITY TO WORK

HARD TOWARD SUCCESS. HOW MANY OF YOU HAVE ANY MONEY YOU HAVE EARNED BY YOURSELF STASHED AWAY IN A BANK FOR COLLEGE OR FOR A RAINY DAY? HOW MANY OF YOU HAVE WAY TOO MUCH FOR WAY TOO LITTLE WORK?

CHECK THE FOLLOWING ITEMS ON THIS "GOODIES LIST" THAT YOU OWN OR YOUR PARENTS PROVIDE YOU:

- [ ] 1. TAPE PLAYER
- [ ] 2. PORTABLE CD PLAYER
- [ ] 3. FANCY BIKE
- [ ] 4. CAR
- [ ] 5. PHONE IN YOUR ROOM
- [ ] 6. VCR
- [ ] 7. NINTENDO
- [ ] 8. COMPUTER
- [ ] 9. ELABORATE AND EXPENSIVE BASEBALL CARDS
- [ ] 10. A MOTORCYCLE
- [ ] 11. A MOTOR BOAT
- [ ] 12. SWIMMING POOL
- [ ] 13. THREE-WHEELER
- [ ] 14. BOOM BOX
- [ ] 15. ELECTRIC KEYBOARD
- [ ] 16. POOL TABLE
- [ ] 17. A VACATION HOME
- [ ] 18. PRIVATE SCHOOL EDUCATION
- [ ] 19. NICE VACATIONS WITH THE FAMILY
- [ ] 20. SOCCER OR TENNIS CAMP
- [ ] 21. RIDING LAWNMOWERS
- [ ] 22. LAWN SERVICE SO YOU DON'T EVEN HAVE TO DO IT
- [ ] 22. HUGE COLLECTIONS OF CDS
- [ ] 23. A ROOM IN THE HOUSE SPECIAL FOR YOU TO PLAY
- [ ] 24. BASKETBALL SET-UP IN YOUR YARD
- [ ] 25. CHARGE ACCOUNT FOR CLOTHES OR EXPENSES
- [ ] 26. A CLOSET FULL OF NICE CLOTHES
- [ ] 27. LAUNDRY SERVICE
- [ ] 28. A CLEANING LADY WHO COMES IN TO HELP
- [ ] 29. SEASON TICKETS TO BASKETBALL OR FOOTBALL
- [ ] 30. A JET SKI
- [ ] 31. SNOW SKIS
- [ ] 32. PARENTS GIVING MONEY FOR GOOD GRADES
- [ ] 33. A SAIL BOAT
- [ ] 34. A RECREATIONAL VEHICLE.
- [ ] 35. MEMBERSHIP IN A TENNIS OR SWIM CLUB

SCORE THREE POINTS FOR EACH ITEM ON THE "GOODIES" LIST.
CHECK YOUR SCORE. HOW DO YOU STAND?

SCORE	RATING
0-10	YOU ARE PROBABLY GETTING BY
11-20	NOT BAD, PROBABLY NOT DEPRIVED
21-30	PRETTY COMFORTABLE, I BET
23-40	COZY
41-50	COMFY
51-60	VERY COMFY
61-70	OUTLANDISH
71-80	OUTRAGEOUS
81-90	INCREDIBLE
91-100	A FOOL TO EVER LEAVE HOME!!!!!
OVER 100	WOW!!!!!!!!!

ALL RIGHT...TAKE YOUR FANGS OUT OF MY ARM! I DIDN'T SAY THAT
YOU ALL HAD TOO MUCH. AND, ANYWAY, IF YOU DO , WHOSE
FAULT IS IT.? ("NO. NO. MOTHER. PLEASE. PLEASE , DON'T GIVE
ME THAT MOPED FOR MY BIRTHDAY——IT WOULD PUT ME WAY
OVER 80 ON THE "GOODIES SCALE" AND I COULDN'T TAKE IT!") YOU
ARE LIKE ANYONE ELSE...YOU ARE GOING TO TAKE WHAT ANYBODY
WANTS TO GIVE YOU.

BUT, WHAT HAPPENS TO THAT WONDERFUL FEELING YOU GET
WHEN YOU WORK HARD AND EARN SOMETHING FOR YOURSELF?
HAVE YOU EVER REALLY DONE IT? EVER WANTED SOMETHING SO
BAD THAT YOU WORKED, SWEATED AND SAVED FOR IT? IF YOU
HAVE, YOU'LL NEVER FORGET THE FEELING. IF YOU HAVEN'T——
WHY NOT?

GO BACK TO PAGE ONE, PARAGRAPH ONE..."LIFE'S A BITCH". THAT,
MY FRIENDS (OR FORMER FRIENDS) IS REALLY THE WAY IT IS. IF
YOU HAVE NEVER HAD TO COME TO GRIPS WITH THAT, YOU ARE
GOING TO BE A BASKET CASE WHEN IT HAPPENS....AND THE
SOONER IT HAPPENS THE BETTER!!!

BUT IT IS NOT SIMPLY A MATTER OF MATERIALISM. HOW MANY
TIMES HAVE YOU GOTTEN A "C" IN A CLASS, WHEN FOR A LITTLE
EXTRA WORK YOU COULD HAVE GOTTEN A "B" AND IF YOU HAD
BEEN WILLING TO WORK YOUR CHOPS OFF IT COULD HAVE BEEN
AN "A"? HOW MANY TIMES HAVE YOU BADGERED YOUR PARENTS
ABOUT A PRIVILEGE, UNTIL THEY FINALLY GAVE IN AND GAVE YOU
YOUR WAY? (HAVE YOU EVER SECRETLY WISHED THAT THEY
WOULD JUST GIVE A STRAIGHT "NO" TO PROVE ONCE AND FOR ALL
THAT THEY ARE TOUGH AND IN CONTROL?)

ANYTHING YOU UNDERTAKE IN LIFE AS A GOAL, AS LONG AS IT IS A HALF-WAY AMBITIOUS GOAL, IS GOING TO REQUIRE HARD WORK AND DELAYED GRATIFICATION. ACCEPT IT! EMBRACE IT! LEARN TO LOVE IT!!! ALTHOUGH THERE ARE NO GUARANTEES IN LIFE, IF YOU EMBRACE IT, YOU'LL HAVE A PRETTY DARNED GOOD SHOT AT BEING A SUCCESS.

DENY THE DIFFICULTY OF LIFE AND I'LL BE SEEING YOU IN A FEW YEARS ON MONDAY MORNING IN YOUR BIG GREEN GARBAGE TRUCK!

EASY STEP #13

A TEAR ROLLED DOWN FROM JENNY'S
EYE, THEN DOWN HER CHEEK AS SHE
SADLY SAID, "THE PROBLEM IS MY MOTHER."

EASY STEP #13

I'VE LOOKED AROUND AND FOUND THE PROBLEM.....

AND IT'S ME!!!

LET ME TELL YOU ABOUT JENNY. SHE WAS TWELVE WHEN I FIRST MET HER. SHE HAD RUN AWAY FROM HOME, GOTTEN WITH A DANGEROUS CROWD AND ENDED UP, ALONE AND SCARED, WHEN A POLICEMAN FOUND HER WALKING THE STREETS IN THE EARLY MORNING. LIKE ALMOST EVERY ADOLESCENT WHO EVER HAD TO GO INTO A HOSPI-TAL..... SHE WAS ANGRY.

SHE STAYED ANGRY FOR FOUR DAYS AND THEN THAT NIGHT I STAYED AT THE HOSPITAL LATE, WITH A NOTION THAT JENNY MIGHT NEED TO TALK. MY HUNCH PROVED RIGHT! HER ANGER WAS STILL THERE BUT AFTER A FEW MINUTES SHE WAS ABLE TO TELL ME, WITH INCREDIBLE CLARITY WHAT IT WAS ABOUT.

I LOOSENED MY TIE AND SHE LOOSENED HER TONGUE.
"THE PROBLEM IS MY MOTHER", SHE BEGAN.

 I THOUGHT TO MYSELF, "WELL, HERE'S ANOTHER TEENAGER NOT READY TO TAKE RESPONSIBILITY FOR HER OWN BEHAVIORS", AND I STARTED THINKING ABOUT GETTING HOME SO THAT I COULD WATCH "MONDAY NIGHT FOOTBALL".

THEN A LITTLE TEAR CAME DOWN OUT OF HER LEFT EYE AND SHE SAID, "YOU KNOW TWO YEARS AGO MY MOTHER HAD A REAL ROUGH TIME. SHE HAD A JOB THAT SHE HATED AND MY FATHER HAD LEFT HER. SHE GOT REAL BAD....REAL DEPRESSED....AND SHE STARTED DRINKING A LOT. I WAS VERY WORRIED ABOUT HER BECAUSE I KNEW HOW BAD SHE WAS, BUT I DIDN'T KNOW WHAT TO DO. I DIDN'T KNOW HOW TO TALK TO HER AND WHEN I TRIED TO IT NEVER SEEMED TO HELP. THEN ONE NIGHT WHEN SHE WAS REAL BAD, SHE TRIED TO KILL HERSELF WITH PILLS.....IF I HADN'T HAD THE STRANGE URGE TO GO INTO HER ROOM IN THE MIDDLE OF THE NIGHT SHE MIGHT HAVE DIED. THE DOCTOR SAID THAT THE AMBULANCE GOT HER TO THE HOSPITAL JUST IN TIME." THEN, SHE STOPPED, ALMOST AS IF SHE FELT SHE WAS TELLING ME TOO MUCH...TRUSTING ME TOO MUCH! BUT SHE CONTIN-UED.

"BUT I'M PROUD OF MY MOTHER. SHE WENT INTO THE HOSPITAL AND SHE DID EVERYTHING THAT IT TOOK TO GET HERSELF BACK

ON HER FEET. SHE LEARNED THAT SHE HAD TO TAKE CARE OF HERSELF AND THAT ONLY SHE COULD BE RESPONSIBLE FOR HER OWN HAPPINESS. SHE LEARNED HOW TO DO THE THINGS FOR HERSELF THAT SHE NEEDED TO DO. WHEN SHE GOT OUT OF THE HOSPITAL SHE WENT TO GROUP THERAPY FOR A LONG TIME AND SHE LEARNED A LOT MORE AND SHE GOT OVER HER DEPRESSION".

THEN JENNY STOPPED AND GAVE ME A LOOK LIKE THAT WISE OLD MAN IN "THE LAST CRUSADE"... (YOU HAVE CHOSEN WELL, MY SON!")... AND THE TEARS CAME AGAIN.

THEN SHE TURNED TO ME AND SAID ,"BUT YOU KNOW THE PROBLEM IS THAT THEY ONLY TAUGHT HER HALF OF WHAT SHE NEEDED TO LEARN. THEY TAUGHT HER THAT SHE HAD TO TAKE CARE OF HERSELF BUT THEY NEVER TAUGHT HER THE OTHER REALLY IMPORTANT PART....THAT SHE WOULD NEVER BE REALLY HAPPY UNTIL SHE LEARNED TO CARE ABOUT OTHERS TOO!

JENNY AND I TALKED FOR A LONG TIME THAT NIGHT. I KNOW I'LL NEVER MISS THAT FOOTBALL GAME, BUT I'LL NEVER FORGET JENNY!

AND SO LET ME USE HER VERY WORDS FOR OUR NEXT IMPORTANT PRINCIPLE:

YOU'LL NEVER BE TRULY HAPPY UNTIL YOU LEARN TO MAKE SOMEONE ELSE HAPPY

HAVE YOU TRIED IT LATELY? HAVE YOU HAD THE EXPERIENCE OF SOMEONE HUGGING YOU AND TELLING YOU HOW MUCH THEY APPRECIATE ALL THAT YOU DO FOR THEM? HAVE YOU HAD ANYONE TELL YOU HOW MUCH OF A DIFFERENCE THAT YOU MAKE TO THEIR LIFE? HAVE YOU GONE AN EXTRA MILE TO MAKE YOUR HOME A PLEASANT PLACE TO BE?

I'M SURE THAT FOR MOST OF YOU...AND HOPEFULLY ALL OF YOU.... THIS HAS HAPPENED WITH A FRIEND. MAYBE A FRIEND THAT YOU HELPED THROUGH A ROUGH TIME. MAYBE, A FRIEND THAT YOU UNDERSTAND BETTER THAN ANY OTHER PERSON IN THIS ENTIRE WORLD. ITS A GREAT FEELING, ISN'T IT?.....QUITE THE OPPOSITE OF WHEN YOU PULLED YOUR FIST OUT OF THAT BUCKET OF WATER TO DISCOVER YOU HADN'T MADE A LASTING INDENTATION!

BEFORE YOU HEAD BACK TO YOUR HOMEWORK OR DRIFT OFF TO SLEEP ON ME, DO THIS PLEASE. GO BACK TO OUR DEFINITION OF A FRIEND AND ASK YOURSELF ONE MORE TIME, "CAN MY PARENT BE MY FRIEND?"

GOOD NIGHT ...SWEET DREAMS!

EASY STEP #14

EASY STEP #14

I'VE LOOKED AROUND AND FOUND THE PROBLEM.....

AND IT'S THEM!!!

AS WE HAVE ALREADY ESTABLISHED, AS IN THE CASE OF JENNY'S MOM, PARENTS AREN'T ALWAYS PERFECT. IN FACT, SOMETIMES THEY ARE A HUGE CHUNK OF THE PROBLEM.

BUT HOW DO YOU TELL YOUR PARENTS THAT THEY ARE PART OF THE PROBLEM?

IN THIS SECTION, I 'M GOING TO TRY MY BEST TO GIVE YOU SOME IDEAS ON HOW TO BREAK THE BAD NEWS TO THEM. TRICKY BUSINESS WITH NO "EL PERFECTO" ANSWERS...BUT LET'S NOT RUN AWAY FROM GIVING IT A SHOT.

TIMING——ALWAYS THINK TIMING FIRST!!! FOURTH QUARTER OF THE SUPERBOWL IS A LOUSY TIME TO TELL YOUR DAD THAT YOU FEEL HE IS DEFICIENT IN SOCIAL GRACES! YOUR MOTHER ISN'T GOING TO BE AT HER BEST FOR TALKING IF SHE'S TRYING TO GET HERSELF READY FOR WORK. MY MOTHER ALWAYS SAID, "NOW, LET'S NOT TELL DAD UNTIL AFTER HE'S EATEN."

WHEN IS THE BEST TIME TO TALK WITH YOUR PARENT? YOU SAY, "UGH!!..... WITH MY PARENT NEVER!"

I SAY, IF YOU HAVE BEEN FOLLOWING ALL THE STEPS AND THEY SEE YOU AS BEING PLEASANT , PRODUCTIVE AND CONSIDERATE OF THEM, ALMOST ANY TIME CAN WORK! TIMING IS USUALLY A MATTER OF SETTING THE MOOD.

PARENTS HATE AMBUSHES! THEY LIKE TO FIGHT ON THEIR OWN TURF, SO TAKE THEM TO THEIR OWN TURF. THEY HATE SURPRISES AND DETEST EMERGENCIES. SO LET THEM KNOW YOU NEED TO TALK TO THEM AND , IF AT ALL POSSIBLE LET THEM THINK THEY ARE SETTING UP THE TIMING. LET'S TAKE AN EXAMPLE OR TWO.

YOU ARE UPSET BECAUSE YOUR PARENTS WON'T TRUST YOU TO

STAY OUT UNTIL MIDNIGHT AFTER THE HOMECOMING GAME. THEY SAY "THE CURFEW IS ELEVEN AND THAT IS IT....TAKE IT OR LEAVE IT!" YOUR FRIENDS CAN ALL STAY OUT UNTIL TWELVE AND YOU THINK IT IS NOT FAIR THAT YOU CAN'T. FIRST, STOP. "FAIR IS WHERE YOU GO ONCE A YEAR TO SEE THE HORSES AND THE COWS........." BUT IT IS WORTH A TRY. HOW DO YOU GET THEM TO LISTEN?

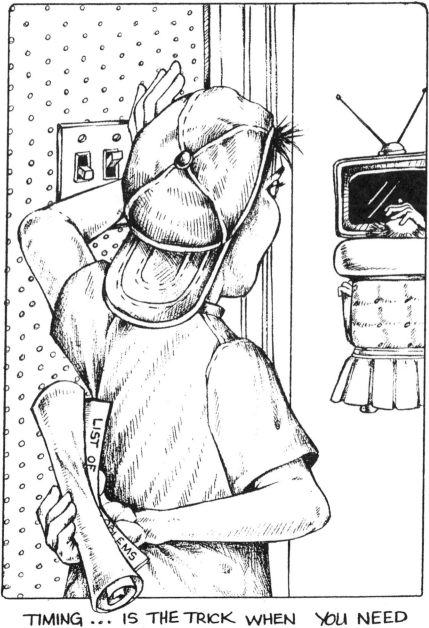

TIMING ... IS THE TRICK WHEN YOU NEED TO TALK WITH YOUR PARENTS.

WHAT ABOUT THIS APPROACH? "MOM, DAD, I REALLY NEED TO TALK TO YOU. WOULD IT BE BETTER FOR US TO DO IT BEFORE I DO MY HOMEWORK OR WOULD IT BE BETTER FOR US TO DO IT AFTER I FINISH MY HOMEWORK?"

"ABRA CADABRA"....YOU ARE A MAGICIAN! YOU HAVE CREATED ONE OF THE GREATEST ILLUSIONS OF ALL TIMES! YOUR PARENTS NOW THINK THEY ARE IN CONTROL! THEY GET TO MAKE THE CHOICE. THEY CAN PICK THE TIME AND THE TURF. NO GUARANTEES THAT YOU ARE GOING TO CONVINCE THEM THAT YOUR IDEA OF CURFEW TIME IS SUPERIOR TO THEIRS....BUT AT LEAST YOU WON'T BE STARTING TO WRESTLE WITH AN ANGRY BEAR.

SPEAKING OF BEARS, THIS MIGHT BE A GOOD PLACE TO TRY OUT THE ANIMAL. "YOU KNOW, MOM, I'M ALMOST FIFTEEN AND YOU MAKE ME FEEL LIKE I'M ONE OF THOSE DOWNY LITTLE DUCKLINGS THAT HAS TO KEEP FOLLOWING ITS MOTHER DUCK AROUND. SOMETIMES, IT FEELS TO ME LIKE YOU DON'T BELIEVE THAT I KNOW HOW TO SWIM YET". BE PREPARED FOR HER TO SAY, "BUT THE WATERS ARE ROUGH OUT THERE...HOME BY ELEVEN, MY DEAR!" BUT AGAIN, SHE MIGHT JUST START TO WONDER TO HER-SELF WHETHER SHE IS BEING TOO PROTECTIVE OF HER DUCKLINGS...AND THAT MIGHT PAY OFF THE NEXT TIME YOU ASK FOR MORE RESPONSIBILITY. THIS, MY FRIENDS, IS WHAT I MEANT EARLIER BY "DELAYED GRATIFICATION"...WORKING TO MAKE THINGS WORK THE NEXT TIME!

WE COULD GIVE MORE EXAMPLES BUT THAT WOULD NOT TAKE US AS FAR AS A LITTLE EXERCISE. GO BACK OVER THESE LAST FEW PARAGRAPHS AND TAKE A LOOK AT HOW WE HAVE USED THE WORDS "NEEDS" AND "FEELING". NOTICE ANYTHING? OK, WHAT IS IT?

YOU, OF COURSE, GIVEN YOUR EXTRAORDINARY IQ AND THIS BEING EASY STEP #14, HAVE NOTED THAT WE HAVE THROWN THESE WORDS AT OUR PARENTS SEVERAL TIMES. "I <u>NEED</u> TO TALK TO YOU." "YOUR MAKE ME <u>FEEL</u> LIKE A DUCKLING." HENCE, WE ARRIVE AT THE NEXT IMPORTANT POINT:

FEELINGS AND NEEDS ARE NOT RIGHT OR WRONG....
THEY JUST ARE!

LET ME GIVE YOU AN EXAMPLE FROM MY OWN VAST PERSONAL EXPERIENCE. JUST A FEW DAYS AGO I CAME INTO MY OFFICE AND TOLD MY SECRETARY THAT I HAD A NEED TO JUMP OUT OF MY OFFICE WINDOW INTO A HUGE VAT OF GREEN JELLO. I TOLD HER THAT I WANTED TO DO IT THE NEXT DAY IF POSSIBLE. MUCH TO MY GREAT SURPRISE, SHE LOOKED AT ME AND SAID, "YOU ARE CRAZY! WHY DON'T YOU GO AND SEE IF ONE OF YOUR PARTNERS HAS AN HOUR FREE TO TALK TO YOU!"

"BUT, YOU DON'T SEEM TO UNDERSTAND. I HAVE THIS NEED", I SAID.

SHE LOOKED AT ME IN HER MERCIFUL WAY AND SAID, "I UNDER-STAND THAT YOU MAY HAVE THAT NEED BUT I'M AFRAID THAT I CANNOT HELP YOU."

I FELT UNDERSTOOD. SHE DIDN'T TRY TO TELL ME I WAS RIGHT OR WRONG....SHE JUST TOLD ME THAT SHE COULD NOT HELP ME TO MEET MY NEEDS. SHE WAS HONEST WITH ME AND I APPRECIATED IT.

LUCKILY, OTHERS IN THE OFFICE NOT ONLY UNDERSTOOD MY NEED BUT WERE ALSO EVEN WILLING TO HELP! ONE HELPED TO MIX THE JELLO AND THE OTHER HELPED ME GET THE WINDOW OPEN WIDE ENOUGH TO JUMP. SO THE NEXT DAY I GOT MY WISH: I WAS ABLE TO DO A ONE AND ONE-HALF GAINER WITH A TRIPLE SOMERSAULT OUT MY WINDOW INTO THE VAT OF GREEN JELLO ..... I WAS EVEN INTERVIEWED ON T.V. (MY BUSINESS FELL OFF CON-SIDERABLY RIGHT AFTER THAT, I MUST, HOWEVER, ADMIT.) (A REMINDER: DO NOT....I REPEAT....DO NOT TRY THIS STUNT IN YOUR OWN OFFICE—I AM A TRAINED PROFESSIONAL. IT CAN BE VERY DANGEROUS IF YOU TRY IT YOURSELF!)

OK, IF I KNOW ME, I'M TRYING TO MAKE A POINT HERE. LET'S TRY TO GRAB HOLD OF IT. MY NEEDS MAY BE ABSURD BUT THEY ARE MINE! TELL ME YOU THINK THEY ARE FAR OUT. TELL ME THEY ARE IDIOTIC. TELL ME THAT YOU CANNOT HELP ME....BUT PLEASE DON'T TELL ME THAT THEY ARE WRONG!. THEY ARE NOT RIGHT OR WRONG..... THEY ARE JUST MY NEEDS. THE SAME IS TRUE OF FEELING. DID YOU EVER SAY TO A FRIEND" I THINK YOU ARE FEEL-ING....." AND HAVE THEM CUT YOU OFF QUICKLY AND SAY, "DON'T

DR. DENNY'S UNDENIABLE DARING DELIGHTFUL (DUMB) DIVE INTO FAME & FORTUNE.

TRY TO TELL ME WHAT MY FEELINGS ARE? HOW DO YOU KNOW
WHAT I'M FEELING?"

SO, YOU NEED TO HELP TEACH YOUR PARENTS ABOUT NEEDS AND
FEELINGS. THEY ARE NOT SCARY. THEY ARE NOT THREATENING.
THEY ARE NOT RIGHT OR WRONG. THEY JUST....... ARE.

LIKEWISE, YOUR PARENTS' THOUGHTS AND FEELINGS ARE NOT
RIGHT OR WRONG..... THEY JUST ARE.

BUT NOT ALL NEEDS AND FEELINGS ARE CREATED EQUALLY. MY
STORY ABOUT THE GREEN JELLO ACTUALLY ENDED QUITE DIFFER-
ENTLY THAN I DESCRIBED. WHAT ACTUALLY HAPPENED WAS THAT
MY SECRETARY CALLED THE POLICE AND THEY CAME IN AND
ARRESTED ME FOR MAKING A PUBLIC SPECTACLE OUT OF MYSELF
AND HOLDING UP TRAFFIC! I WAS MAD AT HER AT THE TIME, BUT I
GUESS I KIND OF THANK HER FOR IT NOW. SAME WITH YOUR
PARENTS! EVEN THOUGH THEY RESPECT YOUR NEEDS AND FEEL-
INGS THEY ARE NOT GOING TO LET YOU DO SOMETHING THAT
THEY THINK WILL BE HURTFUL TO YOU.

IT IS OFTEN VERY DIFFICULT TO CONVEY TO YOUR PARENTS HOW
YOU FEEL WHEN YOU ARE NOT TAKEN SERIOUSLY....THAT IS, WHEN
YOU FEEL THAT YOUR NEEDS AND FEELINGS ARE NOT BEING
RESPECTED. HOW TO BREAK THIS ICE JAM? LET'S TRY TWENTY
MINUTES WORTH OF BRAINSTORMING. BUT FIRST, PLEASE NOTE
SOMETHING. WE HAVE NEVER ONCE TALKED IN THIS SECTION
ABOUT YOUR "WANTS". WE DEALT WITH THEM IN THE LAST
SECTION....AND THEY DIDN'T GET MUCH SYMPATHY FROM ME THEN
AND THEY WON'T GET MUCH FROM YOUR PARENTS EITHER. TALK
NEEDS AND FEELINGS!!!!! I ONCE GOT A FORTUNE COOKIE THAT
SAID, "HELL IS WHERE YOU GO WHERE THEY GIVE YOU EVERY-
THING YOU EVER THOUGHT YOU WANTED" IT HAS TAKEN ME
ALMOST FIFTY YEARS, BUT I THINK I'M STARTING TO UNDERSTAND
WHAT IT MEANS!

LET'S BRAINSTORM......WAYS TO LET YOUR PARENTS KNOW YOUR
NEEDS AND FEELINGS ARE IMPORTANT. GO!

- WRITE SENSITIVE LITTLE SHORT STORIES AND LEAVE THEM
  WHERE YOUR PARENTS CAN SEE THEM...BETTER STILL SHOW
  THEM TO THEM.

- AFTER YOU WATCH A MOVIE WITH YOUR MOM AND DAD, TELL
  THEM HOW IT MADE YOU FEEL.

- AFTER A MOVIE, ASK THEM HOW IT MADE THEM FEEL.

- ASK YOUR MOTHER'S ADVICE ON HOW TO HELP A FRIEND.

- TELL THEM HOW YOU FEEL ABOUT THE HOMELESS.

- TALK ABOUT HOW DISAPPOINTED YOU WERE BY A FRIEND.

- LET YOUR PARENTS KNOW YOU ARE FEELING BLUE...EVEN IF YOU DON'T KNOW WHY (ITS JUST A FEELING, YOU DON'T HAVE TO KNOW "WHY" YOU HAVE IT.)

- TELL YOUR PARENTS YOU ARE THINKING OF TALKING TO THE COUNSELOR AT SCHOOL.

- TRY TO TELL YOUR PARENTS HOW YOU FELT ABOUT A STORY IN THE NEWSPAPER.

- ADMIT THAT YOU ARE CONFUSED ABOUT SOME THINGS AND ' YOU DON'T KNOW WHAT YOU FEEL.

- ASK THEM IF THEY EVER HAD ANY FRIENDS WHO DIED WHEN THEY WERE GROWING UP. HOW DID THEY HANDLE IT?

- LET THEM KNOW THAT YOU WOULD NEVER, NEVER, NEVER BE ABLE TO SHARE <u>ALL</u> YOUR FEELINGS WITH THEM.

- ASK THEM TO TELL YOU THE DIFFERENCE BETWEEN SADNESS AND DEPRESSION. (DON'T EXPECT A CLEVER ANSWER...IT IS A HARDER QUESTION THAN IT SEEMS.)

- TELL YOUR MOTHER THAT YOU WANT TO PRETEND THAT SHE HAS CANCER FOR ONE DAY TO SEE HOW YOU WOULD TREAT HER DIFFERENTLY.

- ASK IF THEY WILL TREAT YOU FOR ONE DAY AS IF THEY THINK THAT THEY WOULD IF YOU HAD "AIDS".

- TELL YOUR PARENTS YOU HAVE ASKED A BLACK FRIEND (OR WHITE OR HISPANIC FRIEND) IF YOU COULD SPEND THE WEEKEND FOR THE EXPERIENCE.

- TELL YOUR DAD HIS SMOKING TERRIFIES YOU.

- DON'T TRY TO LOOK GOOD IN THE MORNING IF YOU CRIED YOURSELF TO SLEEP LAST NIGHT.

- TELL YOUR BIG SISTER YOU ARE JEALOUS OF HER.

- TELL YOUR MOTHER ABOUT YOUR FRIGHTENING NIGHTMARE

- ASK YOUR DAD WHAT IT WAS LIKE IN THE WAR.....(YOU'D BETTER HAVE TIME TO LISTEN BECAUSE HE MAY HAVE A LOT OF STORIES AND HAS ALWAYS BEEN WAITING FOR SOMEONE TO ACT LIKE THEY REALLY CARED).

- LEARN TO FAKE HUMILITY.

- FAKE IT TILL YOU MAKE IT.

NOT BAD. WE COULD GO ON MUCH LONGER. TRY MAKING A LIST WITH A FRIEND (A PARENT?) SOME NIGHT AND SEE HOW MANY YOU CAN GET.

REMEMBER, PARENTS ARE LIKE HORSES, SEALS AND COCKATOOS......THEY ARE TRAINABLE! BUT YOU HAVE TO BE PATIENT AND UNDERSTANDING WITH YOUR PARENTS BECAUSE THIS LISTENING THING MIGHT BE SOMETHING REAL NEW TO THEM....AFTER ALL WHO DID THEY HAVE IN THEIR LIFE TO TEACH THEM ABOUT NEEDS AND FEELINGS?

EASY STEP #15

THE GREAT AMERICAN TAFFY PULL!

EASY STEP #15
THE GREAT AMERICAN TAFFY PULL

WE HAVE TALKED QUITE A BIT ABOUT "PRODUCTIVITY", ESPECIALLY IN SAYING THAT ALL YOU NEED TO MAKE YOUR PARENTS HAPPY IS TO BE PLEASANT, PRODUCTIVE AND TREAT THEM LIKE THEY ARE A MEMBER OF THE HUMAN RACE. BUT, WHAT ARE WE REALLY TALKING ABOUT WHEN WE USE THE TERM PRODUCTIVITY?

AT THE SIMPLEST AND EASIEST LEVEL IT MEANS," WHAT HAVE YOU DONE TO EARN YOUR WAGES TODAY?" (REFER ONCE AGAIN TO YOUR "GOODIES LIST", IF YOU ARE UNSURE ABOUT WHAT YOUR WAGES ARE.) HAVE YOU DONE YOUR JOB WELL ENOUGH?

WHAT IS MY JOB?....... A LOGICAL QUESTION TO ASK YOURSELF!

YOUR JOB IS TO GO TO SCHOOL AND DO YOUR BEST AND TO BE A HAPPY AND USEFUL MEMBER OF YOUR FAMILY. THIS MEANS THAT YOU ARE BEING MOST PRODUCTIVE WHEN YOU GET THE BEST GRADES YOU CAN (PLEASE NOTE WE DIDN'T SAY ..."WHEN YOU GET STRAIGHT "A'S" ON YOUR REPORT CARD!) AND WHEN YOU TAKE OUT THE TRASH AT THE APPROXIMATE TIME YOU ARE ASKED AND WHEN YOU BABYSIT YOUR LITTLE BROTHER WHEN YOUR MOTHER HAS TO GO TO HER AEROBICS CLASS. YOU DO WHAT IS REASONABLE AND WHAT IS EXPECTED OF YOU....AND WITH SOME FREQUENCY YOU STOP AND TELL YOURSELF THAT IN ORDER TO BE REALLY HAPPY YOU NEED TO STOP AND SEE WHAT YOU CAN DO TO HELP SOMEONE ELSE IN THE FAMILY.

SO FAR ....VERY SIMPLE STUFF. YOU ARE MORE PRODUCTIVE IF YOU ARE PASSING YOUR GRADES THAN WHEN YOU ARE FAILING. YOU ARE GOING TO BE MORE PRODUCTIVE WHEN YOU KEEP THE GRASS CUT WITHOUT BEING BADGERED THAN WHEN YOU LET IT GROW UP TO YOUR ARMPITS. IF YOU AREN'T SMART ENOUGH TO HAVE FIGURED OUT THIS BY NOW YOUR BRAIN MUST LOOK A LITTLE LIKE SWISS CHEESE.

BUT LET'S TAKE A JUMP TO A HIGHER LEVEL. CONSULT THE FOLLOWING LIST TO START YOU THINKING:

ANIMAL SPECIES	AGE OF INDEPENDENCE
AMOEBA	0.1 SECOND
STAR FISH	TWO MINUTES
JELLY FISH	SIX MINUTES
GOLD FISH	ELEVEN MINUTES
HERMIT CRAB	SEVENTEEN MINUTES
RATTLE SNAKE	TWENTY-FOUR MINUTES
TORTOISE	THIRTY-SEVEN MINUTES
GREEN LIZARD	FIFTY-NINE MINUTES
CROCODILE	ONE HOUR
WHITE MOUSE	TWO AND-ONE-HALF HOURS
BEAVER	SIX HOURS
HYENA	THIRTY-NINE HOURS
MANATEE	FOUR DAYS
PLATYPUS	THIRTEEN AND ONE-HALF DAYS
DOLPHIN	THREE AND ONE-HALF WEEKS
WARTHOG	NINE AND ONE-HALF WEEKS
GAZELLE	FIVE MONTHS
BABOON	ELEVEN AND ONE-THIRD MONTHS
BLUE WHALE	ONE AND ONE-HALF YEARS
GORILLA	FIVE AND ONE-HALF YEARS
RHINO	FIVE AND ONE-HALF YEARS
ELEPHANT	SEVEN YEARS

AT WHAT AGE DO THESE CRITTERS TURN TO MOM AND SAY..."HEY, MA...I'M OUTTA HERE!"....

{THIS RESEARCH REPRESENTS TWENTY-MINUTES WORTH OF EFFORT. RESEARCH WAS CARRIED OUT IN MY KITCHEN AND ALL "AGES OF INDEPENDENCE", HEREIN DEFINED ARE THE AGE AT WHICH THE OFFSPRING LOOKS AT ITS MOTHER AND SAYS, "HEY, I DON'T NEED YOU. I AM OUTTA HERE!!!", AND ARE, OF COURSE, APPROXIMATIONS}

ONCE AGAIN, YOU ARE REMINDED....I AM A TRAINED PROFESSIONAL. DO NOT...I REPEAT.... DO NOT ATTEMPT THIS RESEARCH IN YOUR OWN KITCHEN!

OK. NOW THE IMPORTANT QUESTION: WHAT IS THE AGE AT WHICH THE AVERAGE AMERICAN HOMO SAPIENS TURNS TO ITS MOTHER AND SAYS, "I'M OUTTA HERE."?

WHAT ARE YOUR GUESSES? EIGHTEEN, WHEN THE LAW DECLARES YOU TO BE AN ADULT....AND YOU GRADUATE FROM CHILDREN'S COURT TO THE REAL THING! TWENTY-ONE WHEN YOUR STATE SAYS YOU CAN HAVE A BEER WITH YOUR HAMBURGER? TWENTY-THREE, WHEN YOU GRADUATE FROM COLLEGE? TWENTY-SIX WHEN YOU MARRY? TWENTY- EIGHT WHEN YOU COMPLETE GRADUATE SCHOOL? THIRTY- FIVE, WHEN YOUR PARENTS KICK YOU OUT OF YOUR BEDROOM?

WELL, ON THE ABOVE LIST, DID YOU NOTE THAT THE "AGE OF SEPARATION" WAS INVERSELY RELATED TO THE RATIO OF BRAIN MASS TO TOTAL BODY VOLUME AND DIRECTLY RELATED TO THE SCORE ON THE "GOODIES LIST". IN OTHER WORDS, IF YOU REALLY HAVE SCORED OVER A SEVENTY-FIVE ON THE SCALE, YOUR PARENTS WOULD HAVE TO BOOT YOU OUT OF THE HOUSE TO GET YOU MOVING.

A COUPLE OF DAYS AGO, ONE OF MY FRIENDS CAME UP TO ME, ALL AGLOW. I ASKED HIM WHAT HE WAS SO EXCITED ABOUT AND HE SAID, " MARTHA AND I JUST BOUGHT A NEW HOME.... AND IT ONLY HAS ONE BEDROOM!"

SO WHAT IS THE POINT OF THIS? YOUR PRODUCTIVITY....YOUR JOB AS AN ADOLESCENT... IS TO BREAK AWAY FROM YOUR PARENTS. TO BE ABLE TO SAY, " HEY, I'M OUTTA HERE." ....AND TO BE PRODUCTIVE ENOUGH TO PULL IT OFF.

LET'S STRESS THE IMPORTANCE OF THIS BY PRESENTING IT AS
YET ANOTHER "GREAT TRUTH" :

YOUR PARENTS HAD YOU SO
THEY COULD GET RID OF YOU

PERHAPS, IT IS KIND OF HARD TO SWALLOW IN THIS FORM....BUT
ITS NOT A LIE!!

AS MY FRIEND WHO WAS SO EXCITED ABOUT THIS NEW ONE BED-
ROOM HOUSE PUT IT, "DON'T GET ME WRONG, I LOVE MY KIDS:
THEY'RE WONDERFUL. BUT, FOR THE LAST TEN YEARS I FEEL LIKE
I'VE BEEN IN ONE HUGE TAFFY-PULL. THEY STRETCH OUT AND
PULL AWAY LIKE THEY ARE GOING TO BREAK OFF ON THEIR OWN
AND THE NEXT TIME I LOOK AROUND ONE OF THEM HAS PULLED
THEMSELVES BACK AND IS STUCK ALL OVER ME AGAIN!"

IS THIS AN UNLOVING FATHER OR JUST A FATHER WHO HAS HAD
CHILDREN WHO HAVEN'T HAD THE DISCIPLINE AND DETERMINA-
TION TO REACH THEIR FULL PRODUCTIVITY?

I DON'T KNOW THE ANSWER FOR SURE.... BUT I KNOW THAT WHEN
HIS KIDS COME TO VISIT THE NEXT TIME THEY'LL BE STAYING AT
THE NEARBY ECONO LODGE!

ARE YOU DOING EVERYTHING THAT YOU CAN TO REACH YOUR
FULL PRODUCTIVE POTENTIAL? I HOPE SO, BECAUSE IT REALLY IS
LIKE THE COMMERCIAL FOR AUTO PARTS SAYS:

PAY ME NOW......OR PAY ME LATER!

THE LESS YOU HAVE WORKED AT IT , THE HARDER IT WILL BE!
YOUR MAJOR JOB AS AN ADOLESCENT IS TO BREAK AWAY FROM
YOUR PARENTS....AND IT IS SUPPOSED TO BE A DIFFICULT
STRUGGLE. YOU ARE NOT AN AMOEBA! YOU ARE NOT AN ORAN-
GUTAN. YOU, THANK GOD, ARE A HUMAN....WITH ALL THE DIFFI-
CULTY THAT GOES WITH YOUR SPECIES. NO OTHER SPECIES HAS
AS DIFFICULT A TIME "BREAKING AWAY" AS WE DO.

ONE OF THE WAYS THAT IT IS MADE POSSIBLE AT ALL IS BECAUSE
OF THE BATTLE THAT PARENTS AND ADOLESCENTS ARE SUP-
POSED TO HAVE WITH EACH OTHER. IF KIDS AND PARENTS WERE

DESIGNED TO LIVE TOGETHER FOR LIFE THERE WOULD BE NO PURPOSE IN DOING ALL THOSE THINGS THAT PARENTS MUST DO TO GET READY TO KICK YOU OUT OF THEIR HOUSE! THERE WOULD BE NO TAFFY PULL....THERE WOULD JUST BE A HUGE LUMP OF MELTED SUGAR IN THEIR LIVING ROOM FLOOR!

IF YOU'RE NOT AN . . . AMOEBA OR AN ORANGUTAN . . . YOU MUST BE HUMAN (WITH ALL THE DIFFICULTIES THAT GO WITH IT.)

EASY STEP #16

OK. TAKE NOTES. NOW, WHO ARE YOU
MY YOUNG FRIEND?

EASY STEP #16

WHAT A BUMMER.......
NO MATTER HOW HARD I TRY, I JUST
KEEP SCREWING UP!

GET YOURSELF READY....THIS IS ANOTHER ONE OF THOSE SEC-
TIONS WHERE YOU ARE GOING TO START LIKING ME AGAIN. (PART
OF WHAT TOOK A LONG TIME FOR ME GROWING UP WAS TO LEARN
THAT YOU COULD BE ANGRY AT SOMEONE, BUT STILL RESPECT
THEM .... AND EVEN GROW TO LIKE THEM.)

I'VE BEEN PRETTY ROUGH ON YOU....TELLING YOU THAT A LOT OF
YOU ARE SPOILED AND LAZY...YOU'VE GOT REASON TO BE AN-
NOYED AT ME, ESPECIALLY IF THAT ISN'T YOU AND YOU STILL
AREN'T GETTING ALONG VERY WELL WITH YOUR PARENTS.

I KNOW THIS HAPPENS, EVEN WHEN PARENTS AREN'T BAD
GUYS...THAT IS, THEY ARE NOT THE REAL PROBLEM EITHER. THEY
ARE TRYING THEIR BEST AND SO ARE YOU, BUT FOR SOME REA-
SON IT JUST ISN'T WORKING AND YOU ARE VERY UNHAPPY ....
SOMETIMES SO MISERABLE THAT NO ONE—NOT EVEN YOUR BEST
FRIEND IN THE WORLD— HAS ANY IDEA OF HOW BADLY YOU ARE
HURTING ON THE INSIDE! IN FACT, YOU HAVE COVERED IT UP SO
WELL THAT YOUR FRIENDS KEEP CALLING YOU FOR HELP AND
ADVICE, BECAUSE EVERYONE THINKS YOU ARE SO COOL AND YOU
HAVE IT SO TOGETHER.

YOU ARE A FAKE AND YOU ARE THE <u>ONLY</u> ONE WHO KNOWS IT.
YOU ARE PUTTING ON A FACE AND PLAYING A ROLE. WHAT ROLE
ARE YOU PLAYING?

JOHN WAYNE	"I'M SO TOUGH, NOTHING BOTHERS ME!
DEAR ABBEY	"KEEP THOSE CALLS AND LETTERS COMING IN!"
PITIFUL PEARL	"I'M NOT ANGRY, I'M JUST HURT!"
JACK THE RIPPER	"JUST STAY OUT OF MY WAY, BUSTER."
BABY DOLL	"IF I CAN'T FIND LOVE AT HOME....."
SPONGEHEAD	"IT DON'T MATTER, MAN, EVERTHING'S COOL"
RUNAROUND SUE	"IT DOESN'T MATTER WHAT PEOPLE SAY ABOUT ME."
BOOKWORM BILLY	"I'LL STUDY SO HARD....
FRIED BRAIN FRED	"YA GOTTA KILL THE PAIN, MAN"
ARNOLD S.	"YOU JUST GOTTA MOW 'EM ALL DOWN"

THERE ARE A MILLION ROLES. PICK ANY, THEY ALL WORK THE SAME. ONE DAY YOU CAN PLAY ONE AND THE NEXT DAY YOU CAN PLAY ANOTHER. EVERYONE CAN PLAY. BUT REMEMBER:

THE REASON FOR THE GAME IS TO HIDE THE PAIN!

SO LET'S GET REAL! NO MORE GAME PLAYING. I'LL BE WHAT I AM AND YOU BE WHAT YOU ARE. I'LL PUT ON MY PSYCHIATRIST'S HAT (AFTER ALL IT TOOK ME TWENTY YEARS TO EARN IT...NOT COUNTING KINDERGARTEN AND THE EXTRA YEAR I HAD TO SPEND IN MEDICAL SCHOOL BECAUSE I FLUNKED MY FIRST YEAR.) AND YOU JUST LIE UPON MY COUCH AND BE WHOEVER YOU REALLY ARE.

THAT'S GOOD. JUST RELAX NOW. WE HAVE A FIFTY- MINUTE SESSION AND THEN I'LL HAVE TO SEE MY NEXT PATIENT! YOU START AND TELL ME WHERE IT HURTS....MY JOB IS TO LISTEN, BUT THAT IS NOT ENOUGH——YOU ARE HERE BECAUSE NOTHING YOU ARE TRYING IS WORKING AND YOU WANT HELP....NOT JUST SOMEONE TO LISTEN AND THEN SEND YOU ON YOUR WAY!

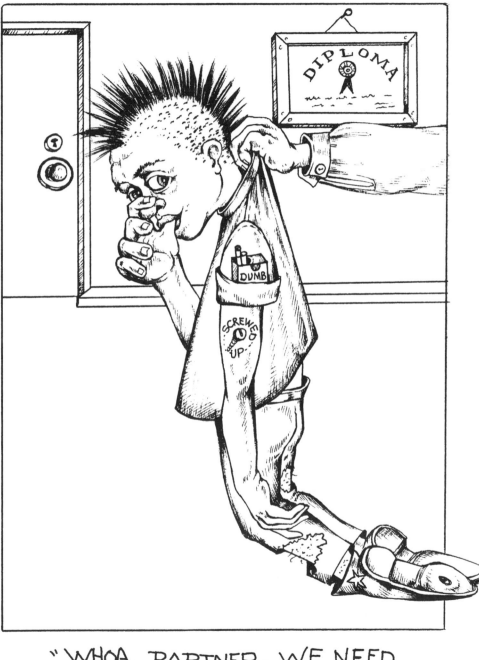

"WHOA, PARTNER. WE NEED TO TALK!"

AS I'M LISTENING TO YOU, YOU HAVE TO UNDERSTAND I'M THINKING...EVEN IF, AT TIMES, YOU THINK I'M NODDING OFF ON YOU! LET ME TELL YOU WHAT I'M THINKING: "DOES THIS SOUND LIKE A PRETTY NEAT KID OR IS THIS KID ALL SCREWED UP? IS THIS KID BLAMING EVERYONE ELSE FOR HER PROBLEMS OR DOES SHE OR HE REALLY HAVE A VERY DIFFICULT SITUATION? IS THIS KID'S SUPEREGO** WOUND TOO TIGHT OR IS IT TOO LOOSE? IS THE PROBLEM WITH THE KID OR WITH HIS PARENTS? IS THERE ANY CHANCE THIS KID IS THINKING ABOUT SUICIDE AS A PERMANENT SOLUTION TO A BUNCH OF TEMPORARY PROBLEMS? (YOU ARE DARNED RIGHT I 'M GOING TO ASK YOU THIS QUESTION STRAIGHT UP IF I HAVE ANY CONCERNS ABOUT HOW TIGHTLY YOU ARE WOUND AT THE MOMENT.) IS THIS YOUNGSTER HAVING TROUBLE IN SCHOOL BECAUSE OF DIFFICULTY CONCENTRATING? IS THIS YOUNG PERSON IN FRONT OF ME TERRIBLY DEPRESSED? DO THIS ADOLESCENT'S PARENTS SEEM LIKE THE KIND WHO ARE GOING TO BE ABLE TO DO WHAT IT TAKES TO IMPROVE THINGS AT HOME? DOES THIS KID SEEM TO LIKE ME ENOUGH THAT HE CAN RELATE TO ME SO THAT I HAVE A CRACK AT BEING ABLE TO HELP HIM?

** IF THE READER DOES NOT KNOW THE MEANING OF THIS FANCY FREUDIAN TERMINOLOGY...........THAT IS TOO BAD!

SO, THESE ARE THE KINDS OF QUESTIONS THAT I'M ASKING MY-SELF. (ISN'T IT THRILLING TO DIVE INTO THE MIND OF A WORLD FAMOUS PSYCHIATRIST AT WORK....WELL, THEY HAVE HEARD OF ME IN THREE STATES!)

BEFORE YOU LEAVE MY OFFICE THERE ARE A FEW THINGS I WANT TO KNOW FOR SURE:

- WHAT ARE THE CHANCES OF THIS KID EVER COMING BACK TO TALK TO ME AGAIN? WE ALL ONLY GET ONE CHANCE TO GIVE A FIRST IMPRESSION, EVEN WORLD RENOWNED-PSYCHIATRISTS!

- HOW MUCH PAIN IS THIS ADOLESCENT IN?.....CAN HE BE EXPECTED TO BE ABLE TO ENDURE IT UNTIL I SEE HIM AGAIN?

- WHAT HAS THIS YOUNG PERSON GOT GOING FOR HIM...HOW STRONG IS HE?

- IS THERE SOMETHING I CAN DO TO HELP RIGHT NOW?

- IS THERE SOMETHING I MUST DO RIGHT NOW?

FORTUNATELY, THERE ARE VERY FEW CASES WHERE WE ARE FACING A TRUE EMERGENCY. YOU HAVE BEEN MISERABLE FOR QUITE A WHILE BEFORE YOU HAVE COME TO ME AND YOU HAVE BEEN DEALING WITH IT PRETTY WELL AND YOU AGREE WE ARE NOT GOING TO BE ABLE TO CLEAN UP THE WHOLE MESS IN ONE SESSION. YOU SEEM TO GIVE SOME HINTS THAT YOU THINK I'M SORTA "OK" AND I DON'T THINK YOU ARE THE BIGGEST JERK I'VE EVER MET. YOU SAY , IF FACT YOU MIGHT NOT MIND COMING BACK TO SEE ME AGAIN. HERE'S WHAT I WANT <u>YOU</u> TO KNOW BEFORE YOU LEAVE:

- YOUR PROBLEMS ARE <u>REAL</u> AND THEY ARE <u>SERIOUS</u> AND <u>VERY MUCH WORTH MY TIME</u>!

- <u>I</u> KNOW WHAT I'M DOING; BUT I CAN'T DO IT WITH OUT YOU.(AND YOUR PARENTS!)

- ALTHOUGH YOUR PROBLEMS ARE BIG, TOGETHER WE CAN FIND ANSWERS.

- AND YOU SURE AREN'T CRAZY!

- I'M ON YOUR SIDE, EVEN THOUGH I'M GOING TO KICK YOUR BUTT AT TIMES.

BEFORE YOU GO OUT MY DOOR, THERE IS ONE OTHER BIG THING THAT I WANT TO ACCOMPLISH.....I WANT TO HAVE SOME IDEA ABOUT WHETHER YOU ARE DEPRESSED?

I WISH I COULD SAY THAT, FORTUNATELY, THIS WAS ALWAYS AN <u>EASY STEP</u>, BUT QUITE FRANKLY IT ISN'T. ARE YOU JUST HAVING A ROUGH TIME AT THE MOMENT OR IS THERE MORE TO IT THAN THAT?

ADULTS SOMETIMES GET DEPRESSED FOR ABSOLUTELY NO "REA-SON" AT ALL. EVERYTHING IN THEIR LIFE SEEMS TO BE GOING WELL...NO CRISES AT WORK, FAMILY LIFE IS FINE, GOLF GAME IS BETTER THAN EVER, BUT FOR SOME REASON THEY JUST GET THE "BLUES" AND THE "BLAHS". NOTHING SEEMS LIKE FUN. NOTHING IS WORTH THE EFFORT IT TAKES. IT'S HARD TO SLEEP. EVERYTHING BUGS THEM. THEY ARE IRRITABLE, SAD, UNFRIENDLY AND THEY DON'T EVEN LIKE TO BE AROUND THEMSELVES. THEY HIDE IN THEIR ROOM BECAUSE THERE IS NOTHING THEY FEEL LIKE DOING AND THEY DON'T WANT TO "INFLICT" THEMSELVES UPON THEIR FRIENDS. THEY THINK IT WILL GO AWAY, BUT IT JUST DOESN'T.

IN MEDICINE WE HAVE COME TO REALIZE THAT SOME ADULTS HAVE CHEMICAL IMBALANCES IN THEIR BRAIN AND THAT THEIR DEPRESSION IS AS MUCH OF A BIOLOGICAL ILLNESS AS DIABETES OR HIGH CHOLESTEROL. WE ARE ALSO MILES AHEAD OF WHERE WE WERE ONLY A FEW SHORT YEARS AGO AND WE NOW HAVE MEDICATIONS, WHICH , AFTER ALL, ARE THEMSELVES NOTHING BUT FANCY CHEMICALS, THAT CAN BALANCE THE CHEMICAL IMBALANCE.

IF ADULTS CAN HAVE A CHEMICAL IMBALANCE WHY CAN'T AN ADOLESCENT?

NOW, BEFORE YOU RUN OFF AND TELL YOUR MOTHER THAT YOU STOLE THE HUB CAPS BECAUSE YOU HAD A "CHEMICAL IMBALANCE", LET ME ADD THE NEXT IMPORTANT PRINCIPLE:

YOU CAN HAVE TICKS AND FLEAS AT THE SAME TIME!

BY THIS I MEAN THAT YOU CAN HAVE A "CHEMICAL IMBALANCE" AND BE A JERK AT THE SAME TIME.   IN FACT, IF YOU WANT TO ACCEPT THE GOOD AND THE BAD OF THE "CHEMICAL IMBALANCE" THEORY YOU HAVE TO REALIZE THAT BEING A JERK MAY ACTUALLY CAUSE A CHEMICAL IMBALANCE! ABOVE I SAID, <u>SOME</u> ADULTS HAVE A PURE CHEMICAL IMBALANCE, BUT IN ACTUAL FACT MOST ADULTS ARE DEPRESSED BECAUSE THINGS ARE NOT GOING WELL IN THEIR LIVES.... THEY ARE NOT MANAGING THEIR LIVES WELL:

IF THIS IS TRUE OF ADULTS, SHOULD IT NOT ALSO BE TRUE OF TEENS?

BUT, BEFORE YOU LEAVE MY OFFICE I WOULD WANT TO KNOW ABOUT YOU. ARE YOU SO STUCK IN THE MUD THAT TALK ALONE IS NOT GOING TO HELP PULL YOU OUT? DO I NEED TO TALK TO YOUR PARENTS, FIRST TO SEE IF DEPRESSION RUNS IN THE FAMILY (IT CAN BE INHERITED MUCH THE SAME WAY DIABETES IS.) AND SECOND TO TELL THEM THAT AS HARD AS YOU ARE TRYING, YOUR GEARS MAY BE STUCK IN REVERSE BECAUSE OF DEPRESSION...... PERHAPS A DEPRESSION SO SERIOUS THAT WE SHOULD CONSIDER HELPING YOU OUT WITH SOME MEDICATION.

THERE ARE MANY OTHER REASONS WHY, TRY AS YOU MIGHT, YOU MIGHT NOT BE AS HAPPY AS YOU COULD BE. WE'LL BE TALKING ABOUT THESE IN BITS AND PIECES IN OUR NEXT EASY STEPS, BUT LET'S GO TO THE NEXT STEP, ANOTHER ONE I KNOW YOU'LL JUST HATE AT FIRST.... TILL YOU COME TO LOVE IT AND ACCEPT IT.

ARE YOU STUCK IN THE MUD SO DEEP; TALK ALONE ISN'T GOING TO PULL YOU OUT ?!?

DEPRESSION . . .

EASY STEP# 17

MR. FEATHERSTONE'S DILEMMA

NO PSYCHIATRIST, IN MY HUMBLE OPINION, COULD KEEP HIS SANITY JUST SEEING ADOLESCENTS THE WHOLE DAY. I'M NO DIFFERENT.....I LIKE TO TALK TO AN OCCASIONAL ADULT FOR VARIETY.

LAST WEEK A DISTINGUISHED-APPEARING GENTLEMAN, LET'S CALL HIM MR. SANDERSON BUTLER FEATHERSTONE III, (SANDERSON BUTLER FEATHERSTONE III, TO HIS CLOSEST FRIENDS!) CAME TO MY OFFICE. HE TOLD ME THAT HE HAD PUT OFF COMING TO A PSYCHIATRIST FOR OVER A YEAR, IN SPITE OF THE FACT THAT HE KNEW HE HAD A NUMBER OF PROBLEMS WHICH WERE GETTING WORSE ALL THE TIME. HE SAID, "I JUST COULDN'T COME IN TO SEE YOU, BECAUSE I WAS AFRAID THAT SOMEONE WHO WORKS FOR ME MIGHT SEE ME! YOU SEE I AM THE PRESIDENT OF A BANK AND I CANNOT AFFORD TO LET ANYONE SEE ME IN A PLACE LIKE THIS!"

HE THEN TOLD ME ABOUT HIS PROBLEMS. "IT SEEMS I CAN'T MAKE ANYONE HAPPY ANY MORE. AT HOME MY WIFE SAYS THAT IT'S MY FAULT THAT SHE IS SO MISERABLE; AND SHE IS RIGHT IN A WAY....I HAVE NOT BEEN A VERY GOOD HUSBAND. AND MY SON IS ON DRUGS AND I KNOW THE REASON....I WANTED HIM TO GO TO COL-LEGE AND FINALLY AFTER A FEW YEARS I FORCED HIM TO DO IT, BUT HE NEVER FINISHED BECAUSE I PUT TOO MUCH PRESSURE ON HIM AND HE HAD TO DROP OUT. MY DAUGHTER IS WONDERFUL, BUT I'M AFRAID THAT SHE IS VERY TIMID AND SHY AND THAT SHE WILL NEVER FIND A HUSBAND BECAUSE SHE IS AFRAID OF ALL MEN. I THINK THAT SHE FEARS THAT THEY WILL ALL TREAT HER LIKE I HAVE TREATED HER....VERY DOMINEERING , I AM EMBAR-RASSED TO SAY."

HE CONTINUED ON WITH HIS STORY." I STARTED THE BANK THIRTY YEARS AGO WHEN IT WAS EASY TO BE A MANAGER, BUT NOW I HATE IT AND AM NOT VERY GOOD AT DEALING WITH MY EMPLOY-EES SO I DO THE THINGS I LIKE TO DO LIKE GOING TO MEETINGS AND I AM INVOLVED IN A LOT OF CIVIC ACTIVITIES...BUT, TO TELL YOU THE TRUTH,I DO IT MOSTLY BECAUSE IT IS EXPECTED OF ME IN MY POSITION AND IT HELPS THE BANK, BUT I DON'T REALLY LIKE DOING IT."

I ASKED HIM WHAT HE LIKED DOING BEST AND HE REPLIED, "TO TELL YOU THE TRUTH, I'VE STOPPED DOING JUST ABOUT EVERY-THING I USED TO LIKE, BECAUSE OF ALL THE RESPONSIBILITIES THAT I HAVE. I USED TO HAVE A FLOWER GARDEN, BUT I DON'T EVEN DO THAT ANY MORE!"

I THOUGHT TO MYSELF, "WHAT A SAD MAN! HE SEEMS TO HAVE EVERYTHING HE COULD EVER WANT, BUT HE ENJOYS SO LITTLE." THEN, SOMETHING STRUCK ME AND I ASKED THIS DISTINGUISHED-APPEARING BANK PRESIDENT WITH HIS GREY HAIR AND PIN-STRIPED, GREY, THREE-PIECE SUIT WHETHER HE KNEW WHAT THE NUMBER ONE CAUSE OF DEPRESSION WAS.

HE HESITATED FOR ONLY THE BRIEFEST SECOND, AND SAID CONFI-DENTLY, AS I SUPPOSE BANK PRESIDENTS HAVE LEARNED TO DO, "WELL, I GUESS IT'S LETTING PEOPLE TAKE ADVANTAGE OF YOU."

THE MAN HAD BEEN QUITE INTIMIDATING TO ME, BUT I TRIED NOT TO SHOW IT AND I JUST SAID, "NO."

THEN HE TRIED AGAIN, "WELL MAYBE IT'S AN UNHAPPY MARRIAGE. DORIS AND I HAVEN'T REALLY COMMUNICATED WITH EACH OTHER IN YEARS."

I STAYED CALM ON THE OUTSIDE, AS I SAW HIM GETTING RED IN THE FACE....BANK PRESIDENTS ARE <u>NOT</u> USED TO BEING TOLD THAT THEY ARE WRONG TWICE IN A ROW ! I SAID "NOPE, TRY AGAIN!"

AT THIS POINT HE STARTED TO STAMMER AND LOSE HIS COMPO-SURE, "WELL, THEN IT IS TAKING ON TOO MUCH RESPONSIBILITY", HE SAID, CONFIDENT THAT HE HAD TO BE RIGHT ON THIS THIRD ATTEMPT.

I STARED HIM DOWN AND SAID, "NO, MR. FEATHERSTONE. WRONG AGAIN!'"

AT THIS POINT HIS FACE WAS PURPLE AND HE SAID, "WELL SINCE YOU SEEM TO KNOW THE ANSWER, WHY DON'T YOU TELL ME?"

I KNEW THAT I HAD MADE ONE OF THE GAMBLES OF MY LIFE AND THAT I WAS IN TOO DEEP TO TURN AROUND. I GATHERED MY COURAGE AND SAID, "WELL, IN MY EXPERIENCE THE NUMBER ONE CAUSE OF DEPRESSION IS STUPIDITY!"

I DON'T MIND TELLING YOU THAT THAT MAN GAVE ME ONE OF THE NASTIEST LOOKS I HAVE EVER HAD AND THEN HE SAID, "YOUNG MAN , ARE YOU TELLING ME THAT I AM STUPID?" AS HE PICKED HIMSELF HALF-WAY OUT OF HIS CHAIR, HIS FACE NOW CANDY APPLE RED.

I SAID, "NO, I'M ONLY SAYING THAT YOUR <u>THINKING</u> IS STUPID!"

HE STORMED OUT OF THE OFFICE AND SAID, " I DON'T NEED TO PAY A HUNDRED DOLLARS AN HOUR TO BE TOLD I'M STUPID."

I SAT THERE FOR A FEW MINUTES THINKING ABOUT HOW MR. FEATHERSTONE III COULD SINGLE-HANDEDLY ASPIRE TO DESTROY MY CAREER.

IF YOU ARE THINKING GARBAGE:
YOU ARE GOING TO END-UP "LIVING" GARBAGE!

A FEW MINUTES LATER THERE WAS A GENTLE KNOCK ON MY DOOR. IT WAS THE BANKER. "YOU KNOW I GOT ALL THE WAY OUT TO MY CAR, CURSING UP A STORM ALL THE WAY AND THEN IT DAWNED ON ME....YOU ARE RIGHT! I'VE BEEN PRETTY DARNED STUPID FOR A LONG TIME." HE LOOKED RATHER SHEEPISH AND SAID, "WOULD YOU MIND IF I USED THE REST OF MY HOUR TO TALK?"

IT IS EASY FOR US TO SEE THE STUPIDITY IN OTHERS. WHY DID THIS BANKER WAIT SO LONG TO GET HELP? WHY DID HE THINK IT WAS HIS JOB TO PLEASE EVERYBODY AND WHY, WHEN SOMETHING WENT WRONG, WAS HE SO EAGER TO BLAME HIMSELF? WHY DID HE STOP DOING ALL THE THINGS THAT USED TO BRING HIM PLEA-SURE? WHY DID HE FEEL A DUTY TO DO THINGS JUST FOR HIS IMAGE? YOU COULD ALSO ASK YOURSELF WHY WAS I SO STUPID AS TO FEEL INTIMIDATED BY HIM IN THE FIRST PLACE? I'M SURE THAT ALL OF YOU CAN IDENTIFY A NUMBER OF OTHER THINGS THAT HE DID STUPIDLY AND PERHAPS, IF YOU WORKED AT IT, EVEN A FEW MORE STUPID THINGS THAT I DID! I'M CONFIDENT YOU CAN DO THIS BECAUSE IT IS SO EASY TO PICK UP ON THE STUPID THINK-ING OF OTHERS.

BUT WHAT ABOUT OURSELVES? WHEN WAS THE LAST TIME YOU CAUGHT YOURSELF IN THE MIDDLE OF SAYING OR THINKING SOMETHING INCREDIBLY DUMB? AS YOU MIGHT IMAGINE BY NOW I COULD EASILY DRAW UP FIVE PAGES OF EXAMPLES OF STUPID THINKING THAT KIDS GET INTO. I'M GOING TO PASS ON THAT, AS YOU FOLKS ARE THE EXPERTS ON THAT ONE!!!

BUT THE SIMPLE FACT IS THAT SOME THINKING IS SUCH GOBBLE-DYGOOK THAT ALL IT CAN DO IS LEAD TO OUR UNHAPPINESS.

"I'LL JUST DIE IF STUART DOESN'T ASK ME TO THE DANCE." " I'M NOT GOING TO TALK TO MY FATHER IF HE DOESN'T LET ME OFF RE-STRICTION TO GO TO THE BASKETBALL GAME THIS WEEKEND." "MY PARENTS ARE SO MEAN — THERE IS NO SENSE EVEN TRYING TO PLEASE THEM!"

STOP AND AND PONDER FOR A FEW SECONDS WHAT YOU ARE THINKING. IF YOU ARE THINKING GARBAGE; YOU ARE GOING TO END UP LIVING GARBAGE. YOU WANT YOUR PARENTS TO STOP AND LISTEN TO YOU AND RESPECT YOU. DO THE SAME FOR YOUR SELF—STEP BACK AND LISTEN HARD TO YOURSELF AND ASK YOURSELF, " IS THERE ANY WAY THAT THIS KIND OF THINKING IS EVER GOING TO LEAD ME TO HAPPINESS. SELF-RESPECT WILL FOLLOW WHEN YOU HAVE LEARNED TO HEAR YOUR OWN STUPID-ITY AND THROW IT AWAY.

INCIDENTALLY, MR. FEATHERSTONE III IS LEARNING TO DO MUCH
BETTER. HE IS MAKING THE MANAGERS UNDER HIM RESPONSIBLE
FOR THE THINGS HE HATES TO DO; HE EVEN TAKES AN AFTER-
NOON OFF A WEEK TO GOLF WITH HIS WIFE AND HE IS PREPARING
TO MAKE A PARACHUTE JUMP.....SOMETHING HE HAS WANTED TO
DO SINCE HE WAS A KID. OH, AND INCIDENTALLY, HE IS THE
"FRIEND" I TOLD YOU ABOUT EARLIER WHO WAS SO EXCITED
ABOUT BUYING THE ONE BEDROOM HOUSE!

MR. FEATHERSTONE III LIVING OUT HIS D-R-E-A-M

ONE MORE THING. HE NOW VOLUNTEERS ONE EVENING A WEEK AT
THE HOMELESS SHELTER—I TOLD HIM JENNY'S STORY AND HE
LEARNED FROM HER THAT ONE OF THE REASONS HE WAS MISSING
HAPPINESS WAS BECAUSE HE WASN'T HELPING OTHERS!

ALL THIS GOES TO MAKE ONE FINAL POINT......A POINT I WAS EVEN-
TUALLY ABLE TO GET ACROSS TO SANDY (STILL MR. SANDERSON
BUTLER FEATHERSTONE III TO MOST OF HIS FRIENDS!)....AND THE
BEAUTY OF THIS WHOLE THING:

STUPIDITY IS NOT
A TERMINAL ILLNESS.

THERE IS A CURE!

EASY STEP #18

HOW TO KNOW WHEN YOU ARE IN DEEP MANURE!

MY DEAR YOUNG FRIEND...(.IT JUST DAWNED ON ME, I'VE STOPPED CALLING YOU "KIDDO". I GUESS BECAUSE IF YOU'VE HUNG AROUND THIS LONG YOU REALLY AREN'T MUCH OF A "KID" SINCE WE'VE BEGUN DEALING WITH PRETTY HEADY STUFF.....MORE THAN A "KID" COULD HANDLE!)

ANYWAY, IF BY THIS POINT YOU NEED SOMEONE TO TELL YOU WHEN YOU ARE IN DEEP MANURE...YOU REALLY ARE IN DEEP MANURE!!!   IF SO, RETURN TO EASY STEP#1.

 THOSE OF YOU WHO KNOW, PROCEED WITH US TO THE NEXT EASY STEP .

THIS IS A SHOVEL ... ENCLOSED: INSTRUCTIONS ON "HOW" TO START SHOVELLING

EASY STEP #19

INSTRUCTION MANUAL: HOW TO START SHOVELLING!

AS I AM MORE INTERESTED IN MY UPCOMING TRIP TO KEY WEST THAN I AM IN MY WRITING , I AM GOING TO TURN THIS SECTION OVER TO TWO OF MY YOUNG FRIENDS WHO ARE JUST ABOUT THE BEST MANIPULATORS I HAVE EVER MET.....IN FACT, THEY ARE SO GOOD THAT THEY ARE ONLY DAYS AWAY FROM MANIPULATING THEIR WAY OUT OF THE HOSPITAL AND BACK HOME TO THEIR FAMILIES AGAIN!!!

HI! I'M LAURA.........AND I'M SHANE!

WELL, WE JUST FIGURED IT OUT! WE'VE BEEN OUT-MANIPU-LATED BY DR. DENNY...ONE MORE TIME! HE'S, LYING ON A BEACH IN KEY WEST (PROBABLY LOOKING LIKE A BEACHED WALRUS!) AND WE END UP DOING HIS WORK FOR HIM!

WE FIGURE IT IS OK BECAUSE WE CAN PROBABLY WRITE THIS SECTION FAR BETTER THAN HE EVER COULD....BECAUSE WE HAVE BEEN THROUGH IT.

ANYWAY, IN OUR OPINION THIS IS THE MOST IMPORTANT PART OF THE WHOLE BOOK....SO WHO IS BETTER TO DO IT THAN US!

WHAT WE NEED TO TALK TO YOU ABOUT IS HONESTY!

THE FIRST FORM OF HONESTY IS BEING ABLE TO ADMIT THAT YOU HAVE A PROBLEM. THIS SOUNDS PRETTY SIMPLE, BUT TAKE IT FROM US, IT ISN'T ALWAYS SO EASY.

TAKE SHANE FOR INSTANCE: "WHEN MY PARENTS TOLD ME THAT THEY WERE GOING TO PUT ME INTO A HOSPITAL TO HELP ME WORK OUT MY PROBLEMS, I TOLD THEM THAT THEY WERE CRAZY AND THEY WERE THE ONES THAT NEEDED TO BE IN A HOSPITAL. THE FIRST TWO WEEKS I WAS IN THE HOSPITAL I WAS SO ANGRY AT MY PARENTS THAT I NEVER WANTED TO GO HOME AGAIN....AND I DIDN'T DO A LICK OF WORK JUST TO PROVE IT! THEN ONE DAY, IN GROUP THERAPY, ONE OF THE OTHER KIDS CONFRONTED ME AND TOLD ME THAT THEY THOUGHT I WAS ACTING LIKE A NASTY, MEAN-SPIRITED, SPOILED, LITTLE KID. MY FIRST REACTION, OF COURSE, WAS TO GET ANGRY AT THE GUY WHO TOLD ME THAT....THEN EVERYONE JUMPED ON ME AND

. . .IS IT A BEACHED WALRUS?. . .IS IT A WHALE?. . .NO-O-O IT'S JUST DR. DENNY ON A BEACH IN KEY WEST! MANIPULATING AS ALWAYS!

BY THE TIME IT WAS OVER I FINALLY HAD REACHED THE POINT WHERE I REALIZED THAT I DID HAVE A PROBLEM....AND I COULD NOT AFFORD TO DENY IT ANY LONGER. ONCE I REALIZED THAT, I COULD START TO WORK AND SOLVING MY PROBLEMS PROVED NOT TO BE AS DIFFICULT AS I THOUGHT IT WOULD BE......BUT FIRST I HAD TO ADMIT THAT I HAD PROBLEMS."

AFTER YOU DISCOVER THAT YOU HAVE A PROBLEM, A SECOND DOSE OF HONESTY IS REQUIRED. YOU HAVE TO ASK YOURSELF WHAT YOUR REAL VALUES ARE. FOR SOME KIDS THAT IS SOMETHING THAT THEY HAVE NEVER EVEN THOUGHT ABOUT BEFORE! BUT WHEN YOU STOP AND REALLY WORK AT IT, IT COMES FAIRLY EASILY. WHAT ARE YOUR VALUES WHEN IT COMES TO STEALING? IS IT ALWAYS WRONG OR WILL YOU TRY TO GET AWAY WITH IT WHEN NO ONE IS LOOKING? SURE, EVERYONE HAS STOLEN AT ONE TIME IN THEIR LIFE....SOME GUM, OR SOME MONEY OR SOMETHING SMALL. BUT WHAT ARE YOUR REAL VALUES AND BELIEFS ABOUT STEALING?

LAURA:"I USED TO GO INTO A STORE AND MAKE A GAME OUT OF TRYING TO SHOPLIFT SOMETHING.....USUALLY SOMETHING I DIDN'T EVEN NEED OR WANT. I CAN'T BEGIN TO EXPLAIN TO YOU WHAT IT FELT LIKE WHEN I GOT CAUGHT ONE DAY AND THEY TOOK ME TO THE POLICE STATION. EVEN BEFORE MY FATHER CAME DOWN TO THE STATION I CAN GUARANTEE YOU THAT I HAD CHANGED MY BELIEFS AND VALUES ABOUT STEALING FOR THE REST OF MY LIFE! LUCKILY FOR ME, MY PARENTS GAVE ME A SECOND CHANCE.....BUT I WAS THE ONE WHO HAD TO REALLY DECIDE WHAT MY VALUES WERE: WHETHER I WAS GOING TO CONTINUE TO BE A THIEF OR NOT."

37 EASY STEPS ... DENNY

SO, WHEN YOU ARE IN DEEP MANURE, THE FIRST STEP IS TO ADMIT YOU HAVE A PROBLEM. THE SECOND STEP IS TO CLARIFY IN YOUR OWN MIND WHAT YOUR VALUES ARE. IT IS OFTEN VERY IMPORTANT TO TAKE ANOTHER STEP BEFORE YOU PROCEED ANY FURTHER AND THAT IS TO PRACTICE YOUR BELIEFS. ONE GOOD WAY TO DO THIS IS TO LISTEN TO OTHERS TALK ABOUT WHAT THEY BELIEVE AND TRY TO DETERMINE WHETHER YOU SHARE THE SAME VALUES WITH THAT PERSON. IF YOU DON'T, YOU DO NOT ALWAYS HAVE TO TELL THEM......AFTER ALL IT IS YOUR VALUES THAT MATTER TO YOU, NOT SOMEONE ELSE'S. ON THE OTHER HAND, AL- THOUGH YOU DO NOT HAVE TO TELL THEM THAT YOU DO NOT SHARE THEIR VALUES, IT IS VERY USEFUL TO PRACTICE EXPRESSING YOUR OWN. ONE WARNING: DON'T BOTHER WASTING YOUR TIME TALKING ABOUT YOUR BELIEFS, IF YOU DO NOT HAVE INTENTIONS OF LIVING UP TO THEM.

YOU CAN'T JUST TALK THE TALK: YOU HAVE TO WALK THE WALK......AND THAT IS THE NEXT STEP! UNLESS YOU ARE A PHONEY, A CON-ARTIST OR A BULL-SLINGER, YOU NEED TO MAKE DECISIONS THAT ARE CONSISTENT WITH YOUR VAL- UES. IF YOU SAY YOU DON'T APPROVE OF DRUGS....THEN YOU HAVE NO REASON TO USE THEM! IF YOU SAY YOU ARE TIRED OF PUTTING YOUR PARENTS THROUGH HELL....THEN YOU HAVE NO REASON TO CONTINUE IT.

THE NEXT STEP IS A NICE ONE......IT IS BASED ON THE PRIN- CIPLE THAT NO ONE IS PERFECT AND THAT IF YOU FAIL IN YOUR EFFORTS, YOU SHOULD AT LEAST LEARN FOR THE NEXT TIME! YOU'LL GET A REASONABLE NUMBER OF OPPOR- TUNITIES FOR THIS, BUT TIME DOES RUN OUT. WHEN YOU TURN EIGHTEEN IT IS A DIFFERENT BALLGAME AND YOU HAD BETTER HAVE IT DOWN PRETTY WELL....BECAUSE PRACTICE ROUNDS RUN OUT.

WHEN YOU CATCH YOURSELF IN A MISTAKE, IT'S TIME TO GO BACK TO STEP #1.

SO THE STEPS THEMSELVES ARE PRETTY EASY:

1. ADMIT YOUR PROBLEM.
2. CLARIFY YOUR VALUES AND BELIEFS.
3. REAFFIRM YOUR VALUES.
4. CHOOSE BEHAVIORS TO MATCH YOUR VALUES.
5. IF YOU MAKE A MISTAKE...LEARN FROM IT!
6. GO BACK AND CHECK YOUR VALUES AGAIN.

APPLYING THE STEPS ISN'T ALWAYS EASY......ESPECIALLY WHEN YOU HANG AROUND WITH FRIENDS WHO HAVE AN- OTHER SET OF VALUES THAT THEY THINK ARE BETTER OR MORE FUN THAN YOUR OWN. BELIEVE IT, COMING FROM US....WE HAVE BOTH FALLEN INTO THAT TRAP. PEER PRES- SURE IS REAL; SOMETIMES YOU HAVE TO CHANGE PEERS!

AT FIRST THIS MAY SOUND A BIT RADICAL....BUT IT MAY
HAVE TO HAPPEN IF YOUR FRIENDS AREN'T GOING TO
CHANGE THEIR VALUES.

MAKE SURE YOU DON'T SET OUT TO BE PERFECT; BUT ON
THE OTHER HAND DON'T SET YOUR GOALS FOR CHANGE TOO
LOW OR YOU WILL NOT ACCOMPLISH ALL THAT YOU ARE
CAPABLE OF ACHIEVING.

ONE OF THE GREATEST MANIPULATIONS IS FREAKING OUT
TEACHERS AND OTHER ADULTS WHO HAVE KNOWN THE
"OLD" YOU. ONE OF OUR FRIENDS WENT BACK TO SCHOOL
RECENTLY AND AFTER A MONTH THE TEACHER CAME UP TO
HIM AND SAID, "OK, WISEGUY! WHAT ARE YOU TRYING TO
PULL OFF! EVERYONE WARNED ME THAT YOU WOULD BE A
NIGHTMARE AND YOU HAVEN'T TRIED A THING YET. WHAT
IS YOUR GAME?" HE SAID THAT THE TEACHER WAS SO
SPOOKED THAT HE ASKED HIM IF HE WAS REALLY WHO HE
SAID HE WAS!

" EXCUSE ME... BUT ARE <u>YOU</u> REALLY WHO
YOU SAY YOU ARE?...I HEARD YOU WERE
A TEACHER'S WORST NIGHTMARE !

THAT BRINGS US TO OUR FINAL POINT.....CHANGE CAN BE
FUN! IF YOU HAVE BEEN TRYING THINGS FOR ONE WAY FOR
A LONG TIME, IT IS FUN TO TRY A NEW APPROACH, ESPE-
CIALLY WHEN THE NEW APPROACH GETS YOU MORE OF
WHAT YOU WANT.

REMEMBER, THINKING YOU WANT TO CHANGE IS NEVER ENOUGH....THAT AND NOTHING ELSE WILL GET YOU NOTHING ELSE!

IT IS LIKE CONFUCIUS SAYS: "MAN WHO CLIMB HILL TO THINK ABOUT CHANGE...NOT ON LEVEL."

SURE, WE'RE GOING HOME SOON AND WE ARE SCARED ... WHAT IF THINGS DON'T GO AS WELL AS WE HAD HOPED? WELL, THEN WE GO BACK TO THE BASICS AND START AGAIN, WITH STEP NUMBER ONE....."WHAT IS <u>MY</u> PROBLEM?"

GOOD LUCK. ENJOY YOUR CHALLENGES! WE'VE ENJOYED OURS....AND HOPE THAT DR. DENNY COMES BACK WITH A SUNBURN AND A BETTER ATTITUDE!

WELL, I'M BACK....WITH A BAG OF ORANGES AND A STUFFED ALLI-GATOR FOR LAURA AND SHANE......WHO FELL FOR MY LITTLE TRICK! I MADE THEM THINK THAT THEY COULD DO A BETTER JOB THAN ME—AND THEY FELL FOR IT! (SORRY, NO SUNBURN.....BUT MY ATTITUDE MAY BE IMPROVED!)

CONFUCIUS SAY,... "MAN WHO CLIMB HILL TO THINK' ABOUT CHANGE .... NOT ON THE LEVEL!

EASY STEP # 20

LITTLE BROTHERS, LITTLE SISTERS....
OTHER CREATURES FROM THE SLIME!

NOW THAT YOU HAVE MASTERED THE "INSTRUCTION MANUAL" AND YOU KNOW HOW TO GO ABOUT IDENTIFYING AND SOLVING PROBLEMS, LET'S USE THESE NEXT FEW CHAPTERS TO TALK ABOUT SOME OF THE MOST FREQUENT PROBLEMS THAT YOU FACE, SUCH AS DEALING WITH YOUNGER BROTHERS AND SISTERS, SELF-ESTEEM, DIVORCE, STEP-PARENTS, SCHOOL ISSUES AND RELATIONSHIPS WITH THE OPPOSITE SEX.

STAY CALM. DON'T PANIC. YOU HAVE SOME PRETTY DECENT TOOLS TO WORK WITH NOW, AND MORE IMPORTANTLY, YOU ARE NO LONGER RUNNING AWAY FROM YOUR PROBLEMS. YOU ARE LEARNING TO FACE THEM STRAIGHT UP! THERE ARE <u>REALLY</u> VERY FEW PROBLEMS THAT DO NOT HAVE SOME KIND OF ANSWERS!

I AM JUST GOING TO PRESUME THAT IF YOU HAVE A YOUNGER BROTHER OR SISTER.....SOMETIMES THEY CAN BE A PAIN! OK. OK. MORE THAN JUST " SOMETIMES", THEY CAN BE A PAIN QUITE OFTEN!

LITTLE BROTHERS , LITTLE SISTERS.... AND OTHER CREATURES FROM THE " SLIME !

LET'S START WITH A FEW SIMPLE FACTS:
      A. THEY ARE NOT GOING TO GO AWAY.
      B. SOME ARE WORSE THAN OTHERS.
      C. IF YOU CAN LEARN TO MANIPULATE A PARENT, A LITTLE
         BROTHER OR SISTER CAN'T REALLY BE THAT BIG A DEAL!

FIRST, A QUESTION! WHY IS THERE FREQUENTLY SO MUCH OF A PROBLEM BETWEEN YOU AND THE YOUNGER KIDS IN THE FAMILY?

I SUSPECT THAT THERE ARE MANY REASONS, BUT THE MAIN ONE IS:

YOUR LITTLE BROTHER OR SISTER WANTS TO BE JUST LIKE YOU
BUT
THEY DON'T WANT TO BE ANYTHING LIKE YOU!

TO YOUR YOUNGER SIBLING YOU ARE BOTH HERO AND ANTI-HERO; ROLE MODEL AND ROLE BASHER; FRIEND AND FOE. AT TIMES THEY THINK YOU ARE COOL AND AT TIMES THEY THINK YOU ARE A WEIRDO.

OF COURSE, A LOT OF THIS DEPENDS ON HOW MUCH YOUNGER THEY ARE THAN YOU. IF YOU ARE SIXTEEN, A THREE-YEAR-OLD SISTER MAY ADORE YOU; A FOURTEEN -YEAR-OLD SISTER MAY THINK YOU ARE A DWEEB! A YOUNGER SISTER MAY BE JEALOUS OF YOU; A YOUNGER BROTHER MAY JUST WANT TO TERRORIZE YOU AND YOUR FRIENDS.....JUST TO PROVE HOW COOL HE IS.

REMEMBER, LITTLE BROTHERS AND SISTERS GROW UP.....AND SOMETIMES THEY CAN EVEN BECOME YOUR FRIENDS!

THE IMPORTANT POINT YOU NEED TO GET HERE IS THAT IT ABSO-LUTELY DRIVES A PARENT UP THE WALL WHEN THEIR OWN CHIL-DREN DO NOT GET ALONG. SO FOR YOUR OWN HAPPINESS LEARN TO DEAL WITH THE SITUATION. TAKE CONTROL OF THE RELATIONSHIP.....DON'T LET IT GET OUT OF HAND.

ONE WAY TO TAKE CONTROL IS TO GIVE YOUR LITTLE BROTHER OR SISTER THE IMPRESSION THAT YOU REALLY CARE ABOUT THEM. THIS CAN BE DONE BEST....WITHOUT WASTING TOO MUCH OF YOUR IMPORTANT TIME....AROUND THE DINNER TABLE. MAKE THEM FEEL THAT WHAT THEY HAVE TO SAY IS IMPORTANT! LISTEN TO THEM AND PICK OUT A FEW POSITIVE THINGS THAT THEY HAVE TO SAY AND DWELL ON THEM. TELL THEM HOW YOU HANDLED YOUR PROBLEMS WHEN YOU WERE THEIR AGE, BUT DO IT WITHOUT PUTTING THEM DOWN OR MAKING FUN OF THEM. MAYBE, YOU CAN EVEN SAVE THEM SOME OF THE HASSLE YOU HAD TO GO THROUGH WHEN YOU FACED THEIR PROBLEM.

AS HARD AS YOU MIGHT TRY, HOWEVER, EXPECT CONFLICT WITH YOUR "KID SISTER" OR "KID BROTHER"——IT'S JUST THE NATURE OF THE BREED! YOU HAVE ALREADY LEARNED A NUMBER OF GOOD TOOLS TO HELP DEAL WITH YOUR PARENTS. HOW CAN YOU APPLY THEM?

FIRST, DON'T THINK OF EVERY FIGHT HAVING TO HAVE A WINNER AND A LOSER. FIND A WAY FOR EVERYONE TO WIN. LET ME TELL YOU ABOUT JODI. SHE WAS FOURTEEN AND HAD GONE THROUGH THREE SOLID MONTHS OF BICKERING AND SQUABBLING WITH HER TWELVE- YEAR- OLD SISTER, HEATHER . HER MOTHER WAS ABOUT TO LOSE HER MIND AND EVEN THREATENED TO SEND ONE OF THEM (OR EVEN BOTH OF THEM) TO THE "PSYCH WARD" IF THEY DIDN'T SHAPE UP. JODI, BEING MORE MATURE AND HAVING READ THIS BOOK, COVER TO COVER, DECIDED SHE NEEDED TO TAKE THE INITIATIVE.......SHE NEEDED TO MANIPULATE HER WAY OUT OF HER PREDICAMENT WITH HER SISTER (AND HER DIFFICULT POSITION WITH HER MOTHER!)

HER FIRST STEP WAS TO TELL HER MOTHER THAT SHE WAS TIRED OF THE WARFARE. THE NEXT STEP WAS TO BEGIN HER PLAN. WHEN HEATHER GOT HOME FROM SCHOOL THE NEXT DAY JODI ASKED HER IF SHE WANTED TO HANG AROUND WITH HER FRIENDS FOR A WHILE. JODI THEN SAID, "OK, I'LL MAKE YOU A DEAL. YOU CAN HANG OUT WITH US TODAY, BUT YOU HAVE TO PROMISE THAT YOU WILL STOP TAKING THINGS THAT BELONG TO ME WITHOUT ASKING."

HEATHER ACCEPTED THE OFFER AND JODI MADE SURE THAT HER FRIENDS DID THESE TWO THINGS:

1. THEY WERE VERY, VERY NICE TO HEATHER.
2. THEY TOLD HER THEY'D LIKE HER BACK IF SHE STOPPED HER STEALING. (YES, THEY CALLED IT WHAT IT WAS!)

HEATHER DIDN'T MUCH LIKE BEING TOLD THAT SHE WAS A THIEF, BUT JODI'S FRIENDS HAD WORKED OUT A WAY TO DO IT SO THAT SHE COULD SWALLOW IT.....THEY TREATED HER LIKE ONE OF THE GANG AND TOLD HER WHAT WAS EXPECTED OF HER IF SHE WANTED TO STAY PART OF THE GANG. CURIOUSLY, HEATHER SOON LOST INTEREST IN HER SISTER'S "OLDER" FRIENDS BUT SHE ALSO EMERGED AS A WINNER AND GOT THE MESSAGE ABOUT HER STEALING.

LISTEN HEATHER...WE'LL LIKE YOU BACK, BUT YOU'VE GOT TO STOP STEALING YOUR SISTERS STUFF. JODI'S OUR FRIEND... FRIENDS WATCH-OUT FOR EACH OTHER.

THERE ARE, OF COURSE, MORE WAYS TO MANIPULATE A SISTER OR BROTHER THAN THERE ARE SHADES OF LIPSTICK. BUT, WHEN IN TROUBLE, REMEMBER........ GO BACK TO THE BASICS! THE SAME PRINCIPLES YOU ARE LEARNING TO USE WITH YOUR PARENTS CAN WORK IN OTHER SETTINGS AS WELL. DEAL WITH YOUR PROBLEMS BEFORE THEY GET TOO BIG. AND, ABOVE ALL , DON'T FORGET TO TAKE CREDIT FOR YOUR MANIPULATIONS.

NOTICE THAT JODI'S FIRST STEP WAS TO TELL HER MOTHER THAT SHE WAS TIRED OF THE WARFARE AND THAT SHE WAS GOING TO MAKE A PLAN TO STOP IT. WELL, WHAT WAS HER LAST STEP? THAT WAS AN EASY ONE. ABOUT A WEEK LATER SHE WANTED TO STAY OUT A LITTLE LATER THAN USUAL AND APPROACHED HER MOTHER, "MOM, HAVE YOU NOTICED THE CHANGES IN HEATHER? MY PLAN SEEMS TO HAVE WORKED! BY THE WAY, WHAT WOULD

YOU THINK ABOUT ME STAYING OUT A LITTLE LATER THAN USUAL FRIDAY TO GO TO THE DANCE AT SCHOOL."

JODI GOT WHAT SHE WANTED....SO DID HEATHER! THAT, MY DEAR YOUNG FRIEND, IS WHAT GOOD MANIPULATION IS ALL ABOUT!

EASY STEP # 21

"ALL MY EXS LIVE IN TEXAS"

OK. THIS IS ANOTHER ONE OF THOSE CHAPTERS THAT COULD GET ME INTO VERY DEEP DO-DO IF IT WERE EVER SEEN BY AN ADULT OF THE SPECIES. I'M ABOUT TO TALK ABOUT ONE OF THE UGLIEST WORDS IN THE ENTIRE ENGLISH LANGUAGE. THERE IS ONLY ONE UGLIER WORD IN THE VOCABULARY! THIS IS SO UGLY THAT I RISK THE WRATH OF THE DEITIES IF I WERE EVEN TO USE THE WORD!

(TO LEARN THE UGLIEST WORD IN THE ENGLISH LANGUAGE, TAKE THE NUMBER OF MEMBERS OF THE "NELSONS" AND MULTIPLY IT BY THE NUMBER OF ORIGINAL "NINJA TURTLES". NOW TRIPLE THAT NUMBER AND ADD THE LEGAL DRIVING AGE. TRIPLE THAT NUMBER AND GO TO THAT PAGE. THE UGLIEST WORD IN THE ENGLISH LANGUAGE IS SPELLED BACKWARDS IN THE LOWER RIGHT CORNER OF THE PAGE!)

BUT, THE SECOND UGLIEST WORD IN THE ENGLISH LANGUAGE IS DIVORCE! IF YOU HAVE ANY DOUBTS ABOUT THE TOTAL UGLINESS OF THIS WORD, FIND SOMEONE YOU KNOW WHO IS DIVORCED. SOMEONE CLOSE TO THE FAMILY FOR SAFETY'S SAKE, AND ASK, "AUNT JANE, IS IT TRUE THAT YOU ARE A DIVORCEE?"

WATCH HER FACE....IT WILL SUDDENLY APPEAR AS IF SHE HAD JUST EATEN A PERSIMMON......OR WHATEVER I PRESUME A PERSIMMON MIGHT TASTE LIKE. HER LIPS WILL WRINKLE UP LIKE

SHE IS TRYING TO SNEEZE AND HER EYES WILL SORT OF CROSS!
SHE WILL PAUSE FOR A MINUTE AND THEN SHE MIGHT BE ABLE TO
SAY, "WELL, YES, MY DEAR. I GUESS THAT IS WHAT YOU WOULD
CALL IT."

IN TRUTH, YOU MIGHT EVEN HAVE BEEN BETTER OFF TO HAVE
USED THE ABSOLUTELY UGLIEST WORD IN THE ENGLISH LAN-
GUAGE, CONSIDERING THE LOOK YOU WILL PROBABLY GET.!!!!

THIS LEADS US TO OUR NEXT IMPORTANT FACT:

DIVORCE **HAPPENS!**

DIVORCE **IS NOT THE WORST THING
IN THE WORLD!**

PICTURE FOR A MOMENT THE FIRST GUY OR GIRL THAT YOU EVER DATED IN YOUR LIFE. NOW SUPPOSE SOMEONE TOLD YOU THAT YOU HAD TO STAY WITH THAT PERSON FOR THE ENTIRE REST OF YOUR LIFE. WHAT WOULD THAT BE LIKE?

WELL, MARRIAGE IS MUCH MORE SACRED AND MUCH MORE IMPORTANT....BUT MISTAKES ARE MADE! WHAT IF THERE WAS NO SUCH THING AS A DIVORCE? WHAT IF EVERYONE HAD TO STAY MARRIED TO THE PERSON THEY CHOSE? IN A WAY THAT MIGHT BE GOOD...IN FACT THERE ARE A FEW COUNTRIES WHERE DIVORCE IS STILL ILLEGAL...BUT IN MANY WAYS IT COULD LEAD TO MISERY FOR MANY PEOPLE.

NOW, HERE COMES ANOTHER POINT OF IMPORTANCE:

THERE HAS NEVER BEEN A DIVORCE THAT WAS <u>CAUSED</u> BY A CHILD.

WHEN A MAN AND A WOMAN CHOOSE TO DIVORCE IT IS BECAUSE THEY ARE NOT BRINGING HAPPINESS TO EACH OTHER AND, NINE TIMES OUT OF TEN, IT IS BECAUSE THEY JUST PLAIN OLD DON'T LIKE EACH OTHER. IT WAS NOT SOMETHING CAUSED BY THE CHILDREN AND IS NOT ANYTHING THAT THE CHILDREN CAN DO ANYTHING ABOUT!

YOU WOULD BE SURPRISED BY THE NUMBER OF KIDS WHO THINK THAT THEIR PARENTS DIVORCE IS THEIR FAULT. "IF ONLY I COULD HAVE BEEN A BETTER KID!" IF ONLY I HAD NOT BEEN SO ANGRY AT DAD ALL THE TIME, MAYBE MOM WOULD HAVE BEEN ABLE TO WORK THINGS OUT!"

THIS IS PURE, UNADULTERATED, POPPYCOCK....YOU WERE NOT EVEN IN THE GAME, HOW COULD YOU HAVE FUMBLED THE BALL?

ADULTS DIVORCE BECAUSE THEY MAKE THE DECISION THAT IT IS WHAT THEY NEED TO DO FOR THEIR OWN HAPPINESS. THEY DON'T DO IT BECAUSE OF THE CHILDREN.....THEY DO IT IN SPITE OF THE CHILDREN! AND MOST PARENTS DO IT WITH A GREAT DEAL OF CARING ABOUT HOW IT WILL AFFECT THEIR CHILDREN. OF COURSE, THERE ARE PARENTS WHO DON'T CARE: BUT MOST PARENTS DO. THEY CARE A GREAT DEAL AND MAKE ELABORATE PLANS WHICH ARE DESIGNED TO TAKE CARE OF THE NEEDS OF THEIR CHILDREN.....WHO THEY KNOW WILL ALWAYS REMAIN THEIR MOST PRIZED POSSESSION.

SOME OF YOU HAVE EXPERIENCED DIVORCE....AND EVERYONE ONE OF YOU HAS A FRIEND WHOSE PARENTS HAVE DIVORCED. (I CAN BE PRETTY DARNED CONFIDENT ABOUT THIS BECAUSE AL-MOST ONE HALF OF THE MARRIAGES IN THE UNITED STATES END UP IN DIVORCE.) THERE ARE PLENTY OF HORRIBLE THINGS ABOUT DIVORCE, BUT THERE ARE SOME THINGS THAT AREN'T SO BAD:

1. BOTH YOUR PARENTS GET THE OPPORTUNITY FOR ANOTHER CHANCE TO FIND HAPPINESS.

2. BOTH YOUR PARENTS GET ANOTHER OPPORTUNITY TO START A NEW RELATIONSHIP WITH YOU!

SOMETIMES A DIVORCE GETS SO BAD THAT THE KID FEELS IT IS NECESSARY TO "TAKE SIDES". "I'VE GOT TO PROTECT MY MOTHER." "POOR DADDY....HE HAS NOWHERE TO GO, NO ONE WHO CARES ABOUT HIM!"

BUT, IN TRUTH, YOU STILL HAVE TWO PARENTS WHO CARE ABOUT YOU VERY MUCH! YOUR JOB IS TO REALIZE THAT AND NOT LET YOURSELF GET MANIPULATED (AFTER ALL YOU ARE THE MANIPU-LATOR!) INTO TAKING SIDES. THIS IS MUCH EASIER SAID THAN DONE I AM SURE....BECAUSE DIVORCE IS FILLED WITH EMOTION.....BUT IT CAN BE DONE AND IT CAN BE DONE FAIRLY EASILY.

(TNEMTNIO)

... SOMETIMES A DIVORCE GETS SO BAD, THE KID FEELS IT'S NECESSARY TO TAKE SIDES... OR FEELS PULLED IN BOTH DIRECTIONS.

THE KEY ELEMENT OF DEALING WITH PARENTS WHO ARE DIVORCING IS <u>TIME</u>. WHEN PARENTS ARE GOING THROUGH A DIVORCE THEY ARE IN A <u>TEMPORARY</u> <u>STATE</u> <u>OF</u> <u>INSANITY</u>! THEY ARE BONKERS! THEY ARE OVERWHELMED AND DON'T KNOW WHICH END IS UP! GIVE THEM TIME AND THEY WILL GET THEIR ACT TOGETHER AND THEY WILL REALIZE ONCE AGAIN THAT THEIR CHILDREN ARE THE MOST IMPORTANT THING IN THEIR LIFE. SOMETIMES ALL YOU CAN DO IS WAIT FOR THEM TO SORT THINGS OUT FOR THEMSELVES.

DON'T EXPECT MOM AND DAD TO BECOME THE BEST OF BUDDIES AGAIN FOR YOUR BENEFIT......REMEMBER THEY GOT DIVORCED FOR GOOD REASONS! (YOU DIDN'T CAUSE IT; GIVE UP THE IDEA YOU CAN CURE IT.) HOWEVER, WITH A LITTLE <u>TIME</u> AND WITH SOME EFFORT ON YOUR PART, IF YOU EVER HAVE TO GO THROUGH A DIVORCE, YOU CAN LEARN TO HAVE A HEALTHY RELATIONSHIP WITH BOTH PARENTS. SOMETIMES, YOU ALMOST HAVE TO LIVE

YOU DIDN'T CAUSE IT... MIGHT AS WELL GIVE-UP THE IDEA YOU CAN CURE IT!

"SEPARATE LIVES" WITH EACH PARENT TO MAKE IT HAPPEN, BUT IT CAN BE DONE.

AVOID TAKING SIDES AND PLACING BLAME AND DON'T GET INTO THE BUSINESS OF PLAYING ONE SIDE AGAINST THE OTHER......THAT CAN BE THE SUPREME FORM OF STUPIDITY! IF YOU WANT TO KEEP BOTH PARENTS AS YOUR FRIENDS.....DON'T DO ANYTHING TO DELIBERATELY HURT EITHER ONE!

ONE WAY THAT YOUR PARENTS MAY FIND HAPPINESS FOR THEM- SELVES IS BY MARRYING AGAIN.....WHICH BRINGS US TO OUR NEXT SECTION.

WHEN PARENTS ARE GOING THROUGH A
DIVORCE THEY ARE IN A TEMPORARY STATE
OF INSANITY. GIVE THEM TIME AND
LOVE 'TILL THEY GET THEIR ACT TOGETHER!

EASY STEP #22

THE FAIRY GOD - DOCTOR!

EASY STEP #22

CINDERELLA! CINDERELLA! WON'T YOU TELL US WHERE THE PARTY'S GOING TO BE!

ONE OF THE FIRST STORIES THAT WE EVER HEAR AS CHILDREN WARNS US OF THE WICKEDNESS OF STEPMOTHERS.....NO WONDER WHEN IT HAPPENS TO US IT IS OFTEN SO DIFFICULT TO SWALLOW!

BUT THERE ARE OTHER MORE IMPORTANT REASONS WHY STEP PARENTS ARE DIFFICULT TO DEAL WITH, OTHER THAT JUST BECAUSE THE STORY OF CINDERELLA IS IMPRINTED ON OUR MINDS. STEP PARENTS DO NOT COME TO US BY OUR CHOICE AND THEY ARE FREQUENTLY EXCESS BAGGAGE.

WHO NEEDS ADDED COMPLICATIONS WHEN YOU ARE IN THE MIDDLE OF TRYING TO FIGURE OUT HOW TO DEAL WITH PARENTS WHO HAVE DIVORCED? IT IS ALREADY A PERIOD OF ADULT INSANITY...WHAT MORE STRESS IS NEEDED?

ALSO, THE PERSON WHO MARRIES YOUR MOTHER OR YOUR FATHER CAN OFTEN BE SEEN AS COMPETITION. THE FIRST THING THAT THEY DO IS KILL OFF YOUR FANTASY THAT YOUR PARENTS MIGHT POSSIBLY GET BACK TOGETHER ONE DAY AND YOU WILL ALL BE ONE HAPPY FAMILY AGAIN. THE OTHER THING THEY DO IS TEST YOUR LOYALTY.....WILL YOUR MOTHER BE HURT IF YOU APPEAR TO LIKE DAD'S NEW WIFE TOO MUCH? WILL YOU STOP BEING DADDY'S GIRL IF YOU TAKE TO YOUR STEPFATHER TOO WELL?

AND THEN WHAT HAPPENS WHEN STEP-BROTHERS AND STEP-SISTERS BEGIN TO APPEAR UPON THE SCENE?

STEP "ANYTHINGS" SEEM TO START OFF WITH TWO STRIKES AGAINST THEM....AFTER ALL THEY ARE SIMPLY NOT THE REAL THING? BUT ARE THEY PEOPLE? LET'S EXPLORE THIS INTERESTING QUESTION A BIT FURTHER IN THIS SECTION, AGAIN DRAWING UPON THE EXPERIENCES OF SOMEONE WHO HAS BEEN THROUGH IT. LET'S LET BRETT TELL HIS STORY:

MY PARENTS' DIVORCE WAS A PRETTY ROUGH ONE. IT WAS ONE THAT CAME AS A SURPISE TO MY BROTHER AND TO ME, EVEN THOUGH WE COULD TELL THAT OUR PARENTS WERE NOT GETTING ALONG WELL. WE WERE AWARE OF THE FREQUENT FIGHTING, BUT WE NEVER THOUGHT THAT THEY WOULD GET DIVORCED.

WHEN THEY FIRST TOLD US THAT THEY WERE DIVORCING, WE WERE MAD AT BOTH OF THEM, BUT THEN AFTER MY FATHER LEFT AND WE SPENT MOST OF OUR TIME WITH MOM WE COULD SEE HOW BADLY SHE HAD BEEN HURT. AND TO TELL YOU THE TRUTH, AT FIRST SHE WAS NOT DOING VERY WELL. IT WAS VERY DIFFICULT FOR US FINANCIALLY AND THERE WERE A LOT OF THINGS WE COULD NO LONGER DO BECAUSE "DAD WAS NOT GIVING US ENOUGH MONEY". DAD, ON THE OTHER HAND APPEARED TO BE DOING QUITE WELL. HE GOT A NEW APARTMENT AND STARTED DATING AND, ALTHOUGH HE DID NOT INTRODUCE ANY OF HIS "DATES" TO US, WE COULD TELL HE WAS ENJOYING HIS "NEW LIFE".

THEN AFTER ABOUT SIX MONTHS HE INTRODUCED CINDY TO US. MY BROTHER AND I HATED HER FROM THE FIRST SECOND WE LAID EYES ON HER. SHE WAS A LOT YOUNGER THAN MOM AND DAD ACTED REAL FOOLISH AROUND HER....TRYING TO ACT LIKE A KID HIMSELF. WE JUST BACKED OFF, THINKING THAT SHE WOULD PROBABLY GO AWAY LIKE THE OTHERS HAD—BUT SHE DIDN'T. JUST BEFORE CHRISTMAS HE BROKE THE NEWS TO US THAT THEY WERE GETTING MARRIED! AT FIRST, WE TRIED TO ACT EXCITED FOR THEM, BUT IT WAS DIFFICULT BECAUSE WE HARDLY KNEW HER AND WE DID NOT PARTICULARLY LIKE HER. THE MORE TIME WE SPENT WITH HER, THE LESS WE LIKED HER.WE TRIED TO BE POLITE WHEN WE WERE WITH HER, BUT FOUND A LOT OF EXCUSES TO STAY AWAY.

MOM STILL WAS NOT DATING VERY MUCH AND WE TRIED TO KEEP HER BUSY. ALTHOUGH SHE NEVER SAID MUCH ABOUT DAD REMARRYING, WE COULD TELL IT WAS HARD ON HER.

FOR THE FIRST YEAR AFTER DAD'S MARRIAGE THINGS WERE FAIRLY GOOD, EVEN THOUGH WE DID NOT GET VERY CLOSE TO CINDY. THEN, DAD TOLD US THAT THEY WERE GOING TO HAVE A BABY AND OUR WORLD WENT CRAZY! THIS WAS TOO MUCH. WE JUST COULDN'T HANDLE IT. WE STARTED GETTING ANGRY A LOT AND BACKED AWAY FURTHER. WE ALSO STARTED RESENTING IT WHEN CINDY WOULD TRY TO TELL US WHAT TO DO WHEN WE WERE WITH HER AND DAD. I REMEMBER TELLING HER ONE TIME THAT I DID NOT HAVE TO DO WHAT SHE SAID, "BECAUSE YOU ARE NOT MY MOTHER". DAD QUICKLY STEPPED IN AND LET ME KNOW OTHERWISE. THINGS GOT PROGRESSIVELY WORSE AND EVENTUALLY WE SPENT AS LITTLE TIME WITH HIM AND HIS NEW WIFE AS WE POSSIBLY COULD.

THEN,ONE DAY WHEN WE WERE VISITING CINDY TOLD ME TO HELP WITH THE DISHES. I SAID I WAS BUSY AND SHE TOLD ME THAT I HAD TO DO IT THEN AND THERE. WORLD WAR III FOLLOWED. EVENTUALLY DAD AND CINDY WERE FIGHTING WITH EACH OTHER AND THEY RETREATED TO THEIR BED-ROOM. THEN WE HEARD CINDY CRYING AND SHE SAID TO DAD, "IT'S NOT FAIR. THEY HAVE NEVER EVEN GIVEN ME A CHANCE. THEY HAVE NEVER EVEN TRIED TO GET TO KNOW ME. YOU ARE GOING TO HAVE TO MAKE A CHOICE WHETHER YOU WANT <u>THEM</u> OR YOUR NEW FAMILY.

LET ME TELL YOU, THAT GOT OUR ATTENTION! WE HAD BEEN PRETTY AWFUL TO CINDY AND WE KNEW IT.

BY THE TIME DAD CAME OUT OF THE BEDROOM WE HAD A PRETTY GOOD IDEA WHAT WE HAD TO DO. DAD HAD A VERY GOOD IDEA WHAT HE WAS GOING TO DO AS WELL...HE TOLD US VERY PLAINLY THAT IF WE DIDN'T ACCEPT CINDY WE DIDN'T ACCEPT HIM EITHER AND WE COULD STAY AWAY.

YOU WOULD NOT BELIEVE HOW QUICKLY WE CHANGED OUR WAYS AND FOUND OUT THAT CINDY WAS A NEAT PERSON. BY THE TIME OUR STEP SISTER WAS BORN, WE HAD FIGURED OUT THAT DAD'S GAIN COULD BE OURS AS WELL.WE ALSO FIGURED OUT THAT:

STEP-PEOPLE ARE PEOPLE TOO!

EASY STEP #23

CATCH YOUR PROBLEMS WHILE THEY ARE SMALL... BEFORE THEY GROW AND... "CASCADE INTO A CATASTROPHE."

EASY STEP #23

WHEN I SAY "NO!", I MEAN "NO!"......

NEVER TAKE "NO!" FOR AN ANSWER!

NEXT RULE:
DON'T EXPECT ADULTS TO BE LOGICAL.

AMONG SOME OF THE CENTRAL AFRICAN CULTURES CHILDREN ARE TAUGHT FROM THEIR EARLIEST DAYS THAT IT IS WRONG TO THINK OF THEMSELVES AS BETTER THAN SOMEONE ELSE OR TO TRY TO HAVE MORE THAN SOMEONE ELSE. THIS CREATES A COMMUNITY IN WHICH A CHILD GROWS UP WITH A WONDERFUL AWARENESS OF THE NEEDS OF OTHERS AND AND A STRONG FEELING OF EQUALITY.

ON THE OTHER HAND, IN SOME SETTINGS THIS CREATES A PROBLEM. FOR EXAMPLE, TEACHERS IN THIS CULTURE HAVE NOTED THAT STUDENTS WHO ARE VERY INTELLIGENT OFTEN DO NOT DO WELL ON EXAMS OUT OF A CONCERN THAT IT IS NOT POLITE TO OUT-SCORE THEIR FELLOW STUDENTS. AS A RESULT, SOME OF THE BRIGHTEST STUDENTS DO NOT EXCEL THE WAY THAT THEY POSSIBLY COULD WERE COMPETITION MORE ACCEPTIBLE IN THEIR CULTURE.

SIMILIARLY, I REMEMBER GROWING UP HEARING THE MESSAGE THAT IT WAS IMPORTANT TO DO AS WELL AS I POSSIBLY COULD IN SCHOOL AND TO EXCEL IF POSSIBLE. AT THE SAME TIME, I HEARD A MESSAGE THAT IT WAS WRONG TO THINK OF MYSELF AS BETTER THAN ANYONE ELSE. I RECALL IN SEVENTH GRADE GETTING VERY GOOD GRADES ON MY FINAL EXAMS, BUT NOT BEING ABLE TO FEEL GOOD ABOUT IT BECAUSE I WOULD BE "THINKING OF MYSELF AS BETTER THAN SOMEONE ELSE". THE NEXT YEAR I "FOUND A WAY" TO BRING MY GRADES DOWN SO THAT THEY WOULD BE MORE LIKE EVERYONE ELSE'S.

I ALSO REMEMBER MY PARENTS TELLING ME: "NO IS NO!" BUT THEN ONE DAY I CAME HOME AND TOLD MY PARENTS THAT I HAD TOLD THE FOOTBALL COACH THAT I WANTED TO PLAY FULLBACK BUT HE TOLD ME "NO, YOU HAVE TO PLAY CENTER". MY FATHER TURNED TO ME AND SAID, "I THOUGHT I TAUGHT YOU NEVER TO TAKE "NO"

FOR AN ANSWER." I WENT BACK TO THE FOOTBALL COACH AND TOLD HIM THAT I WAS NOT GOING TO TAKE "NO" FOR AN ANSWER. HE RESPONDED BY SAYING, "DIDN'T YOUR DADDY EVER TEACH YOU THAT "NO" IS NO"! I PLAYED CENTER THAT YEAR, BUT I DON'T THINK THAT I HAD NEARLY AS MUCH FUN AS I COULD HAVE IF I HAD PLAYED FULLBACK..... BUT I ALSO LEARNED THAT "NO" IS <u>NOT</u> ALWAYS "NO" AND THAT HAS HELPED ME OUT IN A LOT OF OTHER SITUATIONS SINCE.

MANY OF YOU HAVE PROBABLY ALSO HEARD YOUR PARENT SAY, "DO AS I SAY, NOT AS I DO." YOU MAY HAVE ALSO HEARD A PARENT SAY THAT HONESTY IS THE <u>ONLY</u> POLICY AND THEN LATER HEARD THEM TALK ABOUT HOW THEY CHEATED ON THEIR INCOME TAX. OR YOU MIGHT HAVE GOTTEN A LECTURE ABOUT THE DANGERS OF ALCOHOL AND THEN SEEN YOUR FATHER OR MOTHER DRINK TOO MUCH THE NEXT DAY.

I DON'T HAVE AN ANSWER, EXCEPT TO SAY THAT IF YOU ARE AWARE OF THE MIXED MESSAGES YOU CAN SOMETIMES FIND A WAY TO TELL YOUR PARENTS HOW CONFUSING IT IS AND YOU CAN TRY TO REMEMBER ALL THOSE THINGS THAT YOU WOULD <u>NEVER</u> SAY TO YOUR OWN CHILDREN.

BUT THERE ARE SOME MESSAGES FROM PARENTS THAT ARE NOT MIXED AND THEY ARE FREQUENTLY MORE DESTRUCTIVE. A FEW WEEKS AGO I ASKED A GROUP OF TEENAGERS TO TELL ME THE MOST HURTFUL THINGS THAT THEY HAD EVER HAD AN ADULT TELL THEM. THIS IS JUST A FEW OF THE THINGS THEY SHARED WITH ME:

1. "YOU CAN'T DO ANYTHING RIGHT."
2. "I WISH I NEVER HAD YOU."
3. "YOU'LL NEVER AMOUNT TO ANYTHING."
4. "I DIDN'T HAVE TO HAVE YOU."
5. "GET OUT OF MY SIGHT."
6. "YOU ARE STUPID."
7. "YOU ARE NO CHILD OF MINE."
8. "YOU ARE GOING NOWHERE FAST."
9. "WE GOT DIVORCED ON ACCOUNT OF YOU."
10. "IF YOUR FATHER DIES IT WILL BE ALL YOUR FAULT."
11. "YOU ARE THE MAIN REASON YOUR FATHER DRINKS."
12. "I DIDN'T WANT YOU...I WANTED A BOY."
13. "YOU WERE AN ACCIDENT."
14. "YOU ARE A DISGRACE TO THE FAMILY."
15. "YOU ARE JUST LIKE YOUR FATHER."
16. "YOU ARE A LITTLE WHORE."
17. "I WISH YOU WERE DEAD."
18. "YOU ARE NOT WORTH ALL I DO FOR YOU."

19. "GET OUT OF MY HOUSE."
20. "YOU ARE AN AIRHEAD."
21. "IF YOUR FATHER LOVED YOU, HE'D SEND YOU MONEY."
22. "I'M GOING TO GO AND PACK YOUR BAGS FOR YOU."
23. "YOU CAN GO TO HELL."
24. "YOU ARE SUCH AN INGRATE."
25. "YOU ARE AN EMBARRASSMENT."
26. "IF YOU DON'T LIKE IT HERE, GO FIND YOUR DAD."
27. "I COULDN'T CARE LESS ABOUT YOUR STUPID, LITTLE PROBLEMS."
28. " YOU ARE SO PATHETIC."
29. "YOU ARE JUST LIKE YOUR MOTHER."

THESE ARE <u>NOT</u> STATEMENTS THAT I HAVE MADE UP....THESE ARE ALL STATEMENTS THAT ADOLESCENTS SAY THEY HAVE HEARD ABOUT THEMSELVES!

AND ALTHOUGH PARENTS ARE USUALLY ON THEIR "BEST BEHAVIOR" AROUND ME, I'VE HEARD IT MYSELF MANY TIMES. I'VE HEARD A FATHER TELL HIS SON THAT HE IS A ZERO (THE SON IS NOW IN THE MARINES AND DOING FANTASTICALLY.) I'VE HEARD A MOTHER TELL HER SON THAT HE'S GOING TO GROW UP TO BE A CHARLES MANSON. I'VE HEARD A MOTHER CALL HER DAUGHTER A SLUT. AND I'VE HEARD A DAUGHTER PLEAD WITH HER MOTHER TO TELL HER WHETHER SHE LOVES HER......AND I'VE HEARD THE MOTHER REPLY, "I'LL THINK ABOUT IT FOR A WEEK AND LET YOU KNOW!"

THESE ARE WORDS THAT CAN DESTROY THE SPIRIT!

FORTUNATELY, MOST YOUNG ADULTS HAVE STRONG SPIRITS AND , ALTHOUGH ALMOST ALL PARENTS (AND ADOLESCENTS) WILL AT SOME TIME SAY SOMETHING HURTFUL IN THE HEAT OF AN ARGUMENT, THEY QUICKLY RECOGNIZE HOW DAMAGING WORDS CAN BE.

IT IS EASY TO SEE HOW DAMAGING THE WORDS ON THE LIST ABOVE CAN BE. WHAT IS THE YOUNG PERSON HEARING THESE WORDS CAPABLE OF DOING? HOPEFULLY, YOU ALREADY KNOW THE FIRST SEVERAL STEPS: RECOGNIZING THE PROBLEM AND FINDING THE RIGHT TIME AND THE RIGHT PLACE TO TELL YOUR PARENTS HOW IT MAKES YOU <u>FEEL</u> WHEN YOU HEAR IT AND HOW YOUR <u>NEED FOR IT TO STOP</u> . IF THEY CANNOT HEAR YOUR NEEDS, IT IS IMPORTANT FOR YOU TO REALIZE THAT THERE ARE OTHERS WHO CAN: TEACHERS, SCHOOL COUNSELLORS, PASTORS OR CHURCH YOUTH GROUP LEADERS, YOUR FRIENDS AND THEIR PARENTS. PERHAPS, ASKING YOUR PARENTS TO SIT DOWN AND SEE HOW MANY OF THE THINGS ON THE LIST THEY HAVE EVER SAID TO YOU WOULD BE A WAY TO LET THEM KNOW HOW MUCH PAIN IT HAS CAUSED YOU.

THE PROBLEM IS OFTEN A COMPLICATED ONE BUT THE MESSAGE IS SIMPLE. YOU ARE A GOOD PERSON AND YOU SHOULD NOT, AT YOUR AGE, BE READY TO ACCEPT YOUR OWN POWERLESSNESS. WITH SOME OF THE TOOLS YOU ARE ACQUIRING, YOU SHOULD BEGIN TO BE READY TO TAKE <u>ACTION</u> ON YOUR PROBLEMS OR KNOW WHEN TO TURN FOR HELP.

READY...SET..."<u>ACTION</u>"

ONE MORE THING. LET'S TALK ABOUT THE "CASCADE OF CATASTROPHICATION" AND "DE-CATASTROPHICATION" AND I WILL HAVE BLOWN MY WAD ON THIS SUBJECT......I WILL HAVE TOLD YOU EVERYTHING I'VE EVER LEARNED AND I'LL BE RUNNING ON EMPTY.

HAVE YOU EVER SEEN A TINY STREAM AT THE TOP OF A MOUNTAIN THAT PLUNGES DOWN IN A SINGLE LITTLE RIVULET UNTIL IT HITS A

FEW ROCKS AND SUDDENLY STARTS TO DIVIDE AND SPREAD? IT
THEN ENCOUNTERS A FEW MORE ROCKS IN ITS PATH AND SOON IT
SEEMS LIKE A MIGHTY FLOWING RIVER, UNTIL IT FINALLY ENDS IN
WHAT LOOKS LIKE AN OVERWHELMING WATERFALL.

LOOK BACK AT THE TOP OF THE MOUNTAIN. HAS THAT WATERFALL
COME FROM THAT NARROW, GENTLY FLOWING STREAM? OF
COURSE IT HAS....IN FACT IF YOU WENT BACK TO THE TOP AND
MOVED A FEW STONES FROM THE RIVERBED TO STOP THE CAS-
CADE, YOU MIGHT BE ABLE TO STOP IT FROM EVER BECOMING SO
MENACING.

SO TOO WITH PROBLEMS. CATCH THEM BEFORE THEY GATHER
TOO MUCH ENERGY. TAKE PROBLEMS AS THEY COME. LOOK THEM
IN THE EYE AND "MOVE A FEW STONES" SO THAT EACH LITTLE
PROBLEM DOES NOT CASCADE INTO A CATASTROPHE, APPEARING
SO OVERWHELMING...LEARN TO "DE-CATASTROPHIZE"!

WORDS CAN BE SO CRUEL. THEY DEEPLY HURT,
PAINFULLY BURN, AND CAN SCAR FOR A LIFETIME,
WORDS LIKE ..." I WISH YOU WERE NEVER BORN!"

EASY STEP #24

EASY STEP #24

I'M NOT STUCK-UP.....

I'M JUST SHY

I AM GOING TO TELL YOU SOMETHING THAT FEW OF YOU ARE GOING TO BELIEVE: I AM A VERY SHY PERSON!

I CAN GUESS WHAT YOU ARE THINKING—YEAH, AND SO IS MADONNA! BUT, NO! IT IS THE HONEST TRUTH....AND SHYNESS IS A HORRIBLE HANDICAP. I REMEMBER ONE YOUNG LADY, ANGIE, WHO WAS TERRIBLY SHY AND SHE WANTED TO HAVE FRIENDS AT SCHOOL BUT WAS TOO AFRAID TO TALK TO PEOPLE. WITHOUT FRIENDS SHE BECAME VERY BORED, DEPRESSED AND DOWN ON HERSELF. WE BRAINSTORMED AND FOUND A WAY TO HELP HER. WE TOOK HER DOWN TO THE CRAFTSROOM AND SHE MADE A TEE SHIRT THAT SAID:

I'M NOT STUCK-UP....
I'M JUST SHY!

WHEN SHE BEGAN TO WEAR THAT SHIRT SHE DISCOVERED THAT THERE WERE A LOT OF OTHER SHY PEOPLE IN THE WORLD....AND EVEN SOME OF THE PEOPLE WHO WEREN'T SHY BEGAN TO TALK TO HER.

HOW COME SOME PEOPLE ARE SHY AND OTHERS AREN'T?

I HAVE NEVER TALKED TO ANYONE WHO HAD THE ANSWER TO THAT ONE! IN MANY WAYS, IT MUST BE A LOT LIKE NOSES....YOU ARE JUST BORN THAT WAY. BUT I THINK IT IS VERY IMPORTANT TO REALIZE THAT PEOPLE ARE NOT SHY BECAUSE THEY HAVE LOW SELF-ESTEEM. LET ME GIVE YOU A VERY FRESH EXAMPLE: THIS MORNING SOMEONE WE ALL GREW UP WITH, YOUR GENERATION AND MINE, DIED—DR. SEUSS. HE WAS WAS A GENIUS AND A MARVELOUS MAN WHO GAVE US BOOKS (AND LESSONS) AND CHARACTERS—(THE LORAX, THE CAT IN THE HAT, THE GRINCH, THE BROWN BAR-BA LOOTS) — THAT WILL BE ENJOYED BY NOT ONLY MY GRANDCHILDREN BUT ALSO YOURS. BUT HE WAS ALSO A VERY SHY MAN....SO SHY, IN FACT, THAT HE ONLY ALLOWED HIMSELF TO

BE INTERVIEWED ONCE IN HIS ENTIRE LIFE. HE WAS JUST A VERY SHY AND PRIVATE MAN WHO COULD CREATE WONDERFUL CREATURES FROM HIS IMAGINATION BUT COULD NOT TALK ABOUT HIMSELF.

YOU WOULD BE SURPRISED BY THE NUMBER OF OTHER FAMOUS PEOPLE WHO WERE TERRIBLY SHY, INCLUDING ALBERT EINSTEIN, ABRAHAM LINCOLN, QUEEN ELIZABETH AND BABE RUTH. (SO I GUESS YOU AND I ARE IN PRETTY GOOD COMPANY!)

THE FIRST THING TO DO ABOUT SHYNESS IS TO LOOK AROUND AND SEE THAT YOU ARE NOT ALONE. BUT HOW DOES ONE SHY PERSON MEET ANOTHER? WHO GOES FIRST? DO YOU SAY HELLO OR DO YOU WAIT FOR THE OTHER PERSON TO TALK FIRST? ITS A RISKY BUSINESS....BUT MAYBE ITS TIME TO START TAKING RISKS!

JUST BECAUSE YOU ARE SHY IT DOES NOT MEAN THAT YOU CAN NEVER LEARN TO BE A GOOD MANIPULATOR.

ONE THING YOU COULD DO IS START A "SHY PERSONS" CLUB AT SCHOOL......BUT YOU HAD BETTER BE READY TO BE THE ONLY PERSON WHO COMES TO THE FIRST MEETING!

JOINING CLUBS AND OTHER GROUPS IS PROBABLY THE BEST AND EASIEST WAY FOR A SHY PERSON TO BREAK THE ICE. BUT JOIN SOMETHING YOU ENJOY OR THINK YOU WOULD ENJOY. DON'T JUST JOIN ANY GROUP, BECAUSE IF YOU DON'T HAVE THE INTEREST, IT JUST WON'T WORK. BE A GOOD LISTENER AND DON'T BE AFRAID TO VOLUNTEER FOR A COMMITTEE OR TO WORK ON A PROJECT. IF YOU SPEND EIGHT HOURS DOING A CAR WASH OR PLANNING FOR A DANCE, YOU WILL GET TO KNOW OTHER PEOPLE AND THEY WILL GET TO KNOW YOU. JOIN THE BAND...BUT ONLY IF YOU LIKE MUSIC!

EINSTEIN, LINCOLN, QUEEN ELIZABETH, AND
BABE RUTH . . . . ALL SHY PEOPLE .
(AND I MIGHT ADD - NOT BAD COMPANY.)

I KNOW A LOT OF SHY ADULTS....NO, YOU DON'T NECESSARILY "GET OVER" SHYNESS... AND THEY ARE SOME OF THE NICEST PEOPLE I KNOW. ACCEPT YOUR SHYNESS, LIKE YOU HAD TO ACCEPT YOUR NOSE.... THERE MAY BE VERY LITTLE YOU CAN DO ABOUT IT.

ON THE OTHER HAND IF YOU HAVE LOW SELF-ESTEEM...DO NOT ACCEPT IT! WORK ON IT EVERY DAY OF YOUR LIFE....IT IS SOME-THING YOU CAN CHANGE. IT MAY BE SOMETHING YOU WILL HAVE TO LEARN TO CHANGE IF YOU ARE EVER GOING TO BE HAPPY. (SHY PEOPLE WHO I KNOW ARE NOT ONLY NICE PEOPLE , BUT THEY ARE ALSO HAPPY PEOPLE!)

LET'S MOVE TO THE NEXT EASY STEP AND TALK ABOUT THE VERY IMPORTANT SUBJECT OF SELF-ESTEEM.....BUT DON'T MAKE THE MOVE YET, UNLESS YOU ARE READY TO ACCEPT YOUR SHYNESS AS PART OF YOU, SOME THING NOT ALL TOGETHER THAT BAD AND SOMETHING THAT DOES NOT MAKE YOU A LOSER.

37 EASY STEPS ... DENNY

EASY STEP #25

EASY STEP #25

I'M SO LOW.......
I'VE GOT ROAD RASH ON MY NAVEL!

SO, WHERE DOES THIS LOW SELF-ESTEEM COME FROM?

FOR STARTERS, I DOUBT THAT WE ARE BORN WITH IT...EVERY BABY
THAT HAS EVER BEEN BORN THINKS IT IS THE CENTER OF THE
UNIVERSE AND THAT EVERYONE ELSE HAS BEEN PLACED IN THEIR
UNIVERSE TO SERVE THEIR NEEDS! THEY HAVE THIS REINFORCED
BY REALIZING THAT ALL THEY HAVE TO DO IS OPEN UP THEIR
MOUTH AND CRY AND SOMEONE WILL COME RUNNING TO TAKE
CARE OF THEIR EVERY NEED.....LIKE BEING THE KING OF A YOUR
VERY OWN LITTLE LAND! WE CERTAINLY START OUT WITH A
PRETTY GOOD DOSE OF SELF-ESTEEM. BUT LOW SELF-ESTEEM IS
SOMETHING THAT JUST GROWS ON US LIKE A FUNGUS!

AND IT COMES FROM TWO DIFFERENT PLACES: WHAT OTHERS SAY
ABOUT US AND WHAT WE SAY ABOUT OURSELVES.

WE ESTABLISHED BEFORE THAT PARENTS AREN'T PERFECT. BUT,
EVEN IF WE ACKNOWLEDGE THAT PARENTING ISN'T SUCH AN EASY
TASK.....THERE ARE SOME PARENTS WHO SAY PRETTY HATEFUL
AND DESTRUCTIVE THINGS TO THEIR KIDS AND EVEN THE ABSO-
LUTE BEST PARENTS CAN SOMETIMES GIVE VERY NEGATIVE MES-
SAGES TO THEIR CHILDREN. AS KIDS WE BELIEVE A LOT OF
THINGS....ESPECIALLY WHEN THEY ARE REPEATED A LOT OR WHEN
THEY COME FROM PEOPLE WE FEEL WE CAN TRUST.

I REMEMBER WHEN I WAS GROWING UP , IF SOMEONE WOULD SAY

SOMETHING NICE ABOUT ME IN FRONT OF MY MOTHER, MY MOTHER WOULD REPLY, "NOW, DON'T GO SAYING THAT ABOUT HIM....HE' LL GET A BIG HEAD ABOUT HIMSELF!"

IT HAS TAKEN ME A LOT OF YEARS TO REALIZE:

IT IS OK TO FEEL GOOD ABOUT YOURSELF!

NOT ONLY IS IT OK TO FEEL GOOD ABOUT YOURSELF...IT IS ACTUALLY HEALTHY! SOMETIMES I THINK IT IS AMAZING THAT SOME PEOPLE HAVE ANY SELF-ESTEEM AT ALL, WHEN YOU KNOW THEIR EXPERIENCES GROWING UP. HOW DOES A CHILD WHOSE PARENTS HAVE DRILLED IN TO HIS HEAD THAT HE IS NO GOOD AND WILL NEVER AMOUNT TO ANYTHING EVER GAIN SELF-RESPECT AND SELF- LOVE.? HOW DOES THE CHILD WHOSE PARENTS SAY TO HIM, "I'M SORRY I EVER HAD YOU" EVER DEVELOP INTO A HEALTHY ADULT. WELL, IT DOES HAPPEN AND IT HAPPENS BECAUSE EACH OF US HAS WITHIN OURSELVES THE POWER TO OVER-RULE THE NEGATIVES IN OUR LIVES. EACH ONE OF US HAS THE POWER TO SPEAK TO HIMSELF AND GIVE NEW AND POSITIVE MESSAGES TO HIMSELF.

MOST PEOPLE HAVE LOW SELF ESTEEM BECAUSE OF THE STORIES THEY TELL THEMSELVES ABOUT THEMSELVES AND BECAUSE OF THEIR WILLINGNESS TO BELIEVE EVEN THE STUPIDEST STORIES.

LET'S SEE IF WE CAN FIND SOME EXAMPLES....THEY ARE NOT HARD TO FIND, ONCE YOU START LOOKING.

ONE OF THE MOST COMMON EXAMPLES I SEE ARE PEOPLE WHO ALWAYS WANT TO COMPARE THEMSELVES WITH SOMEONE ELSE...AND THEY ALWAYS CHOOSE TO PAINT THE OTHER PERSON AS BEING MUCH COOLER AND MORE FORTUNATE THAN THEM- SELVES. "JENNIE IS SO LUCKY; SHE HAS THE NEATEST PARENTS!" , "MY SISTER IS SO MUCH SMARTER THAN ME", "TROY IS SO LUCKY...HE IS SIX FOOT FOUR AND CAN PLAY BASKETBALL AND STILL GET GREAT GRADES BECAUSE HE IS SO SMART", "TIFFANY IS SO LUCKY, HER FATHER BOUGHT HER A NEW CAMERO FOR HER SIXTEENTH BIRTHDAY....THERE IT WAS RIGHT IN HER DRIVEWAY WHEN SHE GOT HOME FROM SCHOOL!"

I'M SURE YOU CAN ADD A THOUSAND NEW ITEMS TO THIS LIST AND THAT YOU THOUGHT LIKE THIS AT LEAST TEN TIMES TODAY YOUR- SELF.

REMEMBER GROUCHO! THE ONE THING THAT WE CANNOT HAVE IS TO BE SOMEBODY ELSE! WE ARE ALL STUCK. ALL WE HAVE IS OURSELVES AND WE CAN NEVER CHANGE THAT....WE HAD BETTER LEARN TO ENJOY IT AND DO THE BEST THAT WE CAN WITH IT. BUT WHAT GOES INTO DOING THE BEST THAT WE CAN WITH IT?

MAYBE THE FIRST ISSUE IS TO MEASURE YOUR OWN SELF ESTEEM...MAYBE YOU DON'T EVEN NEED THIS CHAPTER....PERHAPS YOU CAN ZOOM RIGHT OVER TO THE NEXT EASY STEP.

LET'S SEE IF WE CAN DEVISE A WAY TO EVALUATE OUR OWN SELF-ESTEEM....OUR OWN PERCEPTION OR FEELING ABOUT OURSELVES, REMEMBERING THAT PERCEPTIONS AND FEELINGS AREN'T NECESSARILY RIGHT OR WRONG.....THEY JUST ARE.

DR. DENNY'S JUSTIFIABLY- FAMOUS SELF ESTEEM QUIZ

		YES	NO
1.	I GET EASILY UPSET BY CRITICISM.	☐	☐
2.	THERE IS ONE THING ABOUT THE WAY I LOOK THAT I ABSOLUTELY DETEST.	☐	☐
3.	I RUN FROM TAKING SIMPLE RISKS.	☐	☐
4.	I AM AFRAID TO LET PEOPLE GET TO KNOW ME BECAUSE THEY MAY FIND OUT TOO MUCH.	☐	☐
5.	I DRESS SO I WON'T STAND OUT IN THE CROWD.	☐	☐
6.	I OFTEN ENVY OTHERS.	☐	☐
7.	I SECRETLY TAKE PLEASURE WHEN OTHERS FAIL.	☐	☐
8.	I FREQUENTLY HIDE MY FEELING FROM OTHERS.	☐	☐
9.	I OFTEN FIND REASONS NOT TO CHANGE.	☐	☐
10.	I THINK OTHERS DO A BETTER JOB THAN I DO.	☐	☐
11.	I SELDOM VOLUNTEER FOR AN ASSIGNMENT.	☐	☐
12.	I HAVE REFUSED A DATE BECAUSE I WAS AFRAID.	☐	☐
13.	I AVOID MEETING NEW PEOPLE.	☐	☐
14.	I OFTEN DON'T GIVE MYSELF CREDIT FOR SUCCESS.	☐	☐
15.	I HIDE WHEN THEY LOOK FOR VOLUNTEERS.	☐	☐
16.	I THINK I'M TOO SKINNY OR TOO FAT.	☐	☐
17.	I SCREW UP MORE THAN OTHERS.	☐	☐
19.	I WISH I COULD BE SOMEONE ELSE.	☐	☐
20.	I HAVE TROUBLE LAUGHING AT MY OWN MISTAKES.	☐	☐

SCORING: GIVE YOURSELF 5 POINTS FOR EVERY "NO" AND ZERO POINTS FOR EVERY "YES"   MY SCORE _____
NOW RATE YOURSELF ON THIS JUSTIFIABLY-FAMOUS RATING

SYSTEM:

100-91   YOU FEEL <u>TOO</u> GOOD ABOUT YOURSELF! A PROBLEM?
90-89   BE CAREFUL ABOUT BEING COCKY!
80-89   SOUNDS HEALTHY
70-79   GREAT!
60-69   GOOD DAYS AND BAD...I BET!
50-59   TOLERABLE, BUT NEEDS SOME WORK!
40-49   LESS THAN HALF FULL; MORE THAN HALF EMPTY!
30-39   WHOOPS.....WORK NEEDED!
20-29   CRAM COURSE NEEDED
10-19   NOBODY SCORES THIS LOW
0-9   CALL FOR AN EMERGENCY APPOINTMENT!

OK, ALL THOSE NEEDING REMEDIAL WORK....LET'S GET TO IT!

FIRST REMEMBER, THIS BOOK IS ABOUT MANIPULATION AND ALL MANIPULATION REQUIRES <u>ACTION!</u> IN FACT, THE KEY TO SELF-ESTEEM IS ACTION!

HOW DO YOU KNOW THAT YOU CAN RIDE A HORSE? BECAUSE YOU HAVE DONE IT! THE SAME IS TRUE FOR JUST ABOUT EVERYTHING THAT YOU CAN THINK OF. HOW DO YOU KNOW YOU CAN COOK? OR DANCE ? OR SING? OR PLEASE YOUR PARENTS? BECAUSE YOU HAVE DONE IT BEFORE!

IF YOU HAVE NEVER BEEN ASSERTIVE, THE WAY THAT YOU CAN PROVE YOU ARE CAPABLE OF BEING ASSERTIVE IS BY DOING IT. RISKING AND DOING IS THE KEY TO ANY CHANGE. AND, OH YES, ALONG WITH ACCEPTING FAILURE AS A PART OF LIFE AND NOT A CATASTROPHE! (TAKE IT FROM SOMEONE WHO CAN'T CARRY A TUNE, IS A LOUSY DANCER AND HAS FLUNKED OUT OF MEDICAL SCHOOL, FIRST TIME AROUND!)

BASIC RULES:

A.   DON'T EXPECT SUCCESS EVERY TIME YOU TAKE A RISK.
B.   YOU DON'T HAVE TO BE PERFECT TO HAVE SELF-CONFIDENCE.
C.   DON'T THINK ABOUT PAST FAILURES
D.   REWARD YOURSELF FOR SUCCESSES
E.   LEARN TO ASK FOR HELP.
F.   REMEMBER, IT IS A GRADUAL PROCESS
G.   LOOK AROUND AND SEE THAT OTHERS ARE HAVING TO RISK TOO
H.   HELP THE OTHER RISKERS AND THEY WILL HELP YOU
I.   KEEP TRACK OF EVERY TIME YOU CATCH YOURSELF BEING THE ONE PUTTING YOU DOWN.

FEE-EE-EE-LINGS WO-O-O

RISKING ISN'T A CATASTROPHE...
TAKE IT FROM ONE WHO CAN'T
CARRY A TUNE, IS A LOUSEY DANCER
& ONCE FAILED-OUT OF MEDICAL
SCHOOL....

ONCE YOU HAVE THE BASIC RULES IT IS A MATTER OF PRACTICE, PRACTICE, PRACTICE.

THE REST OF US CAN ONLY WATCH AND WISH YOU MANY FAILURES SO THAT YOU CAN GROW AND GAIN CONFIDENCE.

ALL RIGHT, TO BED OR BACK TO YOUR HOMEWORK.....YOU'VE DONE ENOUGH WORK FOR ONE DAY—REMEMBER IT HAS TO BE A GRADUAL PROCESS!

BUT, BEFORE YOU LEAVE, HERE IS A LOVELY LITTLE POEM THAT ONE OF MY YOUNG FRIENDS SLIPPED TO ME THE OTHER DAY... HER WAY OF SAYING "THANKS" TO ME, AND TO HERSELF!

I'M A SPECIAL GIFT

A PERSONALITY ALL MY OWN
FOR I AM STRONG
MIST OF SELF-LOVE ENCIRCLE ME
NO ONE CAN BE ME
FOR THERE IS NO OTHER
THERE IS JUST ME
FOR THIS I AM THANKFUL
GOD TRULY BLESSED ME
WITH THE ABILITY TO THRIVE

A FACE OF MY OWN UNIQUENESS
A HEART THAT POUNDS OUT THE LOVE I DELIVER
I HAVE THE GIFT TO TRY
TO SHAPE THE BEST OF WHAT'S BEEN GIVEN
I CAN ACHIEVE
I WILL ALWAYS ARRIVE AT THE DESTINATION
I'VE LONGED TO TRAVEL
WHETHER I HURRY
OR TAKE MY TIME

I WILL SEE THAT GOAL I WORKED TO ACCOMPLISH
I AM FILLED WITH RADIANCE
I AM SEEN BEYOND THE GALAXY
I HAVE THE POWER
THE CONTROL
TO MOLD AND MANIPULATE MY LIFE
TO MY SATISFACTION

MY VOICE
PEOPLE HEAR ME
EXTERIOR AND INTERIOR FEATURES
I WILL NOT BE PASSED OVER
I WILL NOT BE IGNORED
I HAVE SURVIVED
MY OWN WAY
SEE ME STAND TALL

LARISA B.

I'M A "SPECIAL" GIFT
I AM ME ...

NOW MY FRIEND, BEFORE YOU SLEEP, REMEMBER THE EQUATION:
MANIPULATION = ACTION

BEFORE YOU DOZE OFF....MAKE A GOAL FOR TOMORROW: ONE
SPECIFIC MANIPULATION YOU ARE GOING TO MAKE TOMORROW TO
IMPROVE YOUR SELF-ESTEEM.

DON'T FORGET, ONE STEP AT A TIME, BUT EVERY DAY MISSED IS A
DAY YOU'LL NEVER HAVE AGAIN!

EASY STEP # 26

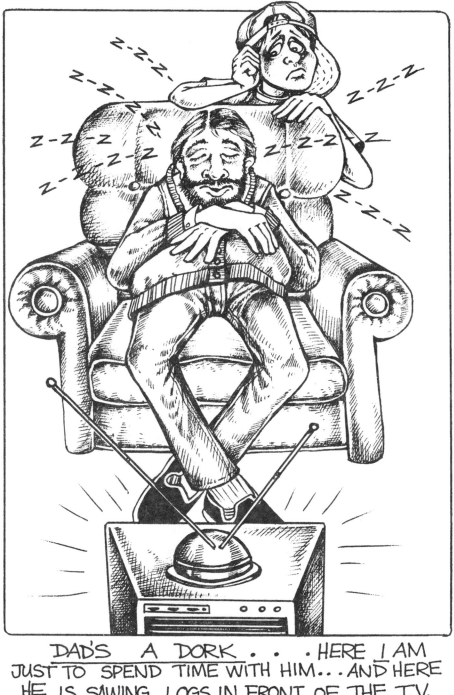

EASY STEP # 26

DAD'S A DORK......I GOTTA GET HIM HELP!

REMEMBER! MANIPULATION EQUALS ACTION....AND SOMETIMES
YOU HAVE TO TAKE ACTION INTO YOUR OWN HANDS. HERE, AN-
OTHER ONE OF MY YOUNG FRIENDS WANTS TO TELL YOU A STORY:

THINGS AROUND MY HOUSE WERE PRETTY BAD AND THEY
WERE GETTING WORSE EVERY DAY. MY MOTHER AND
FATHER HAD GOTTEN DIVORCED ABOUT THREE YEARS
EARLIER AND I THOUGHT THAT I HAD DEALT WITH IT
PRETTY WELL. MY FATHER MARRIED AGAIN AND HIS NEW
WIFE WAS TOLERABLE AND I INHERITED A STEPSISTER WHO
WAS A BIT OF A BRAT, BUT SHE STAYED OUT OF MY HAIR
MOST OF THE TIME. MY MOM SEEMED HAPPY AND WAS
BUSY WITH A LOT OF HER ACTIVITIES....MAKING NEW
FRIENDS AND DATING SEVERAL DIFFERENT MEN WHO
SEEMED TO TREAT HER WELL, ALTHOUGH I NEVER GOT TOO
CLOSE TO ANY OF THEM.

BUT A FUNNY THING STARTED HAPPENING.....EVERY TIME I
WOULD GO OVER TO MY DAD'S HOUSE I WOULD FIND MYSELF
GETTING INTO A FIGHT WITH HIM .... EVEN WHEN I THOUGHT
I WAS TRYING MY BEST NOT TO! SOMETHING SMALL WOULD
USUALLY START IT OFF. I USED TO THINK THAT THE ONLY
REASON HE EVER WANTED ME TO COME OVER WAS TO HELP
HIM CUT THE GRASS. OR I USED TO GET THE IMPRESSION
FROM HIM THAT HE WANTED ME TO COME OVER BUT HE
DIDN'T WANT TO SPEND TIME WITH ME. SOMETIMES HE
WOULD EVEN FALL ASLEEP ON THE COUCH WHILE WATCH-
ING A BASEBALL GAME AND I WOULD HAVE TO FIGURE OUT
WHAT I WAS GOING TO DO WITH MYSELF.

EVENTUALLY IT GOT TO THE POINT THAT I STARTED MAKING
EXCUSES WHY I COULD NOT COME OVER. AND I ALWAYS
HAD LOTS OF EXCUSES....THEY ARE A DIME A DOZEN! EVEN-
TUALLY HE STARTED TO ACT LIKE HE DIDN'T EVEN CARE
THAT I WASN'T COMING OVER. IT GOT SO I ONLY WENT OVER
HOLIDAYS AND SOMETIMES NOT EVEN THEN. ABOUT A
WEEK BEFORE CHRISTMAS WE GOT IN TO A BIG FIGHT AND
NEITHER OF US WOULD BACK DOWN. I CAN HARDLY RE-
MEMBER WHAT IT WAS ALL ABOUT NOW, BUT BOTH OF US
WERE STUBBORN AND NEITHER OF US WOULD SAY WE WERE
SORRY. IT WAS MY YEAR TO SPEND CHRISTMAS WITH MY
DAD BUT I DIDN'T. I WENT HOME WITH MY MOTHER IN-
STEAD.

I THOUGHT THAT MY FATHER WOULD CALL AFTER CHRIST-
MAS AND TRY TO MAKE PEACE, BUT HE NEVER DID AND
FOR THREE MONTHS WE DIDN'T SEE EACH OTHER. HE THEN
CALLED ME ONE DAY AND ASKED ME IF I WANTED TO GO TO
A BASKETBALL GAME AND I SAID YES. AT FIRST WE ACTED
LIKE EVERY THING WAS WONDERFUL.....AS IF WE WERE THE
BEST OF FRIENDS AGAIN, BUT THEN BEFORE THE NIGHT WAS
OVER WE WERE INTO A HUGE FIGHT AND HE DROPPED ME
HOME AND TOLD ME THAT HE DIDN'T WANT TO SEE ME
AGAIN UNTIL I COULD TREAT HIM RIGHT. I TOLD HIM THAT
WAS OK WITH ME BECAUSE I HAD NO DESIRE TO SEE HIM
AGAIN ANYWAY.

AT FIRST I STAYED STUBBORN AND ACTED LIKE I DIDN'T
CARE. ANOTHER HOLIDAY CAME AND HE DIDN'T CALL AND
I ACTED LIKE I DIDN'T CARE....BUT INSIDE IT WAS STARTING
TO BOTHER ME. I AM NOT SURE ANYONE NOTICED IT AT
FIRST. I WAS KIND OF GLOOMY AND MY GRADES STARTED
TO FALL AND THEN ONE DAY I GOT INTO AN ARGUMENT
WITH A TEACHER AND AS A RESULT I WAS SENT TO A
SCHOOL COUNSELOR. I CAN STILL REMEMBER THAT MEET-
ING. I THOUGHT HE WAS GOING TO YELL AND SCREAM AT
ME, BUT INSTEAD HE JUST SAID, "MICHAEL, DO YOU WANT
TO TELL ME WHAT'S WRONG?"

I STARTED CRYING MY EYES OUT.....EVEN THOUGH I
THOUGHT I WAS TOUGH AND SAID, "EVERYTHING'S WRONG"
AND THEN MUCH TO MY SURPRISE I SAID, "I THINK MY
FATHER HATES ME!" BEFORE THAT I HAD ACTED AS IF IT
HADN'T BOTHERED ME...BUT SUDDENLY IT CAME THROUGH
LIKE A WATERFALL AND I COULDN'T STOP CRYING.

THE COUNSELOR SAID SOMETHING THAT SOUNDED KIND OF
STRANGE, "WELL, YOUNG MAN, IT SOUNDS LIKE YOU NEED
TO GET SOME HELP FOR YOUR FATHER!"

I LOOKED AT HIM LIKE HE WAS CRAZY AND SAID, "BUT HE'S THE ONE WITH THE PROBLEM!"

HE REPLIED, "YEAH, MAYBE THAT IS WHY YOU HAVE TO BE THE ONE TO GET THE HELP!"

"BUT HE'S THE ADULT !", I ARGUED.

"THAT DOESN'T MEAN HE KNOWS HOW TO SOLVE THE PROBLEM!" HE SAID.

ANYWAY, THE COUNSELOR ASKED IF HE COULD SET UP A MEETING WITH MY DAD AND ME. I SAID OK, BUT I'M NOT SURE THAT I MEANT IT.

THE FIRST MEETING WAS A TOTAL DISASTER! WE HAD ONLY MADE THINGS WORSE. WE EVEN STARTED YELLING AT EACH OTHER AND HE DIDN'T LISTEN TO A WORD I HAD TO SAY. ALL HE DID WAS DEFEND HIMSELF AND BLAME EVERYTHING ON ME. AT THE END I WOULDN'T EVEN LET HIM DRIVE ME HOME AND I WALKED THE THREE MILES HOME BY MYSELF.

THE COUNSELOR TOLD ME THAT WE HAD TO KEEP MEETING THAT HE THOUGHT THE MEETING HAD GONE WELL. I LAUGHED AT HIM AND TOLD HIM THAT THE ONLY GOOD PART WAS THAT I HADN'T KILLED MY FATHER ON THE SPOT.

THE NEXT MEETING I DIDN'T WASTE TIME....I ATTACKED. I TOLD MY FATHER THAT I THOUGHT HE HATED ME AND THAT I WAS TIRED OF BEING THE ONE PUTTING ALL THE EFFORT IN TO OUR RELATIONSHIP. I TOLD HIM THAT I WAS TIRED OF BEING THE ONE TO BLAME ALL THE TIME AND I WAS TIRED OF TRYING TO PLEASE HIM ALL THE TIME.

MY DAD FIRST SEEMED TO BE GETTING MAD AND THEN HE TURNED TO ME AND SAID, "YOU KNOW, I REALLY BELIEVE THAT YOU LOVE ME BUT I DON'T THINK YOU LIKE ME!"

I KEPT UP MY ATTACK AND SAID, "DAD, SOMETIMES I DON'T EVEN THINK I LOVE YOU! "......I REALIZED WHAT I HAD SAID BUT IT WAS TOO LATE TO TAKE IT BACK!

MY DAD STARTED TO CRY AND THEN HE SAID, "YOU KNOW SON, I DIDN'T KNOW I LOVED MY FATHER UNTIL TWO YEARS AFTER HE DIED...AND THEN IT WAS MUCH TOO LATE TO DO ANYTHING ABOUT IT. I MADE A PROMISE TO MYSELF THAT I WASN'T GOING TO WAIT UNTIL I DIED TO KNOW HOW YOU FEEL ABOUT ME. IF YOU HATE ME I CAN TAKE IT....BUT I WANT TO KNOW WHERE I STAND WITH YOU NOW, NOT AFTER I AM GONE."

THE COUNSELOR THEN SPOKE UP AND SAID, "IT SOUNDS LIKE BOTH OF YOU HAVE THE SAME PROBLEM....YOU BOTH WANT TO KNOW THAT YOU ARE LOVED."

MY FATHER THEN SAID, "I'D SETTLE, FOR NOW, JUST TO KNOW THAT HE LIKES ME!"

SUDDENLY I REALIZED WHERE OUR STUBBORNNESS AND ANGER HAD GOTTEN US. WE WERE LIKE TWO RAMS WITH HORNS LOCKED IN BATTLE AND NEITHER OF US WAS WINNING!

I LAUGHED AND SAID, "I'M WILLING TO TRY IF YOU'LL STOP BEING SUCH A DORK!"

HE HUGGED ME AND SAID, "I'M WILLING TOO, IF YOU'LL STOP BEING SUCH AN INSENSITIVE JERK."

I TOLD HIM WE HAD A DEAL! I'D LIKE TO SAY THE REST WAS EASY, BUT THAT WASN'T REALLY THE CASE. IT TOOK US MONTHS OF HARD WORK TO FIGURE OUT THE TRUTH ABOUT WHY WE HAD BEEN SO ANGRY AT EACH OTHER AND SOME OF THE REASONS WERE THINGS THAT I HAD NEVER THOUGHT ABOUT BEFORE....BUT WE WERE ABLE TO TALK THEM OUT OVER TIME.

DAD'S STILL SELF-CENTERED EVERY NOW AND AGAIN AND I'M STILL A JERK EVERY ONCE AND A WHILE, BUT AT LEAST NOW WE CAN TALK TO EACH OTHER ABOUT IT WHEN IT HAPPENS. I THINK HE ACTUALLY LEARNED TO GROW UP! AND, BY THE WAY, I HAVEN'T MISSED A HOLIDAY IN A LONG WHILE. I'M SURE GLAD THAT I TOOK THE ACTION AND GOT HIM INTO THERAPY!

DAD & I ARE LIKE TWO RAMS; HORNS LOCKED IN BATTLE!

EASY STEP # 27

LEARNING... TOO LATE!

EASY STEP # 27

ARCHEOLOGY 101

THANK GOD, WE ALL GET SECOND CHANCES!

IN THE FIRST EDITION OF THIS BOOK, I WROTE AN "EASY STEP #27" THAT WAS BAD. AND I MEAN BAD. IT WAS LOUSY, STINKY, HOR-RIBLE, EMBARRASSING, IDIOTIC, USELESS, POINTLESS, DUMB, DRAB, DAFT, SICKENING, UNINTERESTING, FLAT, VALUELESS, OFF-THE-MARK, BANAL, SENSELESS, GOOPY, FRIGID, DWEEBISH, COUNTER-PRODUCTIVE, LOQUACIOUS, SELF-AGGRANDIZING, TANGENTIAL, PEDESTRIAN, TEPID, STUPID, NARROW, DISGUSTING, RANCID, WORTHLESS, DEFECTIVE, ABSURD, REDUNDANT, DISOR-GANIZED, BLAND, PUTRID, AND TOTALLY WITHOUT REDEEMING SOCIAL VALUE.

TAKE MY WORD FOR IT… IT WAS NOT GOOD!

THEN, ONE NIGHT AS I SAT IN FRONT OF A ROARING FIRE, SIPPING PRUNE JUICE, IT SUDDENLY CAME TO ME:

WHAT A WORLD WE LIVE IN!
WE ALL GET SECOND CHANCES!

I GUESS IT IS ESPECIALLY TRUE IF YOU ARE YOUNG. HOW MANY TIMES HAVE YOU DONE SOMETHING THAT YOU DID NOT GET A CHANCE TO CORRECT? THINK ABOUT THE BIGGEST FIGHT THAT YOU EVER HAD WITH ONE OF YOUR PARENTS. DID THEY EVER SAY TO YOU, "THAT'S IT! WE'LL NEVER TRUST YOU AGAIN." (AND REALLY MEAN IT… BECAUSE THOSE KINDS OF THINGS SOMETIMES SLIP OUT OF PARENT'S MOUTHS IN THE HEAT OF THE MOMENT. REMEM-BER, THAT DIDN'T EVEN HAVE TO GET A LICENSE FOR THEIR JOB!) HOW MANY TIMES HAVE YOU NOT BEEN GIVEN A SECOND CHANCE?

EVEN ADULTS GET SECOND CHANCES… SO HERE IS MINE TO MAKE A DECENT "EASY STEP #27."

I WANT TO TELL YOU A LITTLE STORY THAT MIGHT MAKE A LIE OUT OF EVERYTHING I JUST SAID AND, HOPEFULLY, WILL CONFUSE YOU INTO SOME DEEPER THINKING ON THE SUBJECT. IS THAT UNCLEAR ENOUGH TO YOU?

THE YEAR WAS 1966. ANCIENT TIMES! LONG BEFORE YOUR BIRTH!

I WAS YOUNG MYSELF AND A PEACE CORPS VOLUNTEER IN EAST AFRICA. I WAS JUST FINISHING MY TWO YEAR TOUR AND WAS EAGER TO GET HOME TO SEE MY FAMILY AND FRIENDS AGAIN. TWO YEARS IS A MIGHTY LONG TIME TO BE AWAY AND, ALTHOUGH I LOVED AFRICA, I WAS EAGER TO GET HOME.

TWO DAYS BEFORE I WAS LEAVING, I WAS RIDING MY BIKE BACK FROM A VILLAGE AND MY CHAIN CAME OFF. I STOPPED TO FIX IT. I HEARD A VOICE ASK, "DO YOU NEED SOME HELP?"

I LOOKED UP AND ACROSS THE ROAD AND UNDER A SHADE TREE, I SAW A SMALL AFRICAN MAN WITH GLASSES AS THICK AS ENGLISH MUFFINS. I TOLD HIM I DIDN'T NEED ANY HELP. HE THEN ASKED IF I NEEDED SOMETHING TO DRINK. I FIXED MY BIKE AND WALKED IT OVER TO HIS HUT AND HE MOTIONED FOR ME TO SIT DOWN. UP CLOSE, I COULD SEE THAT HE HAD ON THE WELL-WORN CASSOCK OF A PRIEST AND HE HAD A BEAUTIFUL GOLD CROSS AROUND HIS NECK.

WE BEGAN TO TALK AS I DRANK THE WATER HE HAD GIVEN ME. THE SUN WAS STARTING TO SET AND THE SKY WAS PINK. I LEARNED HIS NAME WAS PETER AND THAT HE HAD BEEN BORN NEAR WHERE HE NOW LIVED, OVER NINETY-SIX YEARS EARLIER. HE WAS A HUMBLE AND QUIET MAN WHO DID NOT TALK ABOUT HIMSELF EASILY. BUT HE DID TELL ME THAT WHEN HE WAS A LITTLE BOY OF ONLY SIX, ONE DAY SOME ARAB SLAVE TRADERS CAME INTO HIS VILLAGE. EVERYONE YELLED FOR HIM TO RUN. HE HID IN THE REEDS NEAR THE LAKE SHORE BUT COULD SEE THE SLAVERS KILLING THE YOUNG AND THE VERY OLD WHO WOULD NEVER SURVIVE THE SIX HUNDRED MILE WALK TO ZANZIBAR. HE SAW HIS OWN FATHER WHIPPED AND PUT INTO A YOKE FOR THE CARAVAN MARCH. HE SAW HIS MOTHER BEING TIED AT THE WRIST WITH BARK AND BEING FORCED BY WHIP TO FOLLOW. HE DID NOT KNOW WHAT TO DO, BUT KNEW HE WOULD BE ALONE IF HE STAYED BEHIND IN THE VILLAGE. BESIDES, THE SLAVERS HAD BURNED ALL THEIR HUTS AND FIELDS AS IF IT WAS PLAY FOR THEM. THERE WAS NOTHING LEFT OF HIS VILLAGE.

PETER THEN TOLD ME ABOUT THE TRIP THE CARAVAN MADE TO ZANZIBAR, HOW HIS MOTHER WAS DRAGGED FROM HIM TO BE SOLD FOR A HAREM, AND HOW HE HIMSELF WAS AUCTIONED AT THE SLAVE MARKET. THEN HE TOLD ME HOW HE AND HIS FATHER HAD BEEN PUT ON A *DHOW*, AN ARAB SAILBOAT, TO BE TAKEN TO THE MIDDLE EAST.

BUT, BY THEN IT WAS STARTING TO GET DARK AND THE ROAD WOULD BE DANGEROUS. I HAD TO LEAVE AT THIS POINT IN THE

STORY. THAT NIGHT I COULD NOT SLEEP, THINKING ABOUT PETER… WONDERING HOW HE HAD SURVIVED. WONDERING HOW HE HAD LEARNED ENGLISH. WONDERING HOW HE HAD BECOME A PRIEST. WONDERING WHAT HIS LIFE HAD BEEN LIKE.

THE NEXT DAY—MY LAST IN AFRICA—I BICYCLED OUT TO HIS VILLAGE BUT WAS TOLD THAT HE HAD TAKEN A BUS TO THE CITY AND HE WOULD NOT BE BACK FOR TWO DAYS. I HAD MISSED MY OPPORTUNITY TO LEARN THE REST OF THE STORY.

WHEN I GOT HOME I THOUGHT A LOT ABOUT PETER, TRYING TO RECONSTRUCT IN MY MIND THE STORY OF HIS LIFE… BUT, I WAS NEVER VERY SUCCESSFUL.

FOR THREE YEARS I WORKED AND SAVED MY MONEY AND FINALLY HAD ENOUGH TO RETURN. I HAD MISSED AFRICA AND WAS LOOKING FORWARD TO MY RETURN AND SEEING OLD FRIENDS AGAIN. BUT ABOVE ALL, I WAS LOOKING FORWARD TO SITTING ON PETER'S PORCH AND LEARNING THE REST OF HIS STORY FROM HIS OWN LIPS.

WHEN I GOT THERE, I BORROWED A BICYCLE AND PEDALLED TO HIS VILLAGE. IT WAS QUIET AND EERIE. HIS HOUSE LOOKED RUN-DOWN.

I ASKED A MAN WHO LIVED NEARBY WHERE I COULD FIND PETER.

HE SAID, "OH, I AM SO SORRY. YOU ARE TOO LATE. HE DEVELOPED PNEUMONIA AND DIED LAST YEAR!"

I NEVER WOULD SEE PETER AGAIN. I LEARNED AN IMPORTANT LESSON RIGHT THEN AND THERE:

WE ARE NOT <u>ALWAYS</u> GUARANTEED A SECOND CHANCE!

LATER, LIKE AN ARCHEOLOGIST DIGGING IN THE RUINS, I DISCOVERED A LOT MORE ABOUT PETER. SOME OF HIS NEIGHBORS TOLD ME STORIES ABOUT HIS LATER YEARS AS A PRIEST IN THEIR VILLAGES. HIS GRANDSON SHARED MANY OF HIS LETTERS AND PICTURES FROM COUNTRIES HE HAD VISITED WHILE IN THE BRITISH ARMY. I READ WHAT HE HAD WRITTEN ABOUT HIS OWN LIFE, HIS MARRIAGE AND HIS CALLING TO HIS VOCATION. I VISITED THE OLD SLAVE MARKET IN ZANZIBAR WHERE HE HAD BEEN SOLD. I TALKED TO PEOPLE WHO HAD KNOWN HIM IN LONDON, BOMBAY AND OTHER PLACES HE HAD LIVED AND HEARD STORIES THAT HELPED FILL IN THE BLANK SPOTS OF HIS LIFE.

IN THE END, I FELT I HAD COME TO KNOW PETER QUITE WELL…
WELL ENOUGH TO RECONSTRUCT THE STORY OF HIS LIFE AND
WRITE ABOUT HIM. BUT, I NEVER GOT TO KNOW HIM AS I WOULD
HAVE IF I'D HAD THE CHANCE TO SIT ON HIS PORCH AND HEAR THE
STORIES FROM HIS OWN LIPS—JUST ONE MORE TIME.

MAYBE, YOU'LL REMEMBER PETER THE NEXT TIME YOU'RE WITH
YOUR GRANDPARENTS AND WILL REMEMBER TO TAKE A FEW
PRECIOUS MOMENTS TO "DIG INTO" THE STORIES OF THEIR LIVES.
PERHAPS, YOU'LL EVEN SURPRISE YOUR PARENTS THE NEXT TIME
THEY ASK WHAT YOU'D LIKE FOR YOUR BIRTHDAY WHEN YOU
RESPOND, "A TICKET TO GO AND SPEND SOME TIME WITH GRANNY
AND GRANDPA."

BUT DON'T DELAY. THERE ARE INDEED SOME THINGS YOU JUST
DON'T GET A SECOND CHANCE TO DO!

GRANDPARENT IDEAS!

1. ASK THEM TO GO THROUGH OLD PHOTO ALBUMS WITH YOU.

2. TAKE THEM TO A HOBBY STORE AND FIND A PROJECT YOU CAN ALL WORK ON TOGETHER.

3. HAVE THEM SHOW YOU THE SCHOOL THEY WENT TO. ASK THEM WHAT THEY REMEMBER BEST ABOUT THE CLASSROOMS, THE TEACHERS, THE SPORTS TEAMS, THEIR FRIENDS.

4. GO TO THE LIBRARY AND TRY TO FIND BOOKS OR MAGAZINES THAT WERE PUBLISHED WHEN THEY WERE KIDS.

5. GO TO FLEA MARKETS. YOU'LL BE SURPRISED HOW MANY "ANTIQUES" ARE THINGS THEY HAVE ACTUALLY USED.

6. ASK WHAT THEY REMEMBER ABOUT THEIR OWN PARENTS... YOUR GREAT-GREAT GRANDPARENTS.

7. RECORD STORIES THEY TELL YOU; SAVE THEM FOR YOUR OWN GRANDCHILDREN.

8. RENT SOME OLD MOVIES... ONES THEY CAN REMEMBER AS KIDS.

9. TEACH THEM HOW TO ROLLER BLADE. (DON'T LAUGH. THEY MAY NEED A GOOD CHALLENGE.

10. TAKE A RISK. TELL THEM ABOUT PROBLEMS YOU ARE HAVING WITH YOUR PARENTS. IT MIGHT BE TRICKY BUSINESS, BUT THEY MIGHT FIND A WAY TO HELP.

11. VOLUNTEER TOGETHER TO WORK AT THE DOG POUND.

12. SPEND A COUPLE OF YEARS PLANNING A TRIP TOGETHER TO ALASKA.

13. LEARN TO GET EXCITED ABOUT LAWN BOWLING.

14. TELL THEM THAT WHEN YOU VISIT FOR A WEEK, YOU'D LIKE TO WORK WITH THEM ON HABITAT FOR HUMANITY (IF YOU ARE OLD ENOUGH TO SWING A HAMMER OR CLEAN UP A WORK SITE.)

15. ASK THEM TO SHOW YOU HOW THEY DANCED WHEN THEY WERE COURTING.

16. ASK YOUR GRANDFATHER TO TELL YOU ABOUT WHAT IT WAS LIKE WHEN HE WAS IN THE WAR.

17. DON'T FORGET TO ASK YOUR GRANDMOTHER TO TELL YOU WHAT IT WAS LIKE FOR HER WHEN HE WAS AWAY.

18. ORGANIZE THEM AND THEIR FRIENDS TO PLAY SOFT PUCK STREET HOCKEY. (MAYBE ON THE SHUFFLE BOARD COURT WITH ALL THE WEEDS GROWING THROUGH THE CRACKS.)

19. GET THEM TO TELL STORIES ON YOUR MOTHER OR FATHER. SOMETIMES THEY TURN OUT TO BE GOOD FOR BLACKMAIL!

20. TRY TO FIND OUT EVERY PLACE THEY HAVE LIVED IN THEIR LIVES.

21. COUNT THE NUMBER OF PRESIDENTS IN THEIR LIVES.

22. GET EXCITED ABOUT ONE OF THEIR HOBBIES.

23. GET GRANDMOTHER TO TEACH YOU HER FAVORITE RECIPES. PERHAPS YOU CAN MAKE UP A LITTLE COOKBOOK OF HER FAVORITES.

24. MAKE A LIST OF PROJECTS THAT YOU AND YOUR GRANDFATHER ARE GOING TO COMPLETE DURING YOUR VISIT.

25. ARRANGE A MAGICAL MYSTERY TOUR. TAKE THEM SOMEWHERE THEY'VE NEVER BEEN BEFORE.

26. MAKE THEM TELL YOU ABOUT JANIS JOPLIN, THE '54 YANKEES, THE '57 CHEVY, THE FIRST TIME THEY SAW THE BEATLES.

27. SIT AND LISTEN TO A FRANK SINATRA RECORDING WITH THEM. (UGH!)

28. ASK THEM TO TELL YOU EVERYTHING THEY REMEMBER ABOUT THE DAY PRESIDENT KENNEDY WAS KILLED.

29. MAKE A LIST WITH THEM OF THE TEN BEST BOOKS THEY HAVE READ IN THEIR ENTIRE LIFE.

30. MAKE UP SPOOKY STORIES ON A DARK, STORMY NIGHT.

31. RENT THE WIZARD OF OZ OR GONE WITH THE WIND. ASK THEM WHAT THEY REMEMBER ABOUT THE FIRST TIME THEY SAW IT.

32. GO TO A MAGIC STORE. MAKE AN AGREEMENT THAT YOU AND YOUR GRANDPARENT WILL BOTH HAVE TO MASTER A TRICK.

33. ASK YOUR GRANDPARENT IF YOU CAN GO TO THE ATTIC AND RE- TURN WITH ANY FIVE THINGS.

34. GO TO THE STATE FAIR TO SEE THE HORSES, COWS, PIGS AND THE COUNTY'S BIGGEST WATERMELON.

35. TAKE A WALKING TOUR OF THE NEIGHBORHOOD WHERE THEY GREW UP.

36. BUY THEM A CROQUET SET.

37. FIND OUT THE THINGS THAT THEY STILL WANT TO DO IN THEIR LIVES.

38. LEARN WHOM THEY WOULD WANT TO BE STRANDED ON A DESERT ISLAND WITH. (OTHER THAN EACH OTHER.)

39. TRY TO GET THEM TO TELL YOU ABOUT THE BIGGEST FIGHT THEY EVER HAD IN THEIR LIVES. THEN TRY TO GET THEM TO ACT IT OUT.

40. TRY TO FIND A WAY TO TELL THEM THE THINGS YOU LOVE ABOUT THEM THE MOST.

41. ASK THEM TO WATCH MTV WITH YOU JUST ONCE BEFORE THEY DECIDE THAT THEY HATE IT.

42. TELL THEM WHAT IT IS THAT YOU WOULD MOST LIKE TO HAVE OF THEIRS, TO BEST REMEMBER THEM BY.

43. CADDY FOR THEM.

44. SEE IF YOU CAN GET THEM TO TELL YOU ABOUT THE SADDEST DAY OF THEIR LIVES.

45. NEVER LET THEM SAY, "I CAN'T… I'M TOO OLD."

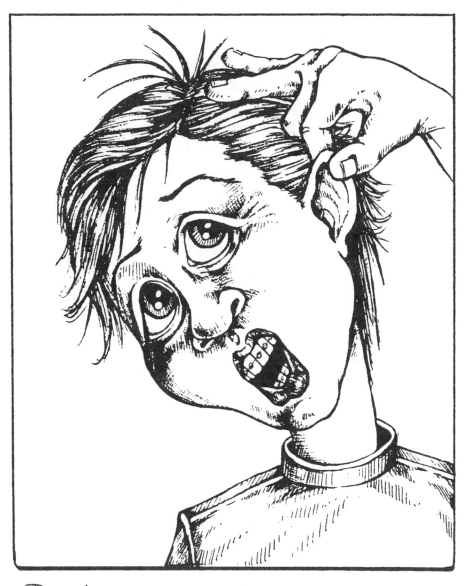

DON'T WAIT TO GET PULLED BY THE EAR. BE READY TO TAKE THE FIRST STEPS!

EASY STEP # 28

EASY STEP # 28

MY TEACHER WEARS LONG UNDERWEAR........ALL YEAR LONG!

I ONCE HAD A JOB I ABSOLUTELY HATED. I HATED TO GET UP IN THE MORNING AND I HATED TO GO TO WORK. I HATED THE THOUGHT I GOT AT NIGHT THAT I WOULD HAVE TO GO BACK TO MY JOB THE NEXT DAY. I HATED THE JOB SO MUCH THAT I DIDN'T PUT A GREAT DEAL OF EFFORT INTO IT AND MY BOSS WAS FOREVER CALLING ME INTO HIS OFFICE TO ASK MY WHY I WASN'T DOING BETTER. MY WORK FELL BEHIND BECAUSE I WASN'T MOTIVATED AND EVENTUALLY I HAD TO START TAKING MORE AND MORE WORK HOME WITH ME AT NIGHT TO MAKE UP FOR WHAT I HAD NOT BEEN ABLE TO DO DURING THE DAY, (MAINLY BECAUSE I SPENT MOST OF MY TIME STARING OUT THE WINDOW AND DREAMING OF WHAT OTHER KIND OF JOB I MIGHT POSSIBLY GET.) EVENTUALLY I QUIT THAT JOB, BUT IF I HAD NOT I AM SURE THAT I WOULD HAVE BEEN FIRED PRETTY SOON, ANYWAY.

I TELL YOU THIS BECAUSE YOUR JOB IS TO GO TO SCHOOL AND I KNOW WHAT IT IS LIKE WHEN YOU HATE YOUR JOB.....IT IS HOR-RIBLE!

NOW, I COULD WRITE A WHOLE LONG BOOK ABOUT SCHOOL.....AND I CAN BE GUARANTEED NO ONE WOULD READ IT BECAUSE IT WOULD BE PRETTY DARNED BORING. INSTEAD, LET ME TRY TO MAKE JUST ONE SIMPLE SHORT POINT IN THIS SECTION.

DO YOU REMEMBER WHEN YOU WERE IN FIRST GRADE AND YOU SAW YOUR TEACHER IN THE GROCERY STORE WHEN YOU WERE SHOPPING WITH YOUR MOTHER? AND YOU TURNED TO YOUR MOTHER AND SAID, "LOOK, THERE IS MRS. JOHNSON! SHE SHOPS IN THE GROCERY STORE!"

AND YOUR MOTHER LOOKED AT YOU AND SAID, "OF COURSE, SHE DOES. SHE IS HUMAN TOO!"

THAT IS WHAT I WANT YOU TO REMEMBER:

TEACHERS ARE HUMAN TOO!

IF TEACHERS ARE HUMAN, THEN EVERYTHING THAT APPLIES TO THE CARE AND FEEDING OF PARENTS SHOULD ALSO APPLY TO

TEACHERS, AS WELL.   AND PLEASING YOUR TEACHERS CAN BE
JUST AS EASY AS PLEASING YOUR PARENTS! REMEMBER, ALL YOU
HAVE TO DO IS BE:

        1. PLEASANT
        2. PRODUCTIVE
        3. WILLING TO TREAT THEM LIKE HUMANS

WHEN I WAS IN SCHOOL ANYONE WHO TREATED A TEACHER TOO
NICELY WAS ACCUSED OF "BROWN NOSING" AND I'LL GUARANTEE
YOU THAT NO ONE EVER WANTED TO BE ACCUSED OF THAT!
INSTEAD WE SEEMED TO HAVE A CONTEST TO SEE WHO COULD
TREAT THE TEACHER THE WORST. ON SOME OCCASIONS I REMEM-
BER BEING SO BAD THAT WE GOT THE TEACHER TO CRY AND WE
EVEN HAD ONE TEACHER WHO WALKED OUT AND REFUSED TO
EVER TEACH US AGAIN. NOW IT IS EASY FOR ME TO SEE HOW
NASTY AND CRUEL WE HAD BEEN, BUT THEN WE ACTED LIKE WE
WERE PROUD OF IT!

SURE, SOME TEACHERS ARE PECULIAR AND SOME ARE EVEN
UNFAIR AT TIMES, BUT LIKE PARENTS, MOST ARE TRYING THEIR
BEST.

I'LL KEEP THIS CHAPTER SHORT (AND FREE OF LECTURES!) IF YOU
DO ME ONE SMALL FAVOR. TRY FOR ONE WEEK TO TREAT YOUR
TEACHER AS A HUMAN BEING AND AS A PERSON YOU WOULD LIKE
TO PLEASE. SEE IF IT MAKES A DIFFERENCE.

BY THE WAY.........THAT JOB I HATED SO MUCH WAS TEACHING!

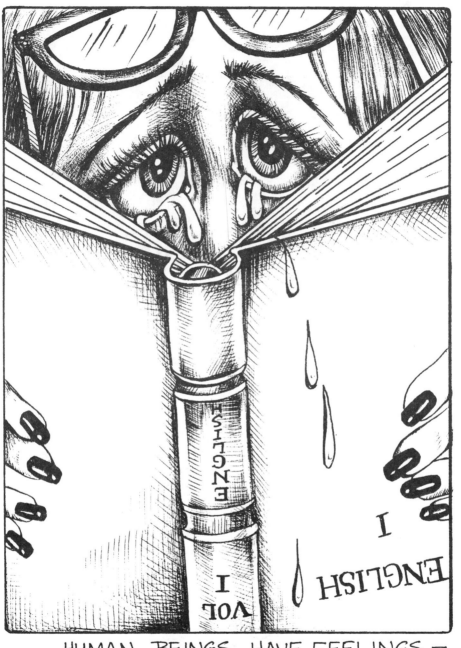

... HUMAN BEINGS HAVE FEELINGS —
TEACHERS ARE HUMAN — THEREFORE...
TEACHERS MUST HAVE FEELINGS...

EASY STEP # 29

EASY STEP # 29
GUNS, CRACK, AND VIOLENCE......
I'M LOSING ALL MY FRIENDS

THIS IS A SECTION THAT I SURE WISH I DID NOT HAVE TO WRITE.
BUT IT IS NECESSARY BECAUSE:

NO ONE CAN HELP YOU IF YOU ARE DEAD!

A FEW SHORT YEARS AGO A CHAPTER LIKE THIS WOULD NEVER
HAVE BEEN NEEDED. WHEN I WENT TO SCHOOL STUDENTS DID
NOT CARRY GUNS AND KNIVES. DRUGS WERE NOT SOLD ON
SCHOOL GROUNDS AND GANGS DID NOT EXIST. POLICEMEN DID
NOT HAVE TO WANDER THE CORRIDORS.

I DON'T NEED TO TELL YOU THAT TIMES HAVE CHANGED....YOU ALL
KNOW IT. MANY, IF NOT MOST OF YOU, HAVE LOST A FRIEND DUE
TO DRUGS OR VIOLENCE. MOST OF YOU HAVE PROBABLY WIT-
NESSED AGGRESSIVE BEHAVIOR IN SCHOOL, ON THE STREETS OR
EVEN AT HOME. CERTAINLY ANYONE WHO WATCHES TELEVISION

GETS ENOUGH OF IT ON THE NEWS AND ON THE PROGRAMS TO LAST A LONG TIME. HOMICIDE IS THE LEADING CAUSE OF DEATH IN YOUNG MEN AND DRUG DEALERS RULE MANY OF OUR NEIGHBOR-HOODS.

WE NOW HAVE TO TEACH OURSELVES AND CHILDREN HOW TO STAY ALIVE.

THE FIRST RULE IS PREVENTION!

ALTHOUGH IT IS BECOMING MORE DIFFICULT TO SIMPLY "STAY OUT OF TROUBLE", THE FIRST RULE HAS TO BE TO "NOT GO LOOKING FOR TROUBLE". YOU ALL KNOW THAT IF YOU CHOOSE TO HANG AROUND WITH A CERTAIN GROUP OF FRIENDS YOU WILL BE AC-CEPTING ALL THE RISKS THAT GO ALONG WITH IT. A LOT HAS BEEN SAID ABOUT "PEER PRESSURE", BUT I KNOW OF FEW SITUA-TIONS IN WHICH SOMEONE WAS <u>FORCED</u> TO BELONG TO A CER-TAIN GROUP. IT IS USUALLY DONE BY CHOICE AND WITH AN AWARENESS OF WHAT YOU ARE GETTING YOURSELF INTO. MAYBE YOU JOIN TO BUILD SELF-ESTEEM? MAYBE OUT OF A FEELING OF DEFIANCE. MAYBE AS A WAY TO FEEL A SENSE OF BELONGING. WHATEVER THE REASON....IT STARTS WITH A DECISION YOU MAKE AND YOU HAVE THE POWER TO MAKE DIFFERENT DECISIONS.

THE SECOND RULE IS TO KNOW THE RISKS!

YOU ALL KNOW THAT OVER 50% OF MURDERS IN OUR COUNTRY ARE COMMITTED BY SOMEONE USING A HANDGUN. BUT DID YOU KNOW THAT IF YOU YOURSELF CARRY A GUN YOU HAVE TWICE AS GREAT A CHANCE OF BEING MURDERED AS AN INDIVIDUAL WHO DOES NOT CARRY A GUN?

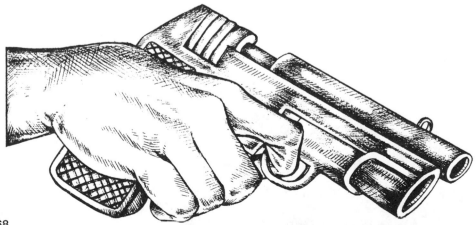

DID YOU KNOW THAT OVER HALF THE VICTIMS OF HOMICIDE HAD BEEN DRINKING AT THE TIME THAT THEY WERE MURDERED?

DID YOU KNOW THAT ALMOST 50% OF MURDERS ARE THE RESULT OF ARGUMENTS, USUALLY BETWEEN PEOPLE WHO KNOW EACH OTHER?

DID YOU KNOW THAT MOST RAPES TAKE PLACE BETWEEN PEOPLE WHO KNOW EACH OTHER?

DID YOU KNOW THAT THERE ARE OVER 50 MILLION HANDGUNS IN OUR COUNTRY?

DID YOU KNOW THAT THE "INNOCENT BYSTANDER" WHO IS MURDERED IS JUST AS DEAD AS THE GUY WHO GOES OUT LOOKING FOR TROUBLE AND GETS KILLED?

THE THIRD RULE IS TO ACT ACCORDING TO THE RISKS!

THERE IS A HUGE DIFFERENCE BETWEEN KNOWING THE RISKS OF DANGER AND ACTING IN A WAY TO AVOID DANGER.

YOU CANNOT AVOID ALL RISKS.....BUT THERE ARE PLENTY THAT YOU CAN! SOMETIMES IT MAY MEAN GIVING UP FRIENDS OR GIVING UP EXCITEMENT, BUT THE DIFFERENCE CAN BE THE DIFFERENCE BETWEEN LIFE AND DEATH.

THEY USED TO SAY THAT TEENAGERS ACTED AS IF THEY THOUGHT THAT THEY WOULD NEVER DIE. I DON'T BELIEVE THAT ANYMORE. I NOW THINK THAT TEENAGERS HAVE TO THINK ABOUT THE CHANCES OF DYING TOO MUCH THESE DAYS! EVEN GOING TO A SCHOOL FOOTBALL GAME CAN BE DANGEROUS BUSINESS. THE RISKS MUST NOT STOP US FROM DOING THE THINGS THAT PEOPLE HAVE ALWAYS DONE IN A FREE NATION, BUT WE CERTAINLY DO NEED TO THINK MORE AND MORE ABOUT HOW TO DECREASE OUR RISKS.

THE FOURTH RULE IS TO KNOW YOURSELF!

EVEN IF YOU ARE NOT LOOKING FOR TROUBLE IT CAN SOMETIMES COME TO YOU OR YOU CAN FIND YOURSELF IN THE MIDDLE OF IT. HOW DO YOU REACT TO THREATS?

ARE YOU THE KIND WHO FEELS ANGER AND IMMEDIATELY BE-COMES VIOLENT TOWARD THE PERSON OR THING THAT MAKES YOU ANGRY? ARE YOU THE KIND WHO KICKS A CHAIR OR PUFFS UP YOUR CHEST AND GETS AGGRESSIVE WHEN YOU ARE CHAL-LENGED? ARE YOU THE KIND WHO WOULD RATHER FIGHT THAN FLEE? ARE YOU THE KIND WHO ACTS BEFORE YOU THINK? IF YOU ARE, I THINK YOU CAN SEE THE DANGERS. <u>THINKING</u> AGGRES-SIVELY MAY NEVER GET YOU IN TROUBLE BUT <u>ACTING</u> ANGRILY AND AGGRESSIVELY COULD GET YOU KILLED.

OR ARE YOU THE TYPE WHO HOLDS YOUR ANGER IN? YOU IGNORE THINGS AND PRETEND THAT THEY DON'T BOTHER YOU. THIS CAN BE POSITIVE IN SITUATIONS THAT ARE MINOR OR TOO DANGEROUS

TO DO ANYTHING ABOUT. ON AN EVERYDAY BASIS, HOLDING YOUR ANGER IN ALL THE TIME MAY LEAD TO FRUSTRATION, DEPRESSION AND TRYING TO HIDE YOUR FEELINGS WITH DRUGS OR ALCOHOL, BUT IN THE TIME OF DANGER IT MAY ENABLE YOU TO BACK AWAY SAFELY AND NOT BECOME A THREAT TO SOMEONE ELSE WHO IS DANGEROUS.

THERE IS NO RIGHT OR WRONG WAY TO DEAL WITH YOUR ANGER, BUT IT IS IMPORTANT TO KNOW YOUR OWN STYLE SO THAT YOU CAN LEARN TO SURVIVE A CRISIS AND PERHAPS SAVE YOUR LIFE.

THE FIFTH RULE IS THAT YOU CAN LEARN AND PRACTICE WAYS TO MINIMIZE YOUR RISKS IN DANGEROUS SITUATIONS.

FIGHT AND FLIGHT ARE ALWAYS <u>CHOICES</u> IN A CONFLICT. MANY PEOPLE GROW UP THINKING THAT FLIGHT IS LIKE ADMITTING DEFEAT AND LOSING FACE. THIS MAY BE SOMETHING IMPORTANT TO LEARN IF YOU ARE A U.S. MARINE, BUT NOT IF YOU ARE A SINGLE KID ON THE STREETS WHO WANTS TO LEARN HOW TO LIVE. THERE ARE OTHER CHOICES.

ALWAYS BE READY TO "THROW A CURVE" WHEN YOU ARE IN A CONFLICT SITUATION. DO THE UNEXPECTED. YOUR OPPONENT PROBABLY EXPECTS YOU TO BE DEFENSIVE OR HOSTILE (READY FOR A FIGHT) OR ELSE FRIGHTENED (READY TO FLEE.) INSTEAD, THROW A CURVE AND PRACTICE BEING CONFIDENT, NON-THREAT-ENING, FRIENDLY AND READY TO JOKE.....ANYTHING TO REDUCE THE RISK.

BE READY TO
THROW
A CURVE ...

PEOPLE WHO STUDY THE MARTIAL ARTS KNOW THE MOST ABOUT THIS. THEIR ENTIRE PRINCIPLE IS TO USE FORCE ONLY WHEN ABSOLUTELY NECESSARY....ONLY IN SELF DEFENSE. IN ORDER TO AVOID GETTING TO THE POINT OF VIOLENCE, THEY TEACH SOME IMPORTANT IDEAS THAT ALL OF US SHOULD PAY ATTENTION TO.

IDEA #1. STAY ON CENTER. STAY IN CONTROL. DON'T LET YOUR FEAR, ANGER OR DEFENSIVENESS THROW YOU OFF BALANCE AND DON'T LET SOMEONE ELSE FORCE YOU INTO FIGHTING. BREATHE DEEPLY, MOVE SLOWLY AND STAY CALM.

IDEA #2. KEEP IT COOL. KEEP YOUR VOICE LOW AND CALM. CALLING SOMEONE NAMES, SHOUTING OR SWEARING IS LIKE THROWING GASOLINE ON A FIRE! KEEP THE SITUATION FROM ESCALATING.

IN A CONFRONTATION — BREATHE DEEPLY... MOVE SLOWLY, STAY CALM, STAY ON CENTER— STAY IN CONTROL.... AND KEEP COOL !

IDEA #3. STAND IN THE OTHER PERSON'S SHOES. IT IS EASIER TO FIGURE OUT THE BEST WAY TO HANDLE A CONFLICT IF YOU CAN RELATE TO THE OTHER PERSON. TRY TO FIGURE OUT WHAT HE OR SHE WANTS, THINKS, AND FEELS. IT IS ALSO A GOOD TIME TO REMEMBER THAT WHAT ANOTHER PERSON FEELS IS NEITHER RIGHT OR WRONG....IT JUST IS! IF YOU CAN DO THIS, IT WILL PUT YOU IN A MUCH BETTER POSITION TO WORK THINGS OUT AND TO MAKE YOUR OWN FEELINGS KNOWN.

IDEA #4. GIVE 'EM A WAY OUT. USUALLY THE OTHER PERSON IS JUST AS INTERESTED IN LOOKING FOR A WAY OUT AS YOU ARE. DON'T BACK THE OTHER PERSON INTO A CORNER WHERE HE OR SHE WILL HAVE TO FIGHT. PROVIDE THEM AS EASY A WAY OUT AS YOU POSSIBLY CAN!

TRY AND PUT YOURSELF IN THE OTHER PERSON'S SHOES; AND TRY AND GIVE THEM A WAY OUT····

IDEA #5. KEEP IT LIGHT. THE LESS SERIOUS YOU MAKE THE SITUA-TION THE LESS LIKELY IT IS THAT IT WILL ESCALATE. MAKE A JOKE—BUT NOT AT THE OTHER PERSON'S EXPENSE— OR FIND SOME WAY TO LET THE OTHER PERSON KNOW THAT THE ISSUE JUST ISN'T WORTH FIGHTING OVER.

IDEA #6. APOLOGIZE AND EXCUSE. SAYING "SORRY" OR "EXCUSE ME" DOESN'T HAVE TO MEAN YOU ARE WRONG AND THAT THE OTHER PERSON IS RIGHT. BUT IT CAN BE A SIMPLE WAY TO DIF-FUSE AN ARGUMENT AND WALK AWAY WITH YOUR PRIDE AND YOUR HIDE INTACT!

KEEP IT LIGHT . . . TELL A JOKE — (BUT NOT A MEAN ONE) . . . OR JUST SAY YOU'RE SORRY. IT DOESN'T MEAN YOU WERE AT FAULT ; AND IT COULD DIFFUSE THE SITUATION.

ONE FORM OF PREVENTION IS TO PRACTICE WHAT YOU WOULD DO IN A PARTICULAR SITUATION. REVIEW THESE RULES FOR SELF-SURVIVAL AND THINK ABOUT THEM SO YOU'LL BE READY. ONE THING I CAN PROMISE YOU IS THAT THEY WILL LOSE ALL OF THEIR EFFECTIVENESS IN A CONFLICT IF YOU HAVE TO PULL OUT YOUR NOTEBOOK TO REVIEW THEM.

REMEMBER......PREVENTION IS SOMETHING YOU MUST PRACTICE!

HOPE YOU'VE LEARNED SOME MORE MANIPULATION AND MORE IMPORTANTLY THAT ALTHOUGH MANIPULATION IS ALWAYS ACTION, IT IS SOMETIMES AN ACTION DESIGNED TO AVOID ANOTHER TYPE OF ACTION........SUCH AS THE ACTION OF GETTING YOURSELF BEAT UP IN A FIGHT!

EASY STEP # 30

SMILE WHEN YOU SEE THOSE FLASHING BLUE LIGHTS!

WE HAVE ALREADY—I WILL ASSUME— ACCEPTED THE NOTION THAT PARENTS AND TEENAGERS ARE NOT EQUAL. NOW LET ME SHARE WITH YOU ANOTHER IMPORTANT PRINCIPLE:

ALL MEN ARE CREATED EQUAL.....

BUT THEY DON'T STAY THAT WAY FOR LONG

THIS IS A PRINCIPLE THAT MANY ADULTS STILL HAVE A PROBLEM WITH. I'LL ADMIT TO BEING ONE!

WHEN I AM DRIVING DOWN THE ROAD, PROBABLY PAYING LITTLE ATTENTION TO MY SPEED, AND I SEE THE FLASHING BLUE LIGHTS IN MY REAR-VIEW MIRROR MY FIRST REACTION IS USUALLY, "WHO DOES THAT GUY THINK HE IS?"

WELL, IT MAY HAVE TAKEN ME A LONG WHILE BUT I THINK I'VE BEGUN TO UNDERSTAND THE ANSWER......"HE THINKS HE IS A

POLICEMAN , AND FURTHER, HE DOES NOT BELIEVE THAT HE AND I
ARE EQUALS!"

I'VE LEARNED THAT TO DOUBT HIS RIGHT TO FEEL HIS SUPERIOR-
ITY LEADS TO A BAD TIME FOR ME! I'VE LEARNED TO SMILE AND
SAY "GOOD MORNING, OFFICER. NICE DAY, ISN'T IT?" HE OWNS THE
HIGHWAY AND THERE IS LITTLE CHANCE THAT I AM GOING TO
CONVINCE HIM OTHERWISE! SINCE ACCEPTING THAT SIMPLE FACT
I HAVE BEEN ABLE TO SMILE AND "PLEASANT" MY WAY OUT OF
THREE POTENTIAL TICKETS. EACH TIME I ACCEPTED THE AUTHOR-
ITY OF THE OFFICER, AND LET HIM KNOW IT WITH MY SMILE, I HAVE
DRIVEN AWAY WITH A WARNING RATHER THAN A TICKET.

THAT WAS NOT ALWAYS THE CASE. I USED TO TRY TO ARGUE THAT
THE POLICEMAN WAS WRONG AND I WAS RIGHT. ONCE I EVEN GOT
INTO AN ARGUMENT WITH ONE OFFICER THAT ALMOST GOT ME
TAKEN TO THE POLICE STATION. ONCE I TOOK MY CASE TO COURT
AND THE JUDGE (ANOTHER AUTHORITY) SIMPLY TOLD ME THAT THE
POLICEMAN WAS RIGHT AND I HAD TO PAY MY TICKET.

I , OF COURSE, TRIED TO TELL THE JUDGE THAT "IT IS NOT FAIR!"
YOU CAN GUESS WHERE THAT LANDED ME! FAIR, AS I HOPE YOU
ALL KNOW BY NOW IS WHERE YOU GO ONCE A YEAR TO SEE THE
HORSES, COWS AND PIGS.

AUTHORITY FIGURES ...YOU HAVE TO
LEARN HOW TO HANDLE EACH OF THEM.

IN MANY WAYS THIS CHAPTER IS A LOT LIKE THE ONE BEFORE IT ABOUT VIOLENCE........YOU HAVE TO TRY TO GET TO KNOW YOUR OPPONENT. THERE ARE MANY PEOPLE WHO HAVE AUTHORITY OVER YOU OR FEEL THAT THEY SHOULD HAVE AUTHORITY OVER YOU: PARENTS, POLICEMEN, TAX COLLECTORS, TEACHERS, JUDGES, BOSSES, DRILL SARGENTS, COACHES, BANKERS, INSUR-ANCE COMPANIES, BULLIES, ROBBERS WITH GUNS AND MOTHER-IN-LAWS. YOU HAVE TO LEARN HOW TO HANDLE EACH OF THEM!

STARTING OFF WITH THE IDEA THAT YOU ARE EQUALS DOES NOT OFTEN LEAD TO YOU GETTING WHAT YOU WOULD LIKE OUT OF AN INTERACTION. HAVE YOU EVER TRIED TO TELL A ROBBER WITH A GUN OR A MOTHER-IN-LAW THAT YOU ARE EQUALS?

THIS LEADS US TO OUR NEXT IMPORTANT EASY STEP:

IT IS A TRULY SUCCESSFUL PERSON WHO HAS LEARNED TO FAKE HUMILITY!

 YOU FAKED HUMILITY WHEN YOU LEARNED TO SAY YOUR WERE SORRY TO THAT BULLY, EVEN THOUGH YOU KNEW THAT YOU HAD NO REASON TO APOLOGIZE TO HIM!

NOW REMEMBER, THERE IS AN IMPORTANT POSITIVE SIDE TO THIS WHOLE THING:

IF YOU WORK HARD ENOUGH.... YOU WILL EVENTUALLY BE MORE EQUAL THAN SOMEONE ELSE.

DELAYED GRATIFICATION MEANS THAT YOU CANNOT EXPECT TO HAVE IT ALL....RIGHT NOW. THE POLICEMAN HAD TO GAIN MY RESPECT BY DOING THE THINGS IT TAKES TO BECOME A POLICE OFFICER...COMPLETING SCHOOL, BEING SUCCESSFUL AT COM-PLETING A VERY DIFFICULT TRAINING PROGRAM AND SWEARING TO CARRY OUT HIS JOB WITH RESPECT FOR THE LAW AND THE CITIZENS HE SERVES. THEREFORE,HE IS DESERVING OF MY RE-SPECT. NOT EVERYONE HAS WHAT IT TAKES TO BECOME A POLICE OFFICER AND NOT EVERYONE IS WILLING TO PUT IN THE HARD WORK IT TAKES OR TO ACCEPT THE RISKS OF THE JOB. I MAY HAVE LEARNED TO FAKE HUMILITY WHEN THE OFFICER STOPS ME, BUT THE WAY THAT I CAN DO IT IS BY ACCEPTING HIS AUTHORITY.

WHAT DO YOU WANT FOR YOURSELF AND ARE YOU WILLING TO

WORK TO GET IT? WHAT DO YOU WANT TO BE DOING TEN YEARS FROM NOW AND DO YOU WANT TO BE IN A POSITION WHERE YOU ARE RESPECTED? IF SO, THE FIRST STEP IS TO RESPECT THOSE WHO HAVE ALREADY EARNED THE RIGHT TO RESPECT AND THE NEXT STEP IS TO GET TO WORK.....THE HARD WORK IT TAKES TO GET YOURSELF INTO A POSITION WHERE YOU WILL BE RESPECTED.

...I AIN'T GOT NO RESPECT!

EASY STEP #31

EASY STEP #31

THINGS TO NEVER, NEVER, NEVER, NEVER
SAY TO YOUR PARENTS!

SOMETIMES GOOD INTENTIONS ARE NOT ENOUGH!

YOU ARE ALL FAMILIAR WITH THE PROBLEM....YOU ARE IN THE PROCESS OF WINNING AN ARGUMENT WITH YOUR PARENTS OR YOU ARE MANIPULATING WELL ENOUGH THAT YOU HAVE A CHANCE OF COMING OUT OF IT WITH A FAIRLY DECENT COMPROMISE WHICH YOU CAN LIVE WITH, AND THEN <u>WHAMMO!!!!</u>, OUT OF NO-WHERE YOU GO AND SAY THE DUMBEST THING THAT BLOWS THE WHOLE DEAL.

THERE ARE SOME THINGS THAT YOU SIMPLY HAVE TO LEARN YOU NEVER, NEVER, NEVER, NEVER SAY TO A PARENT IF YOU WANT TO COME OUT ON TOP OF THE MANIPULATION GAME. THIS SECTION WILL EXPLORE A FEW OF THESE.

BUT, BEFORE WE BEGIN, REMEMBER ONE MORE TIME: PARENTS ARE EASY TO PLEASE....ALL THEY WANT IS FOR YOU TO BE PLEAS-ANT, PRODUCTIVE AND TO TREAT THEM WITH THE RESPECT THAT IS DUE TO THEM AS YOUR PARENT, A FELLOW HUMAN BEING AND AS AN INDIVIDUAL WORTHYOF RESPECT. THE STATEMENTS THAT FOLLOW ARE ALL STATEMENTS THAT CLEARLY INDICATE THAT YOU HAVE NO INTEREST OR UNDERSTANDING OF HOW TO FOLLOW THE SIMPLE PRINCIPLES. THEY ARE KILLERS.....SHOTS TO YOUR PARENT'S HEARTS! THEY ARE NEGATIVE MANIPULATIONS, BOUND TO SET YOU UP AS A LOSER. THEY ARE STATEMENTS THAT WIPE OUT ANY PROGRESS THAT YOU HAVE MADE....THEY ARE THINGS TO SAY TO GUARANTEE YOUR OWN UNHAPPINESS.

HERE WE GO. HERE ARE A FEW GUARANTEED LOSING STATE-MENTS, ALONG WITH GUARANTEED PARENT REACTIONS:

<u>STUPID STATEMENT</u>	<u>WHAT A PARENT THINKS</u>
I'M SORRY YOU EVER HAD ME!	I MIGHT NOT HAVE GONE TO THE TROUBLE IF I KNEW YOU WERE GOING TO BE SUCH A JERK!

BUT DAD, YOU DO THE SAME THING!	MY KID THINKS WE'RE EQUALS. HE'S GOING TO GET A SURPRISE!
I'LL SHOW YOU....	I'LL SHOW YOU CONSEQUENCES!
JIMMY'S MOTHER LETS HIM...	I'LL SHOW YOU I'M ME, NOT JIMMY'S MOTHER!
YOU CAN'T MAKE ME!	OH. WAIT AND SEE!
YOU ARE NOT FAIR.	BEING FAIR IS NOT MY JOB!
YOU'RE SO SELFISH	WAIT TILL YOU WANT YOUR NEXT PAIR OF $100 NIKES
ALL THE OTHER PARENTS LET THEIR KIDS....	I'VE SEEN SOME OF YOUR FRIENDS AND CAN IMAGINE WHAT <u>THEIR</u> PARENTS ALLOW!
YOU ARE SO OLD FASHIONED!	THANKS FOR THE COMPLIMENT!
WHATEVER!	I'LL FIND A WAY TO MAKE HIM CARE!
I'LL NEVER TALK TO YOU IF...	YOU'LL NEED SOMETHING SOONER THAN LATER.
I WISH YOU WERE DEAD!	I WILL BE SOMEDAY...I HOPE MY CHILD CAN SHOW ME HE LOVES ME BEFORE THEN!

WORDS CAN BE <u>KILLERS</u>
SHOTS TO YOUR PARENTS HEARTS.

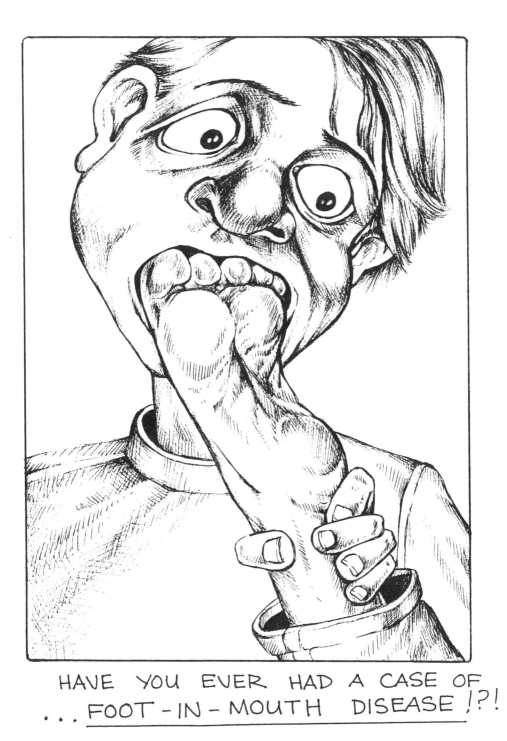

HAVE YOU EVER HAD A CASE OF
... FOOT - IN - MOUTH DISEASE !?!

ALL THE STATEMENTS ABOVE, WHICH YOU WOULD DO WELL TO NEVER, NEVER, NEVER, NEVER SAY TO YOUR PARENTS, HAVE ONE THING IN COMMON....THEY ARE NEGATIVE AND HURTFUL! TO WORK, MANIPULATION ALWAYS HAS TO BE POSITIVE AND HAS TO LEAVE THE OTHER PERSON FEELING BETTER ABOUT THEMSELVES AND ABOUT THEIR RELATIONSHIP WITH YOU. EVERY NEGATIVE STATEMENT AND EVERY ATTACK ON YOUR PARENTS KILLS OFF SOME OF THE LOVE.....YES, LOVE CAN BE KILLED OFF...AND IT LEAVES YOU IN THE "ONE DOWN" POSITION, HAVING TO PROVE THAT YOU DID NOT REALLY MEAN ALL THOSE NASTY , HURTFUL THINGS THAT YOU JUST SAID, RATHER THAN ENJOYING THE BEN-EFITS OF A CARING AND COMFORTABLE RELATIONSHIP WITH YOUR PARENTS. IN OTHER WORDS, THEY WILL LEAD TO YOUR UNHAPPI-NESS AND THAT'S A GUARANTEE!

BE CREATIVE. THINK OF POSITIVE, UNEXPECTED, PSYCHOLOGI-CALLY SOUND THINGS TO SAY THAT ARE GOING TO GET YOUR PARENTS TO THINK RATHER THAN JUST REACT.

CONSIDER A FEW OF THESE STATEMENT BY CONTRAST:

- MOTHER, I FEEL THAT YOU ARE NOT WILLING TO GIVE ME MUCH TRUST. WHAT HAVE I DONE NOT TO GAIN YOUR TRUST?

- I KNOW THAT THINGS ARE DIFFERENT THAN WHEN YOU GREW UP....BUT HAVE YOU EVER THOUGHT THAT I HAVE THE SAME NEEDS THAT YOU HAD WHEN YOU GREW UP?

- DAD, CAN YOU STOP FOR ONE SECOND AND THINK ABOUT HOW YOUR OWN FATHER WOULD HAVE DEALT WITH YOU IN THIS SAME SITUATION.

- MOM, DAD. DON'T YOU REALIZE THAT IF I MESS UP I AM THE ONE WHO IS GOING TO HAVE TO TAKE THE CONSEQUENCES!

- MOM, DAD. DON'T YOU TRUST YOURSELVES AND THAT YOU HAVE DONE A GOOD JOB IN TEACHING ME RIGHT FROM WRONG.

- SOMETIMES YOU MAKE ME FEEL AS IF YOUR GREATEST FEAR IS THAT I AM GOING TO EMBARRASS YOU; MY GREATEST FEAR IS THAT I WILL EMBARRASS MYSELF!

- MOM. LOVE SOMETIMES MEANS LETTING GO!

- AT TIMES, I'M SCARED MYSELF THAT I'M GOING TO SCREW UP, BUT I HAVE TO LEARN TO TRUST MYSELF.

BE CREATIVE WITH YOUR WORDS...
THINK POSITIVE, DO THE UNEXPECTED
<u>THINK</u> RATHER THAN <u>REACT</u>!

- I KNOW IT IS HARD BEING A PARENT....THAT WHY I'M GLAD I GOT YOU, BUT I THINK YOU ARE WRONG IN THIS CASE.

- I KNOW WHEN I'M RAISING MY OWN KIDS I'LL PROBABLY FIND MYSELF TELLING THEM, "MY MOTHER ALWAYS USE TO TELL ME...",BUT RIGHT NOW IT IS HARD, AT TIMES, TO BELIEVE THAT YOU ARE SO WISE.

- I KNOW THAT YOU ARE NOT OUT TO DELIBERATELY HURT ME, BUT AT TIMES IT SURE FEELS LIKE IT.

- I'M VERY ANGRY ABOUT THE WAY THAT YOU ARE TREATING ME....BUT I REALIZE THAT MY ANGER IS MY PROBLEM. I'LL DEAL WITH MY ANGER. WOULD YOU BE WILLING TO GO BACK AND RETHINK WHETHER YOU ARE BEING REASONABLE?

- YOU KNOW, MOM, THE OTHER DAY I WAS SO ANGRY AT YOU THAT FOR A SECOND I WISHED YOU WERE DEAD. IT MADE ME FEEL SO HORRIBLE THAT I NEVER WANT TO FEEL THAT WAY AGAIN, BUT THE FEELING IS STARTING TO COME BACK AGAIN.......WE HAVE TO FIND A BETTER WAY TO DO THINGS!

- MOTHER, I CAN'T GUARANTEE THAT I'LL NEVER DO ANYTHING WRONG.....ALL I CAN TELL YOU IS THAT I WILL NEVER INTENTIONALLY DO ANYTHING TO HURT YOU OR DAD.

OK. I'M SURE YOU HAVE THE IDEA! FOR ME , UNDOUBTEDLY BECAUSE I AM A PARENT, IT WAS AMAZING HOW QUICKLY AND EASILY THE POSITIVE MANIPULATIONS CAME ROLLING OFF MY FINGERTIPS! WOULDN'T IT BE NICE IF THEY WERE THE FIRST THINGS THAT CAME ROLLING OUT WHEN YOU WERE IN THE MIDDLE OF A HOT ARGUMENT WITH YOUR PARENTS! REALISTICALLY, WE KNOW THAT IS NOT ALWAYS GOING TO BE THE WAY IT IS, BUT THE SOONER YOU GET RID OF THE "NEVER, NEVER, NEVER, NEVERS', THE SOONER THERE WILL BE ROOM FOR THE CREATIVE, LOVE-GATHERING POSITIVES.

GET RID OF THE NEVER, NEVER, NEVER, NEVERS ... TO MAKE ROOM FOR THE CREATIVE, LOVE-GATHERING "POSITIVES."

EASY STEP # 32
I RAN AWAY....
THE HIGHWAY SIGN SAID
"WELCOME TO WITCHITA !"

WE TALKED EARLIER ABOUT CONFLICT AND HOW SOMETIMES
FLIGHT IS BETTER THAN FIGHT! FOR SOME TEENEGERS, PROB-
LEMS MAY GET TO THE POINT WHERE FLIGHT SEEMS LIKE THE
BEST POSSIBLE ANSWER. THE FOLLOWING IS A LIST   OF THE
THINGS A TEENAGER NEED TO RUN AWAY SUCCESSFULLY:

1. A BAG WITH A FEW CHANGES OF CLOTHES.
2. A FEW DOLLARS.
3. A BOOK OF PHONE NUMBERS.
4. A ROAD MAP OF THE UNITED STATES.
5. INFORMATION ABOUT HOMELESS SHELTERS.
6. A BLANKET, IF GOING NORTH.
7. A PILLOW, IF YOU'VE NEVER SLEPT WITHOUT ONE BEFORE.
8. A BOTTLE OF VITAMINS, IN CASE THERE IS NO FOOD WHERE
   YOU'RE HEADED.
9. A LIST OF STORIES TO TELL WHY YOU HAD TO RUN AWAY.
10. AN UMBRELLA.
11. PLASTIC TO COVER THE DAMP GROUND WHERE YOU SLEEP.
12. BEEF JERKY.
13. FALSE IDENTIFICATION
14. TOILET PAPER.
15. A BAR OF SOAP AN OPTIONAL EXTRA!)
16. A KNIFE...FOR POTECTION.
17. AN EXTRA PAIR OF SOCKS.
18. STRING (NEVER LEAVE HOME WITHOUT IT!).
19. OINTMENT (OH, THAT WORD AGAIN!).
20. BANDAIDS.
21. TAMPAX (GENDER SPECIFIC).
22. A JOURNAL AND A PENCIL...TO WRITE YOUR BESTSELLER!
23. A FBI WANTED LIST FROM THE POST OFFICE...TO KNOW
    WHICH RIDES <u>NOT</u> TO TAKE!
24. DEODORANT (OPTIONAL).
25. MATCHES.
26. A HAT (GOOD FOR DISGUISE, IF THEY COME LOOKING).
27. A PICTURE OF YOUR DOG (THE ONLY THING YOU SAY YOU'LL
    MISS).
28. TOOTHBRUSH (OPTIONAL).
29. TOOTHPASTE (OPTIONAL).
30. **A <u>DAMNED</u> GOOD REASON FOR LEAVING
    YOUR COZY HOME!!**

EASY STEP # 33

DRUGS.....EVERYTHING YOU NEED TO KNOW!

IF YOU HAVE A DRUG PROBLEM, YOU WOULD NEVER HAVE READ THIS FAR IN A BOOK THAT REQUIRES INTELLIGENCE, CONCENTRATION AND THE ABILITY TO TAKE A LONG HARD LOOK AT YOURSELF AND YOU CERTAINLY DON'T NEED YET ANOTHER LECTURE THAT TELLS YOU DRUGS ARE BAD FOR YOU!

KEEP UP THE GOOD WORK....STAY CLEAN AND GIVE LIFE EVERYTHING THAT YOU HAVE TO GIVE—NATURALLY!

EASY STEP # 34

EASY STEP # 34

LOOKING FOR LOVE IN ALL THE WRONG PLACES!

EVERYONE WANTS TO BE LOVED! WELL, AT LEAST ALMOST EVERY-
ONE WANTS TO BE LOVED! I SUPPOSE IT WOULD BE SAFE TO
EXCLUDE MASS MURDERERS, HERMITS AND "THE JOKER", BUT
EVEN SOME OF THE BIGGEST SCOUNDRELS EVER KNOWN TO HAVE
WALKED THE FACE OF THE EARTH NEEDED TO BE LOVED BY SOME-
ONE! EVEN HITLER HAD A MISTRESS!

YOU ARE NO DIFFERENT—NO NOT FROM HITLER, BUT FROM THE
REST OF US. YOU HAVE A NEED TO BE LOVED!

ONE OF THE BIGGEST DRIVES WE POSSESS IS THE DRIVE TO HAVE
SOMEONE TO LOVE US AND SOMEONE TO TELL US THAT WE MAKE
A DIFFERENCE IN THEIR LIVES. ONE OF OUR TRICKIEST LIFE-LONG
JOBS IS TO REMAIN LOVABLE AND TO BESTOW LOVE ON OTHERS.
IT IS NOT SOMETHING THAT WE LEARN AUTOMATICALLY...IT IS
ANOTHER ONE OF THOSE "TRIAL AND ERROR" THINGS. WE BEGIN
AT HOME AND THEN AS WE GET OLDER WE WE FEEL A STRONG
NEED TO GET SOME OF OUR LOVE FROM OUTSIDE THE FAMILY.

DO YOU REMEMBER THE FIRST TIME YOU WERE IN LOVE? OF
COURSE, YOU DO! IT IS ONE OF THOSE FEELINGS THAT MOST OF
US NEVER FORGET! I REMEMBER MY FIRST LOVE, BUT I'M EMBAR-
RASSED TO SAY I KNOW THAT SHE DOESN'T REMEMBER ME, BE-
CAUSE I NEVER GOT UP THE NERVE TO TELL HER THAT I HAD DEEP,
DEEP FEELINGS FOR HER. (YOU DIDN'T BELIEVE ME BEFORE WHEN

I TOLD YOU THAT I WAS REALLY A SHY PERSON, DID YOU?) I GUESS
I WOULD HAVE TO SAY THAT THE FEELINGS WERE LOVE....AND IT
WAS WONDERFUL AND HORRIBLE ALL AT THE SAME TIME. EVERY
TIME I SAW CLAIRE THAT SUMMER (SEE, I STILL REMEMBER HER
NAME) MY HEART WOULD FLUTTER AND MY HORMONES WOULD DO
CRAZY THINGS. AND I REMEMBER WHAT IT WAS LIKE THE DAY
THAT I SAW HER ON THE BEACH WITH SOMEBODY ELSE! IT WAS
SUCH A DEFEATED FEELING....REAL EMPTY AND IT LEFT ME FEEL-
ING ALONE AND PRETTY WORTHLESS. I WAS FOURTEEN AND IT
FELT LIKE THE WORLD HAD COME TO A SCREECHING HALT! I CAN
STILL EVEN REMEMBER THE COLOR OF THE BATHING SUIT SHE
WORE THAT DAY (ORANGE, IF YOU CARE) AND THE FLAVOR OF THE
ICE CREAM CONE HE BOUGHT HER (CHOCOLATE, IF YOU CARE).
PAINFUL THINGS SEEM TO STICK IN OUR MINDS FOR A LONG TIME!

I REMEMBER WHAT I FELT
LIKE THAT DAY AT THE BEACH WHEN
I SAW CLAIRE WITH SOME-
OTHER GUY!

THE DRIVE TO BE LOVED IS SO STRONG THAT WE HAVE TO BE
CAREFUL OR , AS THE OLD COUNTRY WESTERN SONG SAYS, WE'LL
START "LOOKING FOR LOVE IN ALL THE WRONG PLACES!"

AGAIN, IT WOULD BE EASY TO START LECTURING YOU AGAIN....BUT
I RESPECT YOU TOO MUCH AT THIS POINT TO EVEN THINK ABOUT
DOING THAT! AND ASK ANY PARENT.....LECTURING NEVER WORKS!

DON'T FORGET YOUR VALUES....YOU WORKED HARD TO GET THEM.
YOU'LL , OF COURSE, HEAR FROM SOMEONE YOU CARE ABOUT
THINGS LIKE, "IF YOU CARED ABOUT ME, YOU'D GIVE ME JUST A
LITTLE BIT MORE!" OR, "IT'S OK BECAUSE WE LOVE EACH OTHER!"
ONLY YOU CAN DECIDE WHAT IS RIGHT OR WRONG FOR YOU!
ONLY YOU CAN AVOID BEING MANIPULATED INTO DOING SOME-
THING YOU DO NOT REALLY WANT TO DO. SOMEONE WHO LOVES
YOU WILL RESPECT YOU, WHATEVER YOU CHOOSE AS BEST FOR
YOURSELF.

YOU ALL KNOW HOW QUICKLY SOMEONE CAN GAIN A REPUTATION
AS A SLUT OR AS USER......WHETHER IT IS DESERVED OR NOT.

DO NOT CONFUSE LOVE AND SEX

THIS ONE IS ALL UP TO YOU. HOPEFULLY YOU KNOW YOURSELF
WELL ENOUGH SO THAT YOU TRUST YOUR OWN DECISIONS. MORE
TRICKY....HOPEFULLY YOU KNOW THE OTHER PERSON WELL
ENOUGH TO TRUST THEIR MOTIVES AND THEIR VALUES AND TO
KNOW THAT YOUR LOVE IS NOT BEING MISUSED OR ABUSED.

EASY STEP #35

EASY STEP #35

OK! OK! YOU HAVE WAITED LONG ENOUGH!
HERE IT IS: <u>SEX</u> !!!!

SEX IS BOTH THE MOST WONDERFUL AND THE MOST OVERRATED THING THAT CAN HAPPEN TO THE HUMAN BODY!

ENTIRE BOOKS, I AM TOLD, HAVE BEEN WRITTEN ON THE SUBJECT OF SEX! I'VE NEVER READ ONE COVER TO COVER....BUT I'VE LOOKED AT THE PICTURES. HERE IS WHAT IS IMPORTANT TO KNOW ABOUT SEX IN TERMS OF LEARNING TO MANIPULATE YOUR WAY TO HAPPINESS.

YOU ARE CAPABLE OF MAKING A BABY
MUCH BEFORE YOU ARE CAPABLE OF TAKING CARE OF ONE!

MOTHER NATURE HAS INVENTED SEX AS A PRETTY GOOD THING SO THAT CREATURES WILL WANT TO DO IT AND THE SPECIES WILL CONTINUE TO RENEW ITSELF AND NOT BECOME EXTINCT. IN ORDER TO MAKE SURE THAT THE SPECIES KEEPS RENEWING ITSELF ORGANISMS (FROM THE AMOEBA TO YOU) ARE GIVEN AN OVERKILL IN THEIR ABILITY TO REGENERATE. THERE ARE WOMEN AS YOUNG AS TWELVE AND AS OLD AS FIFTY WHO HAVE BECOME PREGNANT. ON AVERAGE A WOMAN HAS ABOUT THIRTY YEARS OF HER LIFE DURING WHICH SHE CAN GET PREGNANT (LET'S SAY FROM FOURTEEN TO FORTY-FOUR). THERE IS NO GREAT NEED TO HURRY! THEREFORE, IF YOU ARE READY FOR SEX, BUT NOT READY TO START YOUR CHILD-BEARING YEARS, MOTHER NATURE MUST BE TRICKED!

MOTHER NATURE MUST BE FOOLED!

THERE IS NOTHING WRONG WITH TRYING TO TRICK MOTHER NATURE. IN FACT, IF YOU ARE GOING TO SET OUT TO DO IT, YOU HAD BETTER SET OUT TO DO AS GOOD A JOB OF IT AS YOU POSSIBLY CAN!

AGAIN, I STRONGLY DOUBT THAT ANY OF YOU WHO HAVE READ THIS FAR DO NOT ALREADY KNOW ABOUT BIRTH CONTROL PILLS, CONDOMS, FOAMS, DIAPHRAGMS OR OTHER EFFECTIVE WAYS TO PREVENT AN AGGRESSIVE LITTLE WRIGGLER FROM REACHING A BIG OLD EGG, SITTING DUMB AND HAPPY IN A FALLOPIAN TUBE. THE REAL ISSUE....AND THE ONLY ONE I WANT TO TALK TO YOU ABOUT ...IS WHY DO SO MANY BRIGHT, INFORMED YOUNG ADULTS LIKE YOU DO NOT PREPARE YOURSELF TO AVOID PREGNANCY?

IT IS NOT AN EASY QUESTION AND IT IS ONE THAT UNDOUBTEDLY HAS MANY ANSWERS.

IN SOME CASES IT IS FEAR....AND PARENTS DON'T ALWAYS HELP HERE! WHAT WILL MY MOTHER THINK IF I ASK HER IF I CAN GET BIRTH CONTROL? WILL SHE MAKE ME STOP SEEING MY BOY-FRIEND? WILL SHE THINK I AM CHEAP? WILL SHE STOP TRUSTING ME?

WELL, YOUR PARENTS ARE UNIQUE AND ONLY YOU CAN GUESS AT WHAT THEY WILL SAY. BUT, I CAN GUARANTEE YOU THAT THERE IS NOTHING UNIQUE ABOUT WHAT YOUR PARENTS WILL FEEL IF YOU COME HOME PREGNANT!

IN OTHER CASES, I HAVE NOTED THAT YOUNG WOMEN DON'T TAKE PROPER SAFE GUARDS BECAUSE THEY DO NOT WANT TO THINK ABOUT WHAT IT SAYS ABOUT THEM. WHEN I ASKED ONE PREG-NANT FIFTEEN-YEAR-OLD ABOUT WHY SHE DIDN'T USED BIRTH CONTROL, EVEN THOUGH SHE KNEW EVERY KIND THERE WAS TO USE, SHE ANSWERED, "I ALWAYS THOUGHT THAT IF I WENT AHEAD AND GOT BIRTH CONTROL I WOULD FEEL LIKE A WHORE......LIKE SOMEONE WHO WAS ALWAYS READY TO HAVE SEX."

NONSENSE! OUR VALUES COME FROM WITHIN US, NOT FROM WHETHER OR NOT WE CARRY A CONDOM OR TAKE A BIRTH CON-TROL PILL!

EARLIER I SAID THAT SEX CAN BE ONE OF THE MOST WONDERFUL EXPERIENCES OR ONE OF THE WORST. A LOT DEPENDS ON WHETHER IT IS AN EXPERIENCE IN WHICH YOU FEEL A SENSE OF CONTROL OR WHETHER IT IS ONE IN WHICH YOU ARE OUT OF CONTROL. IF YOU ARE OUT OF CONTROL IT WILL LEAD TO WORRY, GUILT, DECREASED SELF ESTEEM, SADNESS AND DEPRESSION. IF YOU ARE MATURE AND IN CONTROL IT CAN LEAD TO GROWTH,

LOVE AND A HEIGHTENED SENSE OF ADULT RESPONSIBILITY. LIKE IN THE CASE OF SO MANY OTHER THINGS WE HAVE TALKED ABOUT IN THIS BOOK, THE CHOICE LIES IN YOUR OWN HANDS.....AND SO TOO DO THE CONSEQUENCES!

ADDENDUM: I HAVE JUST RETURNED FROM TRIP TO AFRICA DUR-
ING THE CHRISTMAS SEASON AND HAVE TO ADD THIS SECTION. I
HAD THE CHANCE TO VISIT HOSPITALS WHERE I SAW MEN, WOMEN
AND CHILDREN DYING FROM AIDS. IN SOME PARTS OF AFRICAN
ALMOST ONE THIRD OF THE POPULATION IS HIV POSITIVE! THIS
MEANS THAT WITHIN SIX YEARS ONE THIRD OF THE POPULATION
WILL BE DEAD...POSSIBLY MORE IF THE EPIDEMIC WORSENS. ONE
THIRD OF THE CHILDREN BORN WILL DIE OF AIDS. ONE THIRD OF
THE MOTHERS WILL BE DEAD. ONE THIRD OF ALL HEALTHY-LOOK-
ING ADOLESCENT WILL BE DEAD! IT IS A NIGHTMARE...AND IT CAN
NOT BE DESCRIBED AS ANYTHING LESS!

IF THERE IS ANYTHING I LEARNED FOR MYSELF IT IS THAT AIDS IS
REAL. EVERYDAY I SAW INFANTS AND ADULTS DIE WHILE ALL WE
COULD DO WAS HELPLESSLY STAND BY. I COULD NO LONGER
THINK OF IT AS A DISEASE THAT JUST HAPPENS TO "SOMEONE
ELSE". IT WAS HAPPENING TO MANY PEOPLE AROUND ME...REAL
PEOPLE. AND IT COULD HAPPEN TO YOU AND IT COULD HAPPEN TO
ME. PLEASE DON'T LET YOURSELF SAY,"IT COULD NEVER HAPPEN
TO ME." WE KNOW HOW AIDS IS SPREAD....YOU KNOW ALL THE
WAYS AS WELL AS I DO. SEX CAN BE DANGEROUS. AIDS IS REAL.
THINK WITH YOUR MIND AS WELL AS YOUR HEART. TEN MINUTES
OF PLEASURE IS NOT WORTH THE RISK OF DEATH. WHETHER YOU
CHOOSE ABSTINENCE OR PROTECTION, YOU MUST BE IN CONTROL
OF YOUR LIFE. AIDS IS REAL...YOU DON'T HAVE TO HAVE BABIES
DIE IN YOUR ARMS TO KNOW IT, BUT, IF I AM GOING TO PRETEND TO
BE YOUR FRIEND, IT IS MY DUTY TO BEG YOU TO REALIZE THAT
"SOMEONE ELSE" COULD SOMEDAY BE YOU IF YOU DON'T TAKE
THE DANGERS SERIOUSLY. PLEASE TAKE THE THREATS AS GENU-
INE AND MAKE EVERY DECISION AS IF IT IS A MATTER OF LIFE OR
DEATH....FOR IT WELL MAY BE.

EASY STEP #36

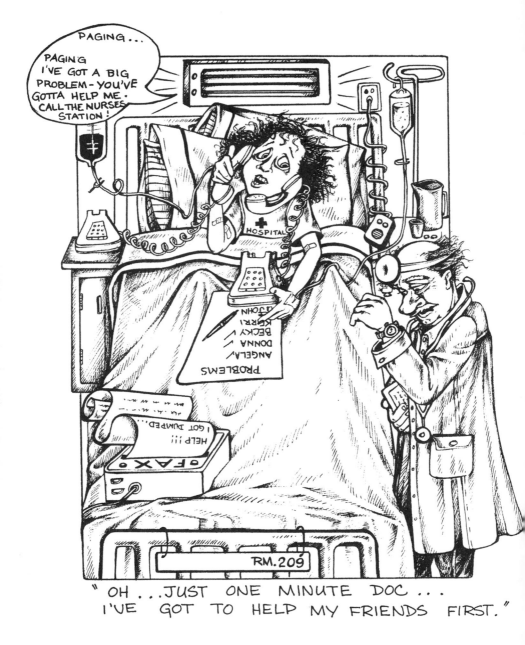

"OH ... JUST ONE MINUTE DOC ...
I'VE GOT TO HELP MY FRIENDS FIRST."

EASY STEP #36

MY FRIENDS ALL NEED ME SO MUCH..... MY TELEPHONE MESSAGE SAYS:

"LEAVE YOUR PROBLEM, I'LL GET BACK TO YOU AS SOON AS I CAN."

LET ME TELL YOU ABOUT TRACY! I FIRST MET HER WHEN SHE WAS IN THE HOSPITAL FOR SURGERY. IT WAS HER FOURTH SURGERY AND ABOUT HER TWENTIETH TIME IN THE HOSPITAL! SHE HAD CROHN'S DISEASE, A CHRONIC INFLAMMATION OF THE DIGESTIVE TRACT THAT CAUSES EXCRUCIATING PAIN AND CAN LEAD TO BLEEDING AND INFECTION. SHE HAD JUST HAD A SECTION OF HER BOWEL SURGICALLY REMOVED AND WAS IN PAIN.

NEVERTHELESS, EVERY TIME I WENT INTO HER ROOM I NOTICED THAT TRACY WOULD BE ON THE PHONE OR THE PHONE WOULD RING WHILE I WAS TALKING TO HER. INTERESTINGLY, I ALSO NOTICED THAT SHE ALWAYS SEEMED TO BE TALKING TO THE OTHER PERSON ABOUT <u>THEIR</u> PROBLEMS.......AND SHE ALWAYS SEEMED TO HAVE SOME PRETTY GOOD SOUNDING ADVICE FOR THEM. SHE SEEMED TO KNOW EXACTLY THE RIGHT THING TO SAY TO EVERYONE WHO CALLED. IT GOT TO THE POINT WHERE I STARTED PICKING UP POINTERS FROM HER ON HOW TO BE A PATIENT AND SYMPATHETIC PSYCHIATRIST!

ONE DAY AFTER SHE GOT OFF THE PHONE WITH A FRIEND WHO HAD A BIG PROBLEM SHE HAD HELPED TO SOLVE, SHE TUNED TO ME AND HAD A LOOK OF PAIN ON HER FACE AND SAID, "MY STOMACH HURTS SO MUCH THAT I DON'T THINK I CAN STAND IT ANY LONGER!"

I ASKED HER, "TRACY, DO YOU EVER TELL YOUR FRIENDS YOUR OWN PROBLEMS?"

SHE REPLIED, "NO, THEY DON'T NEED TO HEAR MY PROBLEMS! THEY HAVE ENOUGH OF THEIR OWN!"

"WELL, THEN, WHAT DO YOU DO WITH YOUR PROBLEMS?", I ASKED.

"I GUESS I JUST SWALLOW THEM." SHE SAID.

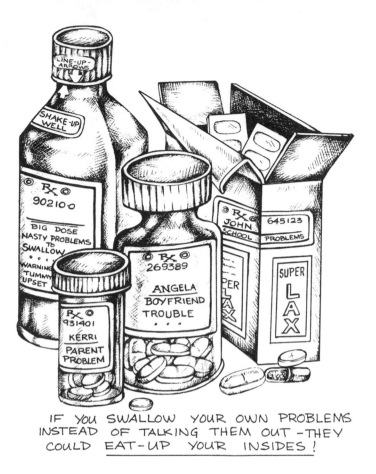

IF YOU SWALLOW YOUR OWN PROBLEMS
INSTEAD OF TALKING THEM OUT —THEY
COULD EAT-UP YOUR INSIDES !

"NO WONDER YOUR GUT ACHES." I SAID, "GIVEN ALL THE GARBAGE YOU SWALLOW!"

SHE LAUGHED BUT SHE ALSO GOT MY POINT.

BUT THEN SHE SAID, "BUT THE BIBLE SAYS: ' LOVE THY NEIGHBOR AS THYSELF'."

"YES, TRACY. BUT THE BIBLE NEVER SAID 'LOVE THY NEIGHBOR BETTER THAN THYSELF', DID IT?"

TRACY HAD A COMMON PROBLEM.....ONE THAT I'VE SEEN TIME AND TIME AGAIN. SHE SPENT MORE TIME TAKING CARE OF HER FRIEND'S NEEDS THAN SHE DID TAKING CARE OF HER OWN. EVERYONE WHO KNEW HER....ALL OF HER FRIENDS...THOUGHT THAT SHE WAS ONE OF THE TOUGHEST AND MOST TOGETHER PERSONS THAT THEY HAD EVER MET! VERY FEW EVEN KNEW THAT SHE HAD PROBLEMS AND SHE HAD A GREAT FEAR THAT SHE WOULD BURDEN THEM IF SHE TOLD THEM ABOUT HER PROBLEMS!

THIS BRINGS US TO OUR NEXT IMPORTANT TRUTH:

FRIENDS ARE PEOPLE YOU
CAN TELL YOUR PROBLEMS TO!

A FRIENDSHIP IS A TWO-WAY STREET. IF YOU FIND THAT YOU ARE
A "GOOD LISTENER" BUT NOT A "GOOD TALKER", SOMETHING IS
WRONG. YOU ARE DOING MORE THAN YOUR SHARE IN THE RELA-
TIONSHIP OR ELSE SOMETHING IS WRONG WITH YOU....YOU ARE
OUT TO PROVE YOUR PERFECTION. YOU ARE OUT TO DEMON-
STRATE THAT YOU ARE TOO GOOD TO HAVE PROBLEMS.

TRACY STARTED TO LEARN HOW TO TELL HER FRIENDS SHE WAS
TOO BUSY TO TALK OR THAT SHE WAS TOO OVERWHELMED BY
HER OWN PROBLEMS TO BE OF HELP AT THE MOMENT. AND A
FUNNY THING STARTED TO HAPPEN......HER FRIENDS BEGAN TO
LISTEN TO HER PROBLEMS AND BEFORE LONG HER RELATION-
SHIPS WERE BACK IN THE SHAPE THAT MADE SENSE.

MAYBE, YOU, TOO , ARE TRYING TOO HARD TO BE TOO NICE!

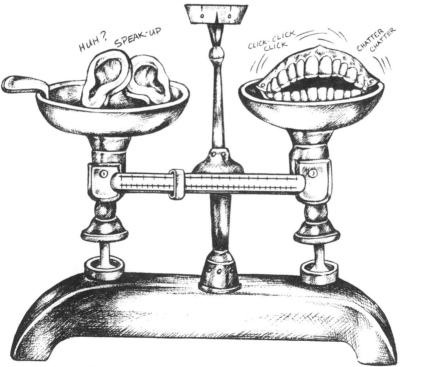

TO BE A GOOD FRIEND—YOU NEED TO CREATE "BALANCE"
BETWEEN BEING A GOOD LISTENER AND A GOOD
TALKER. IN OTHER WORDS—SHARE YOUR PROBLEMS—
DON'T JUST TRY TO SOLVE EVERYONE ELSES.

AT NIGHT WHEN
I TRY TO SLEEP...
I HEAR SKELETONS "RATTLING" IN
MY CLOSET

EASY STEP #37

I CAN'T SLEEP AT NIGHT....
I KEEP HEARING THE SKELETONS
RATTLING IN MY CLOSET

"SHAME! SHAME! SHAME ON YOU!"

THIS SECTION IS ALL ABOUT SHAME.

FIRST, TRY TO THINK OF SOME SHAME THAT YOU HAVE EXPERI-
ENCED IN YOUR PAST. MOST OF US CAN REMEMBER IT QUITE
WELL. A MOMENT OF UTTER EMBARRASSMENT. AN OCCASION
WHEN WE WERE MADE TO FEEL BAD OR GUILTY OR SMALL. A TIME
WHEN WE WERE CAUGHT DOING SOMETHING THAT OTHERS
THOUGHT WAS BAD.

FOR SOME IT MIGHT BE WHEN YOUR MOTHER CAUGHT YOU STEAL-
ING SOME CANDY FROM THE CORNER STORE AND SHE MADE YOU
TAKE IT BACK AND TELL THE MAN AT THE STORE THAT YOU STOLE
IT AND THAT YOU WERE SORRY. FOR OTHERS IT MIGHT BE WHEN
YOU GOT CAUGHT BEHIND THE GARAGE WITH YOUR BOYFREIND
OR WHEN YOU SPLIT YOUR PANTS WIDE OPEN!

THE POSSIBILITIES ARE VAST....BUT IF YOU REMEMBER A SHAME-FUL THING FROM THE PAST AND YOU CAN TALK ABOUT IT, YOU PROBABLY LAUGH ABOUT IT NOW, AS YOU LOOK BACK. AND YOU ARE THE LUCKY ONES.....BECAUSE THERE ARE MANY FOR WHOM SHAME REMAINS A DARK AND UNSPEAKABLE SECRET. OFTEN IT IS EVEN SO SHAMEFUL THAT THE PERSON LEARNS TO ACT LIKE IT NEVER HAPPENED.

BEING ABLE TO FORGET BAD THINGS IS A BLESSING....WHAT WOULD IT BE LIKE IF WE VIVIDLY REMEMBERED EVERY BAD THING THAT HAD EVER HAPPENED TO US?

SOMETIMES, HOWEVER, EVEN THOUGH WE CANNOT VIVIDLY RE-CALL OUR PAST WE ARE HAUNTED BY IT....SOMETIMES TO THE POINT OF UNHAPPINESS.

SOMETIMES THE BURIED MEMORIES WILL JUST NOT GO AWAY. THEY HIDE IN THE NOOKS AND CRANNIES OF OUR MIND AND SI-LENTLY TORTURE US. LIKE GHOSTS THEY FLY IN AND FLY OUT...UNSEEN BUT SCARY.

THE PROBLEM WITH SHAME IS THAT IT OFTEN IS MISPLACED. LET ME GIVE YOU AN EXAMPLE. SARAH WAS FIFTEEN WHEN I FIRST MET HER. SHE HAD BEEN AN EXCELLENT STUDENT AND A JOY TO HER PARENTS BUT ACCORDING TO HER STORY, "I JUST STARTED FEELING REAL BAD ABOUT MYSELF....I DON'T KNOW WHY."

IN FACT, SARAH BEGAN TO FEEL SO BAD ABOUT HERSELF THAT
SHE STOPPED CARING ABOUT EVERYTHING—HOW SHE LOOKED,
HOW WELL SHE STUDIED AND HOW SHE TREATED HER PARENTS.
EVENTUALLY, BY THE TIME I MET HER SHE WAS A VERY DE-
PRESSED YOUNG LADY WHO WALKED AROUND WITH HER HEAD
HUNG LOW.

PORTRAIT OF SARAH
SAD, DEPRESSED, AND SO ASHAMED.

AT FIRST, SHE COULD GIVE NO HINT OF WHAT WAS WRONG WITH HER.......BECAUSE SHE DID NOT HAVE ANY IDEA HERSELF. ONE DAY I BEGAN ASKING HER WHAT SHE REMEMBERED ABOUT HER CHILD-HOOD AND IT WAS AMAZING HOW LITTLE SHE COULD RECALL. SHE HAD A FEW FLEETING MEMORIES, BUT MOST OF HER PAST WAS A BLANK. THEN, A WEEK LATER AFTER I HAD DEVELOPED SOME TRUST WITH HER, SHE SAID TO ME, "YOU KNOW I AM START-ING TO REMEMBER MORE THINGS FROM MY PAST AND IT IS KIND OF SCARY. SOME OF THE THINGS I AM REMEMBERING ARE NOT VERY PLEASANT AND I THINK I MIGHT HAVE BEEN BETTER OFF WHEN I COULD NOT RECALL THEM!"

SLOWLY, OVER THE NEXT SEVERAL WEEKS, AS SHE BEGAN TO FEEL SAFE WITH ME, SHE BEGAN TO TELL ME ABOUT MORE RECOL-LECTIONS FROM HER PAST. THEN, ONE DAY, AS WE WERE TALK-ING, SHE BEGAN TO CRY. I WAITED A MOMENT AND ASKED HER WHAT WAS MAKING HER SAD. SHE LOOKED AT ME AND SAID, "I'M NOT SAD...I AM ASHAMED!" SHE THEN WAS ABLE TO TELL ME IN DETAIL ABOUT THINGS THAT HAD HAPPENED WHEN SHE HAD STAYED WITH HER AUNT AND UNCLE, WHICH SHE HAD DONE QUITE OFTEN WHEN SHE WAS YOUNG. EVENTUALLY SHE WAS ABLE TO TALK ABOUT THE WAY HER UNCLE HAD FONDLED HER AND SHE SAID, " I FEEL BAD BECAUSE I LET HIM DO IT!"

WHEN WE WENT INTO HER PAST A BIT DEEPER WE WERE ABLE TO PUT TOGETHER THAT SHE WAS PROBABLY BETWEEN THREE AND FOUR YEARS OLD WHEN SHE WAS ABUSED BY HER UNCLE. SLOWLY, STEP BY STEP, WE WERE THEN ABLE TO HELP SARAH TO UNDERSTAND THAT THE LITTLE GIRL WHO HAD BEEN ABUSED HAD NO NEED TO FEEL GUILTY BECAUSE IT WAS THE ADULT WHO TOOK ADVANTAGE OF HER AND HE WAS THE ONE WHO HAD THE RESPON-SIBILITY TO KNOW THAT HE WAS DOING WRONG. AS SHE BEGAN TO ACCEPT THE TRUTH, SHE BEGAN TO ACCEPT HERSELF...... IN A WAY THAT SHE HAD NEVER BEEN ABLE TO BEFORE. WITH TIME AND HARD WORK ON HER PART, SHE WAS ABLE TO DEAL WITH HER PROBLEMS AND ERADICATE HER SHAME. AND AS SHE DID, HER DEPRESSION LIFTED AND HER LIFE BECAME JOYFUL ONCE AGAIN.

SARAH WAS PROBABLY ONLY 3
WHEN SHE WAS ABUSED BY AN
UNCLE.

MANY OF US HAVE SKELETONS IN OUR CLOSET....THINGS FROM
OUR PAST THAT WE WOULD RATHER FORGET. SOME SKELETONS
ARE BEST LEFT IN THE CLOSET, BUT SOME ALMOST SEEM TO
RATTLE DELIBERATELY SO THAT WE WILL PAY ATTENTION TO
THEM...ALMOST AS IF THEY KNOW WE WON'T SLEEP SOUNDLY
UNTIL WE CAN LOOK THEM STRAIGHT IN THE EYES.

DO YOU REMEMBER THE FIRST TIME YOU WENT IN TO A HAUNTED
HOUSE? IT WAS TERRIFYING AND I BET YOU HUNG ON TIGHT TO
YOUR PARENT OR A FRIEND. IT IS ONLY NATURAL......SOMETHINGS
ARE TOO SCARY TO DEAL WITH ALL BY YOURSELF. THE SAME IS
TRUE, WITH THE SKELETONS IN YOUR CLOSET....IF YOU KNOW YOU
HAVE TO OPEN THE DOOR TO TAKE A PEEK, IT IS OFTEN VERY
USEFUL TO TAKE SOMEONE ELSE ALONG. THAT IS WHAT HAP-
PENED TO SARAH, AS SHE BUILT TRUST IN ME, SHE WAS ABLE TO
TAKE ME ALONG ON HER JOURNEY INTO THE PAST....AND A JOUR-
NEY THAT WAS SO FRIGHTFUL BECAME A JOURNEY THAT SHE WAS
ABLE TO MAKE!

REMEMBER, THERE ARE PLENTY OF PEOPLE TO TAKE ON YOUR DANGEROUS JOURNEYS—PARENTS, TEACHERS, DOCTORS, COUNSELORS, PASTORS AND FRIENDS. IT IS YOUR JOB TO ADMIT YOUR FEAR AND TO ASK SOMEONE TO JOIN YOU ON YOUR TRIP!

EASY STEP # 38
("THE BONUS")

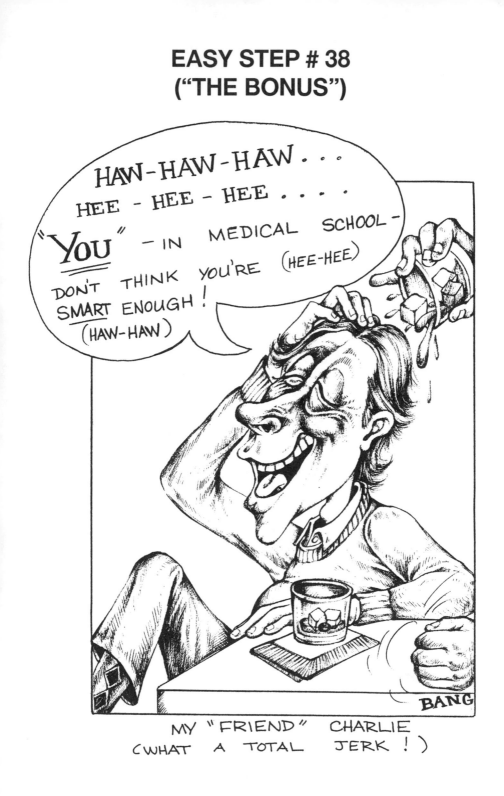

EASY STEP # 38
("THE BONUS")

THE BEAUTY OF ANGER

YOU HAVE PROBABLY NOTICED THAT WE HAVE TALKED A LOT ABOUT ANGER IN THIS BOOK: THE ANGER TEENS FEEL TOWARD THEIR PARENTS AT TIMES, THE ANGER OF PARENTS AND THE ANGER THAT CAN LEAD TO VIOLENCE. AND IN THE WORLD AROUND US THERE IS PLENTY TO BE ANGRY ABOUT—WAR, PREJUDICE, OUR DETERIORATING ENVIRONMENT, INJUSTICE, POVERTY, DISEASE AND OUR MATERIALISTIC WAY OF LIFE. YOU CAN NAME MUCH MORE! REASONS TO GET ANGRY ARE NOT GOING TO DISAPPEAR FROM THE EARTH, WHICH LEADS US TO OUR NEXT IMPORTANT PRINCIPLE:

THERE IS NOTHING WRONG WITH ANGER.

ABOUT TWENTY YEARS AGO, WHEN I WAS IN MY EARLY THIRTIES AND HAD DECIDED THAT I WANTED TO GO TO MEDICAL SCHOOL, I HAD A CHANCE MEETING WITH SOMEONE I HAD KNOWN WHEN I WAS IN THE PEACE CORPS. WE HAD A DRINK TOGETHER AND THE TOPIC SOON TURNED TO MY DREAM OF GOING TO MEDICAL SCHOOL. MY FRIEND CHARLIE STARTED LAUGHING AND SAID, "YOU ARE NOT SMART ENOUGH TO GET INTO MEDICAL SCHOOL. YOU ARE A FOOL FOR EVEN TRYING." HE WAS CRUEL ABOUT IT AND I REMEMBER MY REACTION— I GOT UP FROM THE TABLE AND TOLD HIM THAT HE WAS A FOOL AND THAT I WASN'T GOING TO WASTE ANY MORE OF MY TIME LISTENING TO HIM.

IT TOOK ME FIVE MORE YEARS TO GET INTO MEDICAL SCHOOL, BUT I DON'T THINK I EVER WOULD HAVE MADE IT AT ALL IF I DIDN'T HAVE CHARLIE'S HURTFUL WORDS IN MY EARS. I CAN'T TELL YOU THE TIMES THAT MY ANGER WAS THE ONLY THING KEEPING ME GOING...."I'LL SHOW HIM HOW WRONG HE IS!" "I'LL MAKE A FOOL OUT OF HIM!" "NO IDIOT LIKE HIM IS GOING TO TELL ME WHAT I CAN OR CANNOT ACCOMPLISH!"

IF I EVER RAN INTO CHARLIE AGAIN THE FIRST THING I WOULD WANT TO DO WOULD BE TO TELL HIM THAT I THINK HE IS A @#*&+@!. THE SECOND THING WOULD BE TO SAY THANKS FOR MAKING ME SO ANGRY.......WITHOUT IT I WOULD HAVE NEVER MADE MY DREAM!

I'LL SHOW THAT "JERK" CHARLIE I'M NOT STUPID! I WILL GET THROUGH MEDICAL SCHOOL— NO MATTER WHAT!

THERE IS NOTHING WRONG WITH ANGER....

IT IS ALL A MATTER OF WHAT YOU DO WITH IT!

MANY PEOPLE LET ANGER DESTROY THEM. THEY CHOOSE TO SEE THE WORLD AGAINST THEM AND THE ODDS STACKED AGAINST THEM SO BADLY THAT IT IS NOT EVEN WORTH TRYING. THEY ACCEPT THEIR OWN HELPLESSNESS AND LABEL THEMSELVES AS VICTIMS. THEY BECOME DEPRESSED...AFTER ALL WHAT OTHER DIRECTION IS THERE TO GO WITH SUCH STUPID THINKING! THEY LET THE WORLD PASS THEM BY AND CURSE THEIR FATE. THEY FEEL THE ANGER, BUT TAKE NO ACTION TO CHANGE THEIR LIVES. THEY MANIPULATE THEIR WAY TO UNHAPPINESS AND OFTEN THEY ARE VERY GOOD AT IT, BLAMING OTHERS FOR THEIR PROBLEMS, ALL THE WAY TO THE TRASH HEAP.

IF YOU CAN ACCEPT YOUR ANGER; YOU CAN THEN DO SOMETING WITH IT. AS WE HAVE SAID BEFORE, MANIPULATION ALWAYS

INVOLVES ACTION. THE ONLY USEFUL MANIPULATIONS ARE THE ONES THAT LEAD TO GREATER HAPPINESS FOR YOU AND THE PEOPLE AROUND YOU. THE WONDERFUL CHALLENGE IS THAT NO ONE ELSE HAS THE DESIRE OR THE ABILITY TO MAKE YOUR MA-NIPULATIONS FOR YOU.....IT'S ALL IN YOUR HANDS, TO SINK OR TO SWIM, AND THAT , AFTER ALL, IS WHAT IT IS ALL ABOUT. AS LILY TOMLIN SAYS:

WE ARE ALL IN THIS TOGETHER.....ALONE!

THE JOYS AND THE SORROWS COME FROM THE SAME PLACE: OUR LIVES ARE OURS AND OURS ALONE.....THE CHOICES WE MAKE ABOUT OUR LIVES ARE OURS ALONE.

SPEAKING OF ANGER, I HOPE THAT AT THIS POINT YOU ARE FIND-ING YOURSELF A BIT ANGRY AT ME.....ANGRY AT HAVING BEEN MANIPULATED. AFTER ALL, YOU BOUGHT THIS BOOK TO LEARN HOW TO MANIPULATE YOUR PARENTS, BUT IF YOU HAVE FOL-LOWED ME TO THE END, WE ARE TALKING NOW ABOUT HOW TO MANIPULATE YOURSELF......HOPEFULLY TO HAPPINESS. AND THIS, THEN, IS PERHAPS THE MOST IMPORTANT POINT: THE WAY TO TO MAKE YOUR PARENTS HAPPY , WHEN ALL IS SAID AND DONE, IS THE SAME ROAD THAT YOU MUST TAKE TO MAKE YOUSELF HAPPY. THIS LEADS TO OUR FINAL PRINCIPLES:

LIFE'S A BITCH.......BUT

PLEASING YOUR PARENTS CAN BE ONE OF THE EASIEST THINGS YOU'LL EVER DO.

(AND NOW MY YOUNG FRIENDS
HERE COMES MY FINAL MANIPULATION.)

PLEASING YOURSELF IS <u>THE</u> MOST IMPORTANT THING YOU'LL EVER DO!

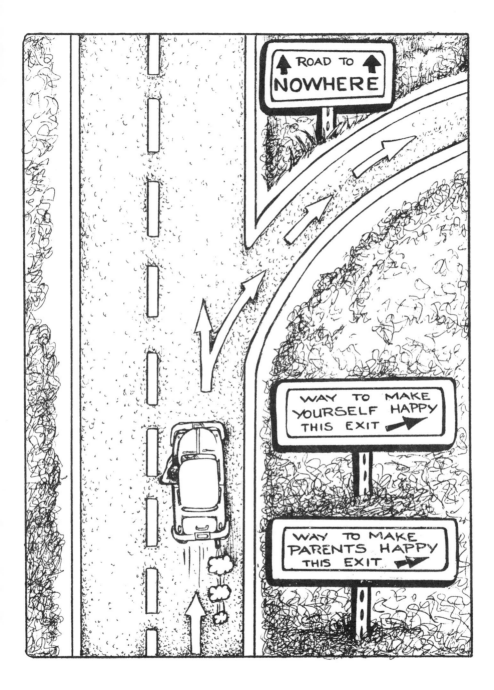

APPENDIX A
RECIPE FOR VEAL OSCAR

1 1/2 POUNDS VEAL CUTLETS, CUT INTO SERVING-SIZED PIECES
1/3 CUP ALL PURPOSE FLOUR
1/8 TEASPOON SALT
1/8 TEASPOON PEPPER
1/8 TEASPOON GARLIC POWDER
1/3 CUPS BUTTER OR MARGARINE, MELTED
1 CUP CHOPPED GREEN ONIONS
2 TEASPOONS WORCESTERSHIRE SAUCE
1 CUP FRESH CRABMEAT
2 (10 OUNCE) PACKAGES FROZEN ASPARGUS SPEARS (OPTIONAL)
BEARNAISE SAUCE
CHOPPED FRESH PARSLEY

FLATTEN CUTLETS INTO 1/4-INCH THICKNESS, IF NECESSARY. COMBINE
FLOUR AND SEASONSING; COOK VEAL IN MELTED BUTTER IN A LARGE
SKILLET UNTIL BROWNED ON BOTH SIDES. REMOVE MEAT, AND KEEP
WARM, RESERVING DRIPPINGS IN SKILLET.

ADD CRABMEAT, GREEN ONIONS, AND WORCESTERSHIRE SAUCE TO
DRIPPINGS IN SKILLET; COOK OVER MEDIUM HEAT, STIRRING OCCA-
SIONALLY, UNTIL MIXTURE IS HEATED.

ARRANGE ASPARAGUS OVER EACH PIECE OF VEAL. SPOON CRABMEAT
OVER THE ASPARAGUS; TOP WITH BEARNAISE SAUCE. SPRINKLE WITH
PARSLEY.

YIELD: 6 TO 8 SERVINGS.

ALTERNATE "37 EASY" RECIPE

CHICKEN BREASTS, AS MANY AS YOU CAN AFFORD
1 CAN CAMPBELL'S CREAM OF ASPARGUS SOUP
SALT AND PEPPER
CHOPPED GREEN ONION, ENOUGH BUT NOT TOO MUCH

TELL PARENTS OSCAR COULD NEVER USE VEAL BECAUSE IT IS A
BABY COW AND HE WOULD NEVER HAVE THE HEART TO DO THAT.
SKIP THE BEARNAISE SAUCE...TELL PARENTS OSCAR FEELS IT IS
NOT GOOD FOR THEIR HEART BECAUSE OF THE CHOLESTEROL. FRY
THE CHICKEN WITH SALT AND PEPPER AND DROP INTO A FRYING
PAN WHERE THE CREAM OF ASPARAGUS SOUP HAS BEEN COOKING.
SPRINKLE GREEN ONIONS ON TOP. SERVE WITH A SMILE.

YIELD: YOUR PARENTS MAY START TO APPRECIATE YOUR FRIEND
OSCAR.

APPENDIX B

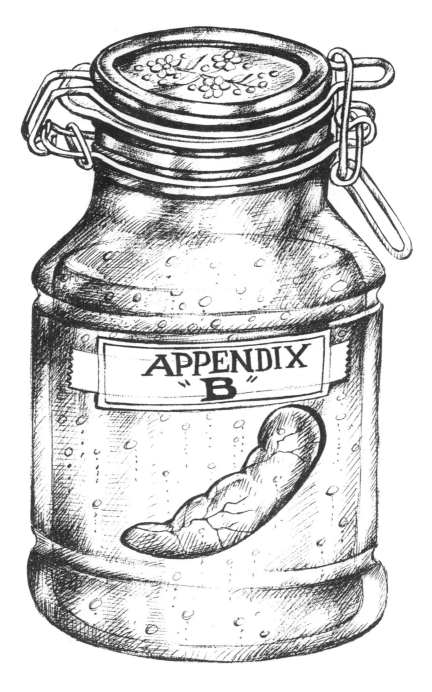

APPENDIX C

PARENT'S CONDENSATION

BASIC PRINCIPLES OF 37 EASY STEPS

1. PARENTS ARE OWED ALL YOUR RESPECT.
2. PARENTS ARE THE DECISION MAKERS IN THE FAMILY.
3. PARENTS KNOW WHAT IS IN YOUR BEST INTERESTS.
4. PARENTS MAKE MISTAKES....BUT THEY ARE IN YOUR BEST INTERESTS.
5. CHILDREN OWE THEIR PARENTS HONOR AND RESPECT.
6. PARENTS WORK HARD FOR YOU...THEIR REWARD IS YOUR RESPECT.
7. IT IS YOUR JOB TO FIGURE OUT HOW TO MAKE YOUR PARENT HAPPY.
8. YOUR LOVE, WITHOUT THE BEHAVIOR TO GO ALONG WITH IT, IS EMPTY.
9. LEARNING TO SAY "I'M SORRY" IS NOT ONLY USEFUL, IT IS ESSENTIAL.
10. THERE ARE FEW MISTAKES SO SEVERE THAT A PARENT CANNOT FORGIVE.
11. LOVING YOUR PARENTS LEADS TO LOVING YOURSELF.
12. PARENTS OFTEN DO KNOW "WHAT IS BEST".
13. WHAT PARENTS ASK OF CHILDREN IS SIMPLE.
14. LOVE IS SHOWN.... NOT SPOKEN.
15. PARENTS MUST BE STERN...YOU WILL SEE WHY SOME DAY.
16. GOOD INTENTIONS ARE NOT ENOUGH...YOU MUST SHOW LOVE.
17. REBELLION IS IMMATURITY; CONFORMITY IS ADULTHOOD.
18. ANGER IS A WEAKNESS...LEARN TO CONTROL IT.
19. YOU ARE YOUR PARENT'S MAIN SOURCE OF HAPPINESS.
20. YOU MUST PREPARE NOW TO TAKE CARE OF YOUR PARENTS IN OLD AGE.
21. DISRESPECT FOR YOUR PARENTS IS THE ROUTE TO FAILURE.
22. PARENTS ARE PARENTS...THEY DO NOT HAVE TO BE RIGHT.
23. YOUR PARENTS SACRIFICED FOR YOU...THEY HAVE GAINED YOUR TRUST.
24. WHEN IN CONFLICT...WEAR YOUR PARENTS' SHOES.
25. AN IMPERFECT PARENT IS BETTER THAN NO PARENT AT ALL.
26. HONOR YOUR PARENTS AND YOUR CHILDREN WILL HONOR YOU.
27. YOUR YOUNGER BROTHER AND SISTER NEED YOU AS A ROLE MODEL.
28. PARENTS SEEK PERFECTION, BUT ARE HUMAN...YOU MUST FORGIVE.
29. ADOLESCENTS DO NOT HAVE A REQUIREMENT TO BE REBELLIOUS.
30. ALMOST ALL CONFLICT CAN BE AVOIDED.
31. PARENTS HAVE "VISION" NO CHILD COULD EXPECT TO HAVE.
32. TEACHERS DESERVE THE SAME HONOR AS PARENTS.
33. IT IS EASIER TO SAY "I'M SORRY" THAN "I DON'T AGREE".
34. NEVER FORGET....WITHOUT YOUR PARENTS YOU WOULD NOT EXIST.
35. YOUR PARENTS LOVE YOU, EVEN WHEN YOU DON'T BELIEVE IT.
36. ANGER WILL DESTROY ANYTHING YOU ATTEMPT.
37. YOU WILL MISS YOUR PARENTS WHEN THEY ARE GONE....AND IT WILL BE TOO LATE TO TELL THEM.

APPENDIX D

DEAR DOCCO,

OK. I'LL ADMIT THAT I MIGHT HAVE LEARNED A FEW THINGS FROM YOUR BOOK, AND MAYBE I GRINNED (SLIGHTLY) AT SOME OF YOUR CORNY JOKES. AS A MATTER OF FACT YOUR BOOK BECAME SOMEWHAT OF A COMFORT, LIKE AN OLD FRIEND, AFTER THE FIRST FEW CHAPTERS.

I DO, HOWEVER, HAVE ONE MAJOR CRITICISM. I WAS VERY ANGRY ABOUT YOUR ABRUPT AND IMPERSONAL ENDING. IN THE BEGINNING YOU TOOK A LOT OF TIME FOR US TO GET TO KNOW EACH OTHER AND YOU GAINED MY TRUST AND FRIENDSHIP....I EVEN LET YOU GET AWAY WITH CALLING ME "KIDDO" (UGH!). AND THEN.....AND THEN <u>NOTHING!</u> YOU LEFT WITHOUT SAYING GOODBYE. WHY? HOW COULD YOU DO THAT TO ME?

SINCERELY,

HURT READER

P.S. I AM SORRY THAT I COULD NOT CONTROL MY PARENTS. THEY SNUCK INTO MY ROOM AND STOLE MY BOOK WHEN I WAS ASLEEP. NOW, IF <u>THEY</u> START TRYING TO CALL ME "KIDDO" I <u>REALLY</u> WILL BE MAD AT YOU!

DEAR HURT READER,

THANK YOU SO MUCH FOR YOUR KIND LETTER. I AM VERY PLEASED THAT YOU ENJOYED 37 EASY STEPS AND FOUND IT USEFUL. I AM EVEN READY TO FORGIVE YOU FOR LETTING IT SLIP INTO YOUR PARENTS HANDS. (DIDN'T YOU HAVE A PILE OF OLD CLOTHES AND "STUFF" TO HIDE IT UNDER?) BUT, IT SOUNDED LIKE IT MIGHT HAVE LED TO SOME RATHER INTERESTING CONVERSATION BETWEEN YOU AND YOUR PARENTS.

MY DEAR HURT READER, I MUST ADMIT, AT FIRST YOUR COMMMENTS ABOUT BEING ANGRY AT ME PERPLEXED ME. BUT AFTER THINKING IT OVER I REALIZED YOU HAVE A VERY GOOD POINT. SAYING GOOD-BYE IS VERY IMPORTANT BUSINESS AND I'M AFRAID THAT I DID NOT DO A VERY GOOD JOB OF IT. MAYBE, IT WAS BECAUSE I WAS TOO EAGER TO FINISH AND TO GET ON WITH OTHER THINGS OR MAYBE IT WAS BECAUSE SAYING GOOD-BYE IS NEVER EASY. BUT I THINK THE REAL REASON IS THAT I HAD NOT

REALIZED HOW SUCCESSFUL WE HAD BEEN IN SETTING UP A FRIENDSHIP. MAYBE, I WAS A BIT INSECURE AND I HAD NOT BEEN ABLE TO REALIZE WHAT I GOOD JOB I HAD DONE IN REACHING YOU....ALL MY READERS-TO-BE (HURT AND UNHURT) SEEMED SO FAR AWAY WHEN I WAS WRITING.

I DID WORK HARD TO BECOME YOUR FRIEND....AND YOU DESERVE MORE IN THE WAY OF A GOOD-BYE, ESPECIALLY SINCE SAYING GOOD-BYE IS ONE OF THOSE THINGS THAT WE OFTEN ONLY GET A SINGLE CHANCE TO DO!

I NEEDED TO TELL YOU THAT I'M GOING TO MISS YOU AND THAT I TRUST YOU. I THINK WE BOTH KNOW THAT SOMETIMES LIFE CAN BE VERY COMPLICATED AND VERY DIFFICULT....BUT IF YOU BREAK IT DOWN TO ITS SIMPLEST PARTS IT CAN BE SOMETHING THAT WE CANNOT ONLY DEAL WITH, BUT IT CAN ALSO BE SOMETHING THAT CAN BRING US IMMENSE JOY—EVEN THE MOST DIFFICULT PARTS. IF I'VE HELPED TO SEE THAT, THEN YOU ARE WELL ON THE WAY TO MAKING YOURESLF A PRETTY NIFTY ADULT. IT IS RATHER SAD TO THINK THAT I WILL NEVER KNOW HOW THE "LITTLE CONVERSA-TIONS" IN THIS BOOK AFFECT EACH OF YOU THAT READ IT OR HOW IT MIGHT HELP TO CHANGE A LIFE. FROM THE INSIGHT THAT YOU HAVE GIVEN ME, I HAVE THE JOY OF KNOWING THAT YOU ARE GOING TO BE ALRIGHT. MAYBE, AVOIDING SAYING GOOD-BYE IS MY WAY OF TELLING YOU THAT I AM GOING TO MISS YOU AND THAT THERE IS A CERTAIN KIND OF SADNESS THAT I MAY NOT HAVE A FURTHER ROLE IN YOUR LIFE. I, TOO, WILL MISS YOU.

BUT THERE IS A FINAL THOUGHT. IN THE FUTURE, OTHER PEOPLE YOU CARE ABOUT MAY LEAVE YOU LIKE I LEFT YOU, WITHOUT SAYING GOOD-BYE. MAYBE THAT IS AN IMPORTANT LESSON AND ONE THAT YOU WILL REMEMBER THE NEXT TIME YOU SEE YOUR MOTHER OR YOUR FATHER OR YOUR SISTER OR BROTHER OR A FRIEND OR A GRANDPARENT...... AND THAT MIGHT BE JUST THE RIGHT TIME TO HUG THEM AND TELL THEM YOU LOVE THEM AND APPRECIATE THEM FOR WHO THEY ARE....FOR THE OPPORTUNITY TO SAY A FINAL "GOOD-BYE" IS NOT AN ABSOLUTE GUARANTEE.

THANKS FOR BEING SO HONEST AND TELLING ME HOW ANGRY I GOT YOU. I THINK I'VE LEARNED WHAT YOU WANTED ME TO LEARN AND PERHAPS YOU WERE ABLE TO EXPERIENCE THE "BEAUTY OF ANGER" IN A WAY THAT YOU CAN CARRY WITH YOU LONG INTO THE FUTURE. THANKS FOR TAKING THE TIME TO TEACH ME.

WITH TRUST AND AFFECTION,

DOCCO (UGH!)

APPENDIX E.

DEAR DR. DENNY,

YOU REALLY KNOW WHAT YOU ARE TALKING ABOUT, BUT WHAT I WANT TO KNOW IS—HOW DID YOU KNOW?

I COULD NOT BELIEVE EASY STEP # 32! I RAN AWAY LAST CHRISTMAS AND ENDED UP IN WICHITA! I WAS SO SHOCKED WHEN I READ "MY STORY" IN YOUR BOOK THAT I COULD NOT BELIEVE IT.

MY BOY FRIEND AND I RAN AWAY TOGETHER AND THE PLACE WE HEADED FOR WAS KANSAS, BECAUSE WE FIGURED IT WAS THE LAST PLACE ANYONE WOULD LOOK FOR US.

WE DIDN'T HAVE QUITE EVERYTHING ON YOUR "LIST", BUT WE HAD QUITE A FEW. I DIDN'T HAVE ANY PHONE NUMBERS AND I DIDN'T EVEN THINK ABOUT HOMELESS SHELTERS BECAUSE I WAS GOING TO "MAKE IT ON MY OWN". I DIDN'T HAVE MUCH FOOD AND DIDN'T THINK ABOUT VITAMINS BECAUSE I WANTED TO GET SKINNY.

I HAD A PEN AND NOTEBOOK AND KEPT A JOURNAL BECAUSE I WANT TO BE A WRITER. WHEN I READ THE JOURNAL NOW IT'S PRETTY SCARY, BUT I GUESS I THOUGHT I WAS COOL AT THE TIME.

AS FAR AS THE "DAMNED GOOD REASON FOR LEAVING MY COZY HOME" IS CONCERNED, I REALIZE NOW THAT I DID NOT HAVE ONE—UNLESS IT IS WAS THE DEPRESSION THAT I AM FINALLY LEARNING TO DEAL WITH.

WITCHITA WAS THE END OF A MUCH LOOKED FORWARD TO TRIP ACROSS THE COUNTRY. I ARRIVED THERE AROUND NINE IN THE MORNING AND FOOLED AROUND ALL DAY. MY BOYFRIEND AND I GOT BORED AND SLEPT IN THE PARK FOR A WHILE. AROUND THREE IN THE MORNING—FRIDAY THE 13TH—WE WENT TO A PHONE BOOTH TO CALL SOMEONE WE THOUGHT COULD HELP US WITH MONEY BECAUSE WE WERE DOWN TO OUR LAST DOLLAR AND VERY HUNGRY. SUDDENLY I FELT A COP TOUCH MY SHOULDER AND ASK US WHY WE WERE BREAKING CURFEW AND I KNEW WE WERE IN TROUBLE, BUT TO BE HONEST, I THINK I FELT A BIT RELIEVED.

THEY KEPT US IN THE JUVENILE HALL FOR A WEEK, SEPA-RATED FROM EACH OTHER, AND I'D NEVER LIKE TO LIVE THAT

WEEK AGAIN. FINALLY, THEY MADE ARRANGEMENTS FOR US
TO RETURN HOME BY BUS, AND I'LL TELL YOU, HOME DID LOOK
MIGHT COZY ONCE I GOT THERE.
I WISH I HAD READ YOUR BOOK BEFORE I RAN AWAY AND GOT
INTO ALL THE PROBLEMS THAT FOLLOWED BUT I'M THANKFUL
TO HAVE IT AS I WORK ON ALL THE REST OF MY PROBLEMS.
THANKS SO MUCH.

SINCERELY,

ANNIE

DEAR ANNIE,

THANK YOU FOR YOUR KIND LETTER. I MUST TELL YOU I HAVE NO
IDEA WHY I PICKED WITCHITA....IT COULD HAVE JUST AS EASILY
HAVE BEEN DES MOINES,SALT LAKE CITY OR MEMPHIS OR ANY
OTHER CITY OUT THERE. I GUESS I USED THE SAME LOGIC AS YOU:
WHERE WOULD BE THE LAST PLACE.....? (I'D BETTER STOP OR I
WON'T SELL ANY BOOKS IN WITCHITA!)

ANNIE, I'M NOT SURE READING MY BOOK AHEAD OF TIME WOULD
HAVE CHANGED YOUR PLANS IN ANY WAY. I DOUBT THAT BACK
THEN YOU WERE READY TO FOLLOW ANYTHING OTHER THAN YOUR
IMPULSES, BUT IT SOUNDS TO ME LIKE YOU ARE A VERY
DIFFERENT PERSON NOW! I HOPE THAT YOU ARE TAKING PLEA-
SURE IN WORKING ON YOUR PROBLEMS AND THAT YOU ARE MAK-
ING THINGS AT HOME WORK FOR BOTH YOU AND YOUR PARENTS.
IT SEEMS THAT WHEN THAT POLICEMAN TAPPED YOU ON THE
SHOULDER YOU WERE MORE THAN READY TO ADMIT YOU HAD
PROBLEMS. WHAT MATTERS NOW IS WHERE YOU GO FROM HERE!
FROM YOUR LETTER, IT SEEMS THAT YOU ARE MORE THAN READY
TO MOVE AHEAD.

MAY ALL YOUR MISTAKES BE ONES THAT YOU LEARN FROM....AND
REMEMBER, A LIFE WITHOUT MISTAKES IS NOT A LIFE LIVED TO THE
FULLEST. (BUT, PLEASE. NO MORE WHOPPERS!)

BY THE WAY, HOW ARE YOU COMING WITH YOUR NOVEL? I'D LOVE
TO READ IT AND SEE HOW YOU ARE PUTTING ALL YOUR CREATIVE
ENERGIES TO WORK.

THANKS AGAIN FOR YOUR KIND LETTER. I'LL BE LOOKING FOR-
WARD TO HEARING MORE FROM YOU.

FONDLY,

DR. DENNY

APPENDIX F.

DEAR DR. DENNY,

THERE WERE A LOT OF PARTS IN YOUR BOOK THAT I LIKED BUT
THERE WERE TWO THINGS I DID NOT LIKE. YOUR SECTION ON
SEX REALLY DIDN'T SAY TOO MUCH AND I CERTAINLY DID NOT
LEARN ANYTHING NEW. BUT WHAT I REALLY DID NOT LIKE
WAS THE DRAWINGS THAT SHOWED PEOPLE WHO CHOOSE TO
EXPRESS THEIR OWN INDIVIDUALITY AS MESSED UP, LIKE THE
CARTOON OF THE YOUNG MAN WITH THE SPIKED HAIR BEING
DRAGGED OUT OF YOUR OFFICE BY THE COLLAR. I DON'T THINK
THAT WAS VERY FAIR.

ADULTS ALWAYS SEEM TO JUDGE PEOPLE BY THE WAY THEY
LOOK AND I AM VERY DISAPPOINTED THAT YOU ACTED LIKE
YOU UNDERSTAND TEENAGERS, BUT YOU DID THE SAME THING.
GOOD PEOPLE COME IN ALL SIZES, SHAPES AND APPERANCES.

BUT, THANK YOU FOR WRITING THE BOOK.
SINCERELY,

KELLY

DEAR KELLY,

LIGHTEN UP! IF YOU LOOK CLOSELY YOU WILL SEE THAT I AM AN
"EQUAL OPPORTUNITY" OFFENDER. AND, LET'S FACE IT, THERE
AREN'T THAT MANY THINGS LEFT IN THE WORLD TO LAUGH AT! IF
ONE GOES TO ALL THE TROUBLE TO MAKE THEMSELVES UNIQUE
BY SPIKING THEIR HAIR OR DYING IT PINK THEY WILL MOST LIKELY
DRAW ATTENTION...THE REST OF US CAN RESPECT THAT PERSON'S
RIGHT TO THEIR INDIVIDUALITY, BUT WE ARE ALSO ENTITLED TO
OUR RIGHT TO A SMILE WHILE WE DO IT.

THANKS FOR WRITING. I LOVE YOUR ASSERTIVENESS, BUT MAYBE I
NEED TO ADD ANOTHER EASY STEP: BEING ASSERTIVE DOESN'T
ALWAYS MAKE YOU RIGHT.

KELLY, SORRY, I TURNED OUT TO BE AN ADULT.....BUT THAT IS NOT
RIGHT OR WRONG, IT JUST IS. JUST AS IT IS PART OF ME, MY HOPE
FOR YOU, KELLY, IS THAT YOU WILL CONTINUE TO CHERISH YOUR
OWN UNIQUENESS AND WATCH IT GROW.
FONDLY,

DR. DENNY

AND, OH. ABOUT THE SEX..... PLEASE BEAR WITH ME, I'M STILL
DOING THE RESEARCH!

APPENDIX G

ONE LAST AND FINAL PIECE OF ADVICE, IF ALL ELSE FAILS:

DO NOT HESITATE TO RESORT TO

BLATANT KISSING-UP!

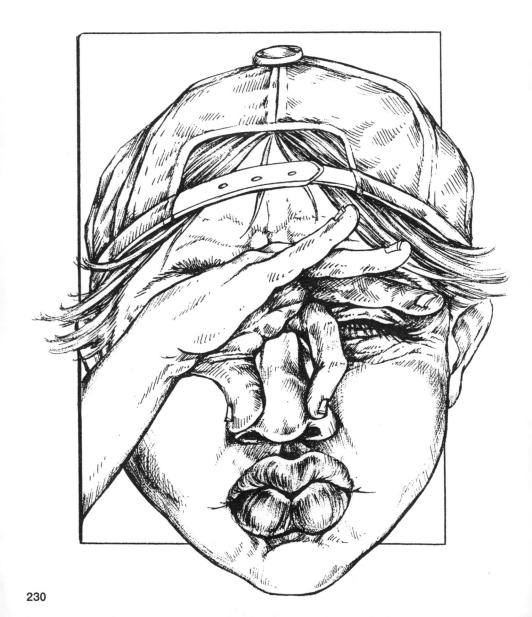

ABOUT THE AUTHORS

KEVIN M. DENNY HAS BEEN A NEWSPAPER BOY, A SODA JERK, A TELEGRAM DELIVERY BOY, A HIGHWAY REPAIRMAN, A PEACE CORPS VOLUNTEER, AN ANTHROPOLOGIST, A DEMOGRAPHER AND UNEMPLOYED. HE HAS LIVED IN AFRICA AND AFGHANISTAN AND, AFTER A SERIES OF CREATIVE MISADVENTURES, BEGAN MEDICAL SCHOOL AT THIRTY-SIX...AND AGAIN AT THIRTY-SEVEN!

HE LIKES IRISH MUSIC, VELVEETA CHEESE, THANKSGIVING, SUNDAY NAPS, AFRICAN MASKS, PROFESSIONAL WRESTLING, "THE AMERICAN GLADIATORS", WARTHOGS, TRAVEL, BASEBALL, FLEA MARKETS AND A GOOD BOOK .

HE HATES DANCING, BALLET, OPERA, NINTENDO, ILL-BEHAVED KIDS, SNOBS, LIMA BEANS, CHRISTMAS, KNOW-IT-ALLS, LAZY PEOPLE AND SCIENCE FICTION.

HE HAS FOUR SONS EMERGING FROM THEIR ADOLESCENCES AND IS A CHILD PSYCHIATRIST WHO HAS DIRECTED AN ADOLESCENT HOSPITAL UNIT FOR NINE YEARS. HE CURRENTLY LIVES IN A SLEEPY LITTLE TOWN HE REFUSES TO NAME.

ANDREA EVANS WINTON HAS RECENTLY MOVED TO MARIPOSA, CALIFORNIA WHERE SHE RAISES OSTRICHES, WORKS FOR THE OLDEST NEWSPAPER IN THE NATION AND ATTEMPTS TO SHUCK HER NORTH CAROLINA ACCENT. SHE GREW UP DEVOURING MAD MAGAZINE AND MICHAELANGELO WITH IMPUNITY AS SHE HONED HER ARTISTIC ASPIRATIONS AND TALENTS.

SHE DRAWS ON A MULTITUDE OF REAL LIFE EXPERIENCES FOR HER ILLUSTRATIONS, BEING THE MOTHER TO SEVEN CHILDREN AND A GAGGLE OF GRANDCHILDREN.

ANDREA, WHO STUDIED AT THE BROOKS INSTITUTE OF FINE ART IN SANTA BARBARA, FINDS HER CURRENT RETURN TO CARTOONING TO BE A PLEASANT DIVERSION FROM HER MORE USUAL DETAILED STUDIES IN WESTERN AND GRAPHIC ART.